TREACHEROUS WATERS:
KINGSTON'S SHIPWRECKS

DISASTERS ON LAKE ONTARIO

Every Autumn, Lake Ontario, in common with the other Great Lakes, takes its toll of life and property. The eastern end of the lake has always been the scene of these late Autumn disasters. This is due to the fact that there is here located the widest expanse of the waters of the lake and also dangerous shores with but few harbors....

Just as long...as the old wooden sailing and steam craft operate, there will be wrecks and loss of life. Probably there have been few better sea boats on the lakes than were some of these trim sailing vessels in their prime, but their best days are gone. It needs good sailors and good bottoms to weather nasty autumn gales on the Great Lakes as there is no sea room, as sailors call it, to ride out a gale. There is only one thing to do, and that is to make shelter, and these old craft are not always capable of doing that....

---from an editorial in the *Daily Intelligencer* (Belleville, near Kingston, Ontario), Saturday, December 2, 1922.

Books by Cris Kohl:

Dive Southwestern Ontario!

Shipwreck Tales: The St. Clair River (to 1900)

DIVE ONTARIO! The Guide to Shipwrecks and Scuba Diving

DIVE ONTARIO TWO! More Ontario Shipwreck Stories

Treacherous Waters: Kingston's Shipwrecks

TREACHEROUS WATERS:

KINGSTON'S SHIPWRECKS

by
Cris Kohl

ILLUSTRATED WITH PHOTOGRAPHS,
MAPS, AND DRAWINGS

Published by Cris Kohl,
Chatham, Ontario, Canada

Published by
Cris Kohl,
16 Stanley Avenue,
Chatham, Ontario, Canada N7M 3J2
Telephone: (519) 351-1966
Fax: (519) 351-1753

NOTE: Photo credits are shown in terms of the author's source for the photograph rather than a specific photographer who might have taken it, except where the photographer is known and specifically named.

Printed and bound by BookCrafters, Chelsea, MI

First Edition: June, 1997

Cover photograph: *Technical diver, Barb Marshall of Stevensville, Ontario, on one of several deep dives that day, glances up at an immense, silhouetted paddlewheel of the steamer,* Comet, *which sank in an 1861 collision (story on pp. 33-36). This early but well-preserved shipwreck rests in about 85' (25.5 metres) of cold Lake Ontario water several kilometres west of Kingston.* PHOTO BY CRIS KOHL.

ACKNOWLEDGEMENTS

The author sincerely thanks the following individuals, listed alphabetically, for information and assistance that led to the completion of this book: Robert Aucoin, Kingston area (Elginburg) artist; Marcel Blanchette of Black River, Ontario, commercial artist; Kathy Everson of Trenton, Ontario, journalist, photographer, and underwater model; diver and historian Joan Forsberg of High Lake, Illinois, who offered proofreading, strong words, and other inspiration; Pat Kelly of Oshawa, Ontario, diver and underwater model; Dani Lee of Brossard, Québec, diver and underwater model; Ian and Barb Marshall of Stevensville, Ontario, technical divers/instructors and underwater models; Marcy McElmon of Trenton, Ontario, scuba instructor and underwater model; Gary Moore of Trenton, Ontario, sailboating diver; Earl Moorhead, Archivist, the Marine Museum of the Great Lakes, Kingston, Ontario; Ken Mullings of Trenton, Ontario, diver and marine historian; Doug Pettingill of Picton, Ontario, diver, marine historian, and shipwreck locater; Spencer Shonicker of Kingston, Ontario, diver and charterboat operator; Jim, Pat, Sherry, and Jim Jr. Stayer of Lexington, Michigan, divers, marine historians, and shipwreck locaters; Lloyd Shales of Kingston, Ontario, diver, shipwreck locater, researcher, and retired diveshop/charterboat operator; James Taylor of Picton, Ontario, commercial diver; Guenter Wernthaler of Ottawa, Ontario, diver and shipwreck locater; and George Wheeler and Susan Yankoo of Point Traverse, Ontario, divers and charterboat operators. For anyone I may have inadvertently overlooked, please forgive me; I do thank you for your assistance.

The generous co-operation of the following institutions and their helpful staffs is also gratefully acknowledged: the Province of Ontario Archives, Toronto; the Public Archives of Canada, Ottawa; the Marine Museum of the Great Lakes, Kingston; the Marine Museum at South Bay, Ontario; the Belleville (Ontario) Cemetery; the Belleville (Ontario) Public Library; the Kingston (Ontario) Public Library; the Picton (Ontario) Public Library; the Metropolitan Toronto (Ontario) Public Library; Preserve Our Wrecks (P.O.W.) of Kingston, Ontario; the Great Lakes Marine Collection of the Milwaukee Public Library, Milwaukee, Wisconsin; the Institute for Great Lakes Research (Bowling Green State University), Perrysburg, Ohio; the Great Lakes Historical Society, Vermilion, Ohio; and the Lake Carriers Association, Cleveland, Ohio.

Lastly, the author sincerely thanks all his relatives and other friends for their encouragement, support, and help that led to the completion of this project, and for tolerating the many hours of travel, patience, seclusion, and absence necessitated by the research, field work, photography, and writing of the text.

The Maritime Conservation Organization called
Preserve Our Wrecks (P.O.W.)

Preserve Our Wrecks (P.O.W.) was formed in the Kingston, Ontario, area in 1981 by scuba divers upset at the unauthorized salvage and damage done to a popular local shipwreck. P.O.W. is a group of concerned individuals who volunteer their time towards the preservation of shipwrecks in the Kingston area for the benefit of all. They install permanent moorings adjacent to the wreck sites in order to prevent anchor damage by visiting boats, and they work with charterboat operators in maintaining these moorings. They also perform volunteer underwater archaeological surveys on Kingston area shipwrecks and help educate divers about the histories and non-renewabilities of these shipwrecks.

For more information about this valuable organization's work, or on becoming a member of this team and supporting its worthy cause, write to Preserve Our Wrecks, c/o Marine Museum of the Great Lakes, 55 Ontario Street, Kingston, Ontario Canada K7L 2Y2.

CONTENTS

INTRODUCTION

Kingston's maritime history generally ranges from the construction of the largest warships ever employed on the Great Lakes to the scuttling of a steel passenger ferry and a former scuba charter boat as scuba dive sites, with literally thousands of nautical events occurring in between.

The eastern Lake Ontario and the beginning of the St. Lawrence River area around Kingston, Ontario, is dotted with shoals, reefs, points of land, and islands of varying sizes, all navigational challenges that, among the over 200 cases described in this book, were often not overcome by ships and their masters. Nature in the form of inclement weather (or, being less polite, "severe gales" and "ferocious storms") often prompted the demise of ships and sailors not adequately suited for that challenge. Human error often resulted in vessel collisions, some with severe loss of life and property. Fire on board a ship produced particularly terrifying meetings of opposite elements, again frequently resulting in much loss of life and the destruction of the vessel to the waterline. In many instances, vessels simply grew old and weary, losing first their working capability and then their watertight integrity. Abandoned for years in the Kingston area's backwaters, many of these broken workhorses were eventually, in major "clean-ups," deposited into local "ships' graveyards" in deep enough water and far enough away to be out of sight, if not out of mind.

All of these stories, and more, are offered in this book.

After the opening chapter, which outlines the Kingston area's significant maritime background, the book follows specific shipwreck occurrences in chronological order. One chapter covers the early, pre-1870 losses, with subsequent chapters covering one decade each right up to 1930. The modern era total losses, since 1930, are covered in a single chapter, since that was the time when "shipwreck production" slowed down dramatically. The concluding chapter is called "A Potpourri of Shipwrecks," describing as best as possible stories and histories which lack significant or satisfactory documentation, or vessels that were wrecked for only a short period of time before being restored and returned to service, often to be scrapped years later or to become shipwrecks in another part of the Great Lakes. Some published vessel histories incorrectly finalized those ships' careers at their initial sinkings! In quotations, I have retained the original spelling, punctuation, and grammar, regardless of how incorrect they were.

I have had a lot of fun in the past 15 years exploring these shipwrecks, photographing them, and researching their stories. In the process, I have made many friends and acquaintances. This is my attempt to share some of that fun and good fortune with you. Please accept this book's offer of friendship.

Cris Kohl,
Chatham, Ontario, Canada

Chapter One

Kingston's Maritime Background

Kingston, Ontario, nestled strategically in the northeast corner of Lake Ontario at the point where the lake empties into the St. Lawrence River, is rich in history, particularly maritime history.

Surprisingly, Lake Ontario was not the first of the five Great Lakes to be discovered; that honour goes to Lake Huron, which French explorers first viewed in the year 1609. However, it was not long afterwards, in 1615, that Lake Ontario, originally referred to as Lake Iroquois (after the predominant First Nation tribe in that region) was traversed by Etienne Brulé, and later that same year, by famed French explorer, Samuel de Champlain.[1]

The Kingston site is the location which was selected by the French explorer, René Robert Cavelier de LaSalle, for an important meeting in 1673 between the Iroquois chiefs and the Governor of New France (Québec), Frontenac. To impress the Indians and to tap the fur trade in the Lake Ontario region, LaSalle constructed a stockaded fort at the site. Two years later, LaSalle ordered the fort rebuilt out of stone, naming the important site Fort Frontenac.[2] This site served as a defended port of trans-shipment, a clearinghouse for supplies heading to the western French forts and for furs brought up in canoes, bateaux, and lake schooners from the western frontier regions.

This area established its trendsetting maritime significance early. At Fort Frontenac, in 1678, LaSalle constructed the first commercial vessels that ever plied Great Lakes waters, two twin-masted schooners of about 45' (13.5 metres) length each. Thus began the Kingston area's claim to maritime history fame. A little-known fact is that one of these two vessels, named the *Frontenac* (LaSalle recognized the importance of making and maintaining important political allies!) became the first recorded shipwreck on the entire Great Lakes when it sank on January 8, 1679 near Thirty Mile Point on the present-day U.S. side of Lake Ontario.[3]

The far-more-famous sailing vessel, *Griffon,* also constructed by LaSalle and built at Niagara near the shores of Lake Erie in the spring and early summer of 1679, sailed on her maiden voyage on August 7th that year, and thus entered the history books as the first commercial vessel on the upper Great Lakes, that is, upstream from Niagara Falls. The *Griffon* disappeared in September, 1679, with all hands and a cargo of furs which had been loaded while in Lake Michigan.[4] Unquestioned evidence still eludes sleuths attempting to solve this greatest of all Great Lakes mysteries ("Where is the wreck of the *Griffon?"*) and for that inexplicably attractive reason, history and the general public have been prone to overlook the less dramatic demise of LaSalle's earlier vessel on Lake Ontario!

The Eastern Great Lakes

LAKE CARRIERS ASSOCIATION, CLEVELAND, OHIO

The Kingston area again played an important marine role during the Seven Years' War (1756-1763) between Britain and France. Keep in mind that Fort Frontenac (Kingston) was part of New France (Québec) prior to that war, and that the American colonies were still British, and not yet the United States of America. In 1727, the British converted their seven-year-old trading post at Oswego, New York, due south of Fort Frontenac across Lake Ontario, into an armed fortification subsequently named Fort Oswego. Immediately at the start of the Seven Years' War, French troops swooped down upon this fort, burning it to the ground, destroying seven British ships, and taking 1,600 prisoners. To put it mildly, this upset the British, and two years and 11 days later, British Col. John Bradstreet and his army tasted revenge by capturing Fort Frontenac. French dominance of the Great Lakes conclusively ended a year later when the British captured Fort Niagara in July of 1759.[5]

In 1783, the old Fort Frontenac area was settled by United Empire Loyalists from New York State. "Loyalists" were faithful British subjects who suffered political persecution, tar-and-feathering, imprisonment, and sometimes death in the Thirteen Colonies during the time of the American Revolution because they wished to remain loyal to Britain rather than live in the rebellious new country which was eventually named the United States of America. The Loyalists had their properties confiscated by the new country when they fled to Canada, transporting only the possessions they could carry with them.

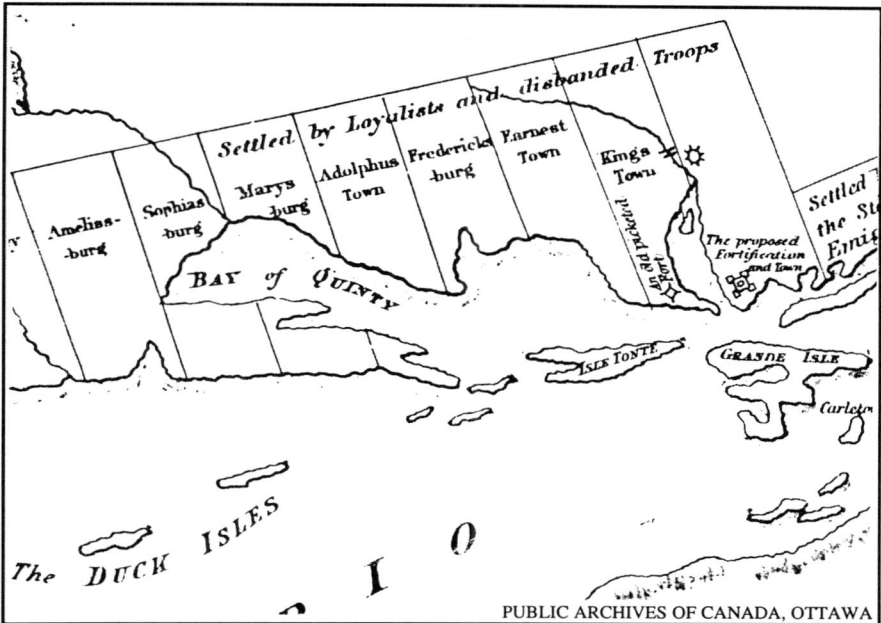

This 1790 map portion of the Royal Townships and Cataraqui Townships clearly indicates how unclear the geography of eastern Lake Ontario appeared to mapmakers and settlers in that era. On this map, the enormous "Duck Isles" are southwest of Prince Edward County, where, in reality, no islands exist at all! The small Ducks Islands lie to the southeast of the "Bay of Quinty." Amherst Island was then called "Isle Tonte", while present-day Wolfe Island appeared as "Grande Isle." "Carleton I." retains that name, even though today it lies within the U. S. A. The site of Kingston has the inscription, "An old picketed Fort," while today's Fort Henry site is earmarked as "The proposed Fortification and Town" (using that older English grammar rule of capitalizing all nouns, even common ones). The 11 townships to the east of Kingston are described as being "Settled by Loyalists lately from the States of America and Emigrants from Scotland." Toronto is described on this early map as being "formerly an Indian Village, now abandoned." My, how times change!

By the 1830's, general maps of Upper Canada referred to present-day False Ducks Island and Timber Island as "The Drakes," while Main Duck Island and Yorkshire Island were called "The Ducks," a combination more appropriate to satisfying today's sensitive, new-age males and females. "Amherst I." and "Wolfe I." had already received their name changes, but Salmon Point was called "Wicked Point," for good reason, and tiny Pigeon Island, a major threat to navigation, was boldly named on maps. By the late 1800's, the only cartographical bird named in that locale was "Duck Island," referring to today's Main Duck Island, while Point Petre replaced "Wicked Pt." (today's Salmon Point) as the main landmark and/or major potential hazard to navigation in that area worthy of inclusion on the Rand McNally & Co. map of the province. Pigeon Island was no longer specifically named on general maps of Ontario by the late 1800's, but its deadly presence was duly indicated.

In the eastern Lake Ontario region at old Fort Frontenac, these new settlers from the American colonies renamed their community "Kingston" in honour of Britain's King George III. Their skills quickly tamed this wild frontier.[6] Bills recently introduced in Canada's Parliament would allow descendents of these Loyalists to sue individuals or businesses in the United States that have been using their ancestors' confiscated properties.[7]

The Provincial Marine naval vessels, *Duke of Kent* and the brig, *Earl of Moira,* slid down the launchramps at Kingston on May 28, 1805, as a prelude to further tension between Great Britain (Canada) and the United States. The Americans built the brig, *Oneida,* 40 miles (60 kilometres) away at Oswego in 1808. In 1809, the Provincial Marine launched the *Royal George* at Kingston; the Americans built one of the largest merchant ships on Lake Ontario in 1810 at Oswego, the *Charles and Ann.*[8] The potential arms race was in full swing!

This race for Great Lakes sea strength erupted heatedly with the declaration of war between Great Britain and the United States on June 18, 1812. Merchant ships were seized and converted to military vessels; the Kingston dockyard furiously engaged Sackets Harbor, New York, in a shipbuilding race, both sides producing ocean-calibre vessels. These new behemoths were rendered impotent two years later when the War of 1812 ended with the signing of the Treaty of Ghent on December 24, 1814.[9] Naval armaments limitations began in 1817.[10]

The fort which had seen construction at Point Henry at Kingston during the War of 1812 to protect the dockyard was rebuilt on a larger scale in 1832-36 (this is the present Fort Henry which serves primarily as a public attraction). When that war ended, so did armed conflicts between Canada and the United States. Today both sides proudly point to the "longest undefended border in the world."[11]

Economic competition replaced wartime confrontations. Being only a generation removed from their physical dislocation from the United States, Kingston area Loyalist business interests pooled their resources in 1816 to build the first steamship on the Great Lakes.[12] It was no secret that they competed with business interests in Sackets Harbor, New York. The Kingston steamer, named (surprise! surprise!) the *Frontenac,* displacing 740 tons and measuring 150' (45 metres) in length, was launched at Ernesttown just west of Kingston on September 7, 1816.[13]

The entrepreneurs of Sackets Harbor launched the first American steam-powered vessel on the Great Lakes in early 1817,[14] and they named it (surprise! surprise!) the *Ontario.* This smaller vessel, of 240 tons and a length of 110' (33 metres), was also not as fast or as well-equipped as her Canadian rival, the *Frontenac,* which was soon nicknamed the "Palace Steamer."[15]

Both trendsetting vessels, which spawned many offspring in both countries, ran locally for years, but became obsolete and were dismantled by 1832.[16]

The new invention, a steam-powered ship named the Frontenac, *received much promotion and business from the Kingston area where she was built and launched in 1816.* MARINE MUSEUM OF THE GREAT LAKES, KINGSTON, COLLECTION.

In 1842, Kingston launched the very first iron ship on the Great Lakes, a 150-ton vessel named the *Mohawk,* a sidewheel steam gunboat of the Royal Navy. This 99' (30-metre) vessel, converted to a bark, reportedly foundered with the loss of all hands in Lake Huron off Port Aux Barques, Michigan, in 1868.[17] Forty years after the *Mohawk's* launch, a much larger iron-hulled ship, built at Cleveland in 1882 and named the *Onoko,* was enthusiastically received as the first iron ship on the Great Lakes. She sank in Lake Superior in 1915.[18]

Aerial view of Kingston and a small portion of its harbour. This entire scene is surprisingly quiet in terms of dockside or vehicular activity. If the picture were taken from an aeroplane, it could be circa 1920; if, as a colleague suggested, it were taken from the topmast of a passing ship, then it could have been taken much earlier, but it would have been a pretty tall topmast by comparison to the masts in the foreground! MARINE MUSEUM OF THE GREAT LAKES, KINGSTON, 982.19.282.

Kingston shipyards launched numerous vessels over the years; most prolific was the Calvin family's shipbuilding interest at Garden Island, located about two miles (three kilometres) off Kingston's harbour. Between 1839 and 1903, they constructed 62 vessels running to 225' (67.5 metres) in length, and including such Kingston area shipwrecks as the tug, *Frontenac,* and the steamer, *Simla.*[19] Nearby Belleville, Deseronto (Mill Point), Napanee, Picton (Hallowell), Port Milford, and Cherry Valley also built commercial vessels.

The awareness by local residents in the Kingston-Belleville-Picton area of maritime influences in their daily lives prompted some aspiring literary types, particularly in the bleak months of late fall and winter, to wax poetic. The realization that water travel posed a potential for calamity is reflected in this ode to the simple lifeboat, which appeared in an early, local newspaper:

THE LIFE BOAT

by Miss Agnes Strikeland

The life-boat! The life-boat! when tempests are dark,
She's the beacon of hope to the foundering bark,

When, midst the wild roar of the hurricane's sweep,
The minute-guns boom like a knell on the deep.

The life-boat! the life-boat! the whirlwind and rain,
And white-crested breakers, oppose her in vain;
Her crew are resolved, and her timbers are staunch,
She's a vessel of mercy...God speed to her launch.

The life-boat! the life-boat! how fearless and free
She wins her bold course o'er the wide rolling sea!
She bounds o'er the surges with gallant disdain,
She has stemm'd them before, and she'll stem them again!

The life-boat! the life-boat! she's manned by the brave,
In the noblest of causes commissioned to save;
What heart but has thrilled in the seaman's distress,
At the life-boat's endeavors, the life-boat's success!

The life-boat, the life-boat! no vessel that sails,
Has stemm'd such rough billows, and weathered such gales;
Not e'en Nelson's proud ship, when his death strife was won,
Such true glory achieved as the life-boat has done![20]

The east side of modern, downtown Kingston still yields a view of 19th-century, gray limestone buildings which were constructed near the waterfront at the height of the city's marine participation. The construction of the railroads eventually overshadowed Kingston's significant role as a maritime centre. PHOTO BY CRIS KOHL.

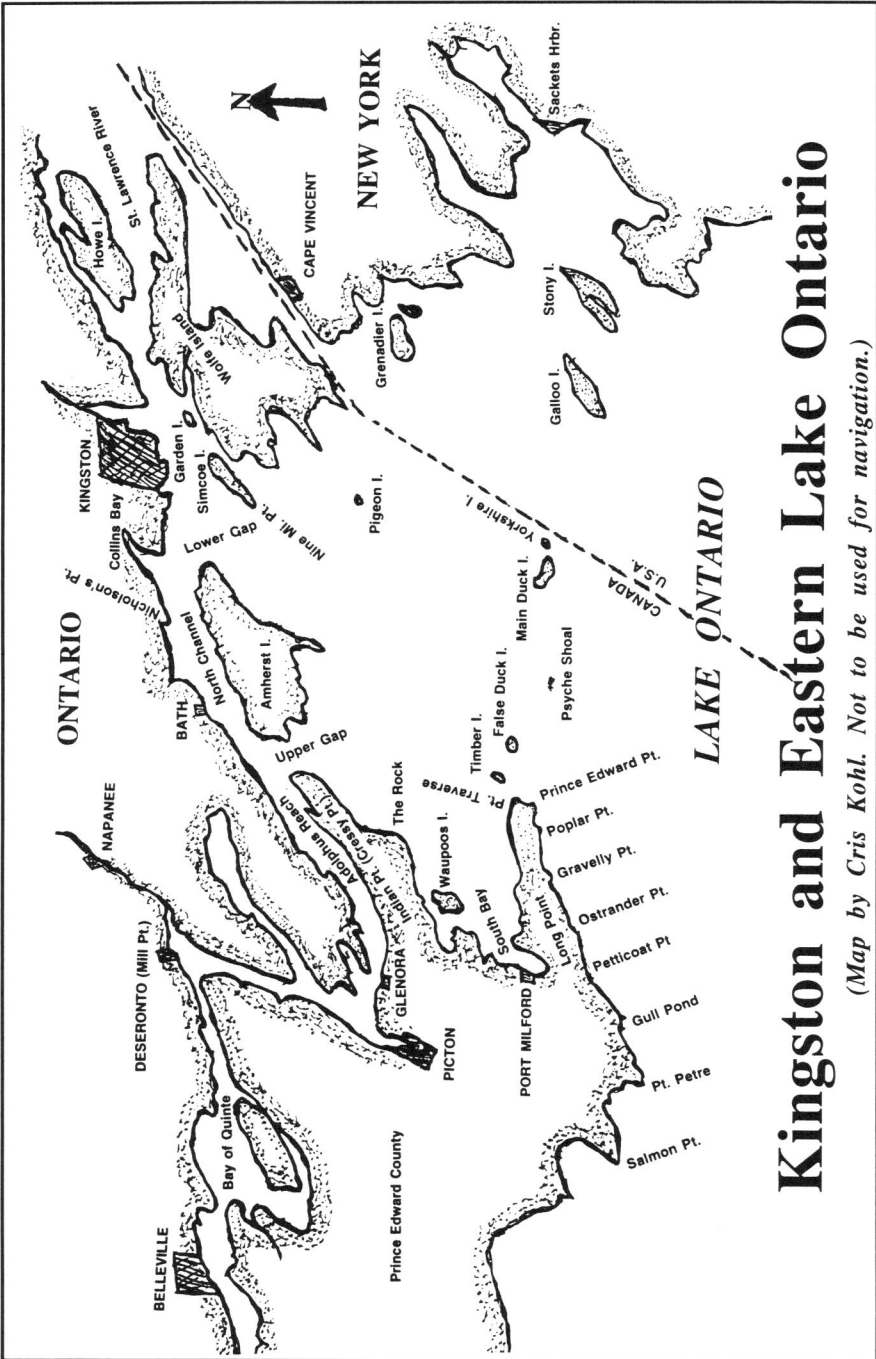

Kingston and Eastern Lake Ontario

(Map by Cris Kohl. Not to be used for navigation.)

Safety of passengers and crew has always been the number one priority of any responsible vessel that ventured forth to sea. Besides ensuring that the vessel remained safe and sturdy, the availabity of succor, should disaster strike, was a consolation for which many seafarers kept their fingers crossed. Some took it a step further, and wrote to the proper authorities to establish whatever could humanly be done to safeguard the loss of life and property on the Great Lakes. In both the United States and Canada, particularly in the former, the inception of local, land-based lifesaving stations in areas dangerous to navigation emerged. Sometimes local opinion on marine safety matters were publicly aired in the press:

Cause of Disasters.

Ottawa, Nov. 8.---Letters have been received by the Department of Marine and Fisheries, from lake ports, pointing out the cause of steamboat disasters, which are in brief: Overloading; a bad system of loading; light freight sometimes being placed in the hold, and cattle and heavy freight above; the employment of inexperienced lads as sailors and the faulty construction of propellors. One of the writers, who has had experience on the lakes, expresses his readiness to give his testimony on these points at any time.[21]

At a time when steam was quickly replacing wind as the propulsion method of most Great Lakes vessels, government evaluation of marine calamities and the education of the public and the operators hoped to reduce accidents, as this local newspaper item from 1882 indicates. Captain John Donnelly was the head of the family that was then already becoming the most famous and respected "wreckers" (shipwreck salvagers) in the Kingston area. He praised the American system of lifesaving stations, which had been in operation on the Great Lakes since 1876:

LIFE SAVING STATIONS

Recommendations Made to the Minister of Marine and Fisheries --- Suggestions of Capt. John Donnelly

Repeatedly the necessity of life saving stations has been pointed out, up to this time without result. We are encouraged to make one more effort to secure protection for our vesselmen and their property, remembering that we have succeeded in other agitations and that there may be virtue in an oft-told tale. About two years ago, during the session of Parliament, Captain John Donnelly, then in the service of Messrs. Calvin & Breck, chanced to be in Ottawa, and he had occasion to discuss with the Hon. J. H. Pape, Minister of Marine and Fisheries,.... The veteran wrecker then took the opportunity to state the great need there was of life saving stations along the Prince Edward County coast, the most dangerous perhaps upon the chain of lakes. Captain J. Donnelly's opinions were considered of some value, and his recommendations were endorsed....It was represented that three stations, fully equipped, were absolutely required --- one at South Bay, one at Salmon Point, and one at Presque Isle. Had these been erected, as it was expected they would be, a score of lives would have been saved....

THE AMERICAN STATIONS.

The American Government has been accused of parsimony in connection with a service in which men exhibit heroism that is not surpassed upon the battlefield, and yet they granted last year $500,000 for the maintenance of life stations and have added to their number and efficiency to such an extent that the expenditure next year must be $750,000. On Lake Michigan alone some ten new stations are to be established and those on this lake [Ontario] and the river [St. Lawrence] greatly improved. There are three not far from Kingston, to the usefulness of which several vesselmen last evening bore testimony. These are at Oswego, Port Ontario and Sandy Creek, the whole within a distance of 30 miles. This season they have saved more Canadians than Americans, a circumstance which our Yankee cousins will not appreciate so highly when it has been so lately made apparent that there is not a reciprocity of favours on the part of this country. On the opening of navigation the Sandy Creek party took the crew off the schooner, Nellie Theresa, abandoning the vessel, but after a channel had been dredged outside of her, she was pulled off the beach by the Dominion Wrecking Company. On Thursday last the Oswego men came to the timely relief of the schooner Annie M. Foster, but on the same day, the schooner

Folger went to pieces in sight of land, the fishermen of Prince Edward viewing the catastrophe and proving unable to render the perishing crew assistance in the absence of

PROPER BOATS AND EQUIPPAGE.

The American crews as a rule number five; they live in comfortable houses, are always watchful, and are very prompt in coming to the aid of vessels in distress. When not otherwise engaged, they are drilling and have become so expert in the use of the mortar that they can throw a line a great distance and with remarkable precision. Their boats are flat-bottomed, and so constructed that they can be hauled safely and with great facility upon the shore, and ride the surf as the metallic boats will not....

The Salmon Point Lighthouse, by Prince Edward County artist Marcel Blanchette. Capt. Donnelly, in 1882, stated that "At no time is it safe to sail within two miles of Salmon Point, and in a blow it is unsafe to get within three miles of it."[22] Salmon Point is a treacherous stretch of nightmarish real estate, from a navigator's point of view, and many vessels ended their careers on the rocks around this lighthouse. Mr. Blanchette, a talented artist capable of capturing that classic style of turn-of-the-century nautical artwork in pen and ink (see also his drawing of the Oliver Mowat-Key West *collision in chapter eight of this book), offers this and other examples of his wide range of artwork (he did an enormous, outdoor, historic mural in Picton!) for sale as prints. Contact him at Black River, Ontario K0K 2P0, telephone (613) 476-6585.*

NOT PROPERLY LIGHTED

Mariners have another complaint to make
--- that there is insufficient light on Salmon
Point. The little, red light is visible 7 miles
distant on a bright night, but totally
invisible during a storm. There is neither
signal gun nor bell, and the vessels in the
blackness rush upon the shoals and are lost.
A signal gun should be placed on Salmon
Point and fired every hour during the stormy
weather. A better light should be provided.
Even the wreckers dread doing any work
along the Prince Edward coast, as there are
no harbors where safety can be had in the
event of a blow....[23]

*The Point Traverse Life Saving Station operated from April 20, 1883 (the year after
Captain John Donnelly so vigorously agitated for the establishment of these units on
the Canadian side of Lake Ontario) until 1900, when it was moved west to
Wellington. This lifeboat, which was built in Buffalo, New York, hung in a swing of
tackles in a shed just to the west of the Life Saving Station directly at Point Traverse.
In an emergency, the lifeboat was winched down onto the horsedrawn wagon, the men
clambered aboard, and rode the bumpy way to the nearest access point to the vessel in
distress. The man standing is Life Saving Station Captain Leroy Spafford.[24] Before
and after this Station existed, commercial fishermen in the area often risked their
lives to save the victims of wrecked vessels. AUTHOR'S COLLECTION.*

One sombre, yet romantic, vision of the shipwrecked sailor has traditionally
been of the desperate, last-minute attempt to cram a message into a bottle: some
words hastily scribbled onto any available scrap of paper, stuffed into the glass,
the neck sealed tightly with a cork, and this last, pitiful attempt at
communication with the outside world thrown into the pounding waves as the
ship was breaking to pieces. Presuming the message was found and relayed, it

was hoped the relatives and friends of the deceased would find some consolation in knowing about the victim's final moments. Kingston area shipwrecks had a smattering of bottled messages, whether real or spurious. The following account appeared in the Kingston *British Whig* newspaper on May 19, 1880:

Is it a Hoax!

The following letter, enclosed in a small bottle, was picked up today on the shore of a bay at the head of Lake Ontario:

"April 15---Lake Ontario schr. 'Fire Fly' of Kingston, mast gone and sinking. Crew mostly all lost. Poor hopes of rest. Only two survivors now. Yawl broken. No chance of escape. If any person should find this bottle, please write my friends and oblige.

Yours respectfully,
(signed) Thos. Brown,
Captain.
Address Mrs. T. Brown at Kingston."

The above note bears no mark of the year in which it was written. The original can be had by addressing Agent, Montreal Telegraph Company, Jordan station.

Two days later, after the local reporter had had an opportunity to ask sailors some questions, the following brief item appeared in the same newspaper:

Mariners here know nothing of a vessel named 'Fire Fly,' said to have foundered on the lake. Mr. Thomas Brown referred to in the message found in the floating bottle as one of the crew is also unknown. Some one has been perpetrating what he evidently considered a joke.

Likely not a joke was the message found in a bottle several months after the local schooner, *Picton,* sank in about 200' (60 metres) of eastern Lake Ontario with no survivors during a storm on June 29, 1900:

Have lashed Vessy to me with heaving line so will be found together.
J. Sidley, Picton

Jack Sidley was the owner and captain of the doomed vessel, *Picton,* and Vessy was his 12-year-old son who had accompanied his father on this voyage because the ship was shorthanded.[25] The father, abandoning hope for survival, at least found solace in the likelihood that his and his son's bodies would be located together. However, cadavers that descend to a depth of 200' (60 metres) in the cold waters of Lake Ontario will likely never rise "before the Resurrection." These bodies were never found. Future underwater explorers might locate the skeletal remains, bound together by thick, rotting ship's rope, of a father-and-son team that was able to sadly share a dramatic portion of their final moments of life with the rest of the world by means of a message in a bottle.

At Consecon, Ontario, near Picton, a bottle with a message inside was picked up along the shore on December 21, 1902. It read:

> **August 28th, 1902. Seven miles off the south shore of Lake Ontario about 5:45 p.m. Witnessing a severe gale; mast broke; rudder gone.**
> **(Signed) Wesley Hutchinson, John Sandon, Toronto**[26]

The other side of the note was signed by "George Hyams," who apparently was also on board. No commercial vessel reported having any difficulties on Lake Ontario at that time. The likelihood of three fellows, out for a summer sail in a small, perhaps 20' (6-metre) long sailboat, encountering storm conditions and damage such as those described, is certainly possible. However, local papers did not report anything further about the authenticity of the note or details of any story behind it, so it is hoped that, during some time between August 28th and December 21st, 1902, these three men solved their difficulties and made it safely back to shore.

"Wrecking" was a legitimate and honourable profession around the Great Lakes and elsewhere in the world in the 1800's and early 1900's. Attempts to carry on that antique calling in the 1980's and 1990's have resulted in some spectacular wrangling and ugly complications, legal and otherwise.

The most famous "wrecker," or salvager of wrecked ships, in the Kingston area, as mentioned earlier, was a man named Captain John Donnelly, who ran his own company. In 1880, the media, always ready to dramatically report to the public on individuals who did not conform to lives of quiet desperation, found this man to be a colourful figure in an otherwise drab world. As they put it, "Captain Donnelly is the best wrecker in the Dominion [of Canada]. If he cannot succeed in saving a vessel, it is about useless for any other person to try it."[27]

Thirty-eight years later, his son and namesake, Captain John Donnelly, received similar hero-worship treatment by making front-page news in Kingston, this time with a published photograph, a part of newspaper technology developed since his father's time. His salvaging of 19 vessels in the year 1918, as well as how the vocation of wrecking had changed recently, was described:

The Donnelly Salvage and Wrecking Company Have Successfully Floated Nineteen Vessels on Lake and River.

...The work in marine salvage on Lake Ontario and the St. Lawrence river between Port Dalhousie and Montreal has changed greatly in the last decade. Formerly the majority of the accidents were to the old-time sailing vessels that plied Lake Ontario, either in the barley or timber trade from Canadian to American ports, or the wheat trade from Chicago to Kingston, or the square timber trade from the upper lake ports to Garden Island, where the cargoes were unloaded, made up into rafts, and floated down the St. Lawrence river and rapids to Quebec, where they were reloaded and sent to the European markets. Most all of this trade is a thing of the past.

In the fall of the year, snow storms caused great destruction to the grain fleet by stranding. Fully ten sailing vessels have been stranded in one snow storm, on the south side of Amherst Island, by one vessel following the lights of the vessel ahead, the master saying to his crew, "Well, I cannot see where we are going, but I guess the master of that vessel can," and then came to grief.

The modern steel freighters that run over the same course all season can time the distance run so exactly that many of them see no land marks until they are close into the harbors.

When the sailing vessels went ashore on Lake Ontario laden with grain, very little thought was given of salvaging the cargo. Steam pumps were placed on board and the cargo was pumped overboard until the boat was lightened enough to be pulled off by a wrecking tug. Now a lighter with a clamshell outfit is placed alongside the wreck and about two tons of wet grain a minute is hoisted out and put in the lighter. The grain is reconditioned by drying, and used for feed purposes.

The work requiring the greatest wrecking skill years ago was the salvaging of the passenger steamers of the Richelieu and Ontario Navigation Company after they had grounded in the rapids. In some cases the hull was so badly damaged that the boat was not worth saving, and after the wreckers had removed the machinery out of the wreck, pontoons were built on board the boat and put down in the hold, chained in position, and pumped out, which gave buoyancy enough to float the wreck out of the channel. The placing of wooden sheeting over the iron plating of the bottom of these steamers reduced the number of accidents very greatly.

The Donnelly Salvage and Wrecking Company of Kingston has been connected with this work for the past fifty years without failure. The late Capt. John Donnelly, father of the present head of this company, was master wrecker and partner of Calvin & Breck, of Garden Island, in their salvage work from the early fifties up till 1888, when the Donnelly Salvaging and Wrecking Company was incorporated.

The salvaging of the steamer Rosedale by this company, when she went ashore on Charity Shoal, Lake Ontario, late in November, twenty-one years ago, in three days after the failure of the underwriters to release her, was one of the best pieces of salvage work done in this vicinity up to this time....

For the past few years the master mind of the Donnelly Wrecking Company has been John Donnelly, one of the leading marine men of Canada, who also holds the Queen's University degree of mining engineer. He has had great success in all his marine ventures, and the list given above shows that he has had a busy season.[28]

Years ago, there was more to be salvaged from these waters than shipwrecks! Logging was a major industry in this locale many years ago, and the recovery of sunken logs, well-preserved even after many years of immersion, has been an active moneymaker for a number of commercial divers, particularly since the end of World War II. A few ambitious loggers in the Bay of Quinte area thought of this career potential as early as 1911:

Sunken Logs

On the shore of Lake Ontario, in the Bay of Quinte, the most peculiar lumbering operations in the country are now in progress.

Hundreds of logs of oak and black walnut, many of them 50 or more feet long, are being brought up from the bottom of the bay with grappling hooks operated by powerful engines and hoisting apparatus stationed on barges.

Some of the logs have been submerged over twenty-five years, but when brought to the surface are found to be in as perfect a state of preservation as the day they went to the bottom.

Forty years ago, the shores of the Bay of Quinte were lined with great primeval forests of pine, oak and black walnut. The pine first attracted the lumbermen and was the timber really sought for, but every tree went down before the woodman's axe during the winter months.

In the ten or fifteen years required to denude the country of its forests, the bottom of the bay and the adjacent coves became carpeted with logs that today are worth a high price.

It was not until this summer that plans were devised for raising the sunken logs. Divers were sent down to see if there were a sufficient number to make hoisting operations profitable. The reports brought up were so favorable that scows were equipped with the necessary machinery and the hoisting work is now in full swing.

Some days a scow or barge and its crew will bring up hundreds of dollars worth of logs and on two different days, the returns reached the $1,000 mark.

An investigation is now being made in several other rivers along the banks of which lumbering operations were conducted on a large scale years ago.[29]

Speaking of divers, hardhat divers existed in the Kingston area for quite a while before the advent of scuba diving in the 1940's, and, like today's self-contained adventurers, surface-supplied underwater explorers in the 1920's were willing to experiment with different gasses. This article, which appeared in the Belleville *Daily Intelligencer* on November 20, 1926, describes hardhat divers in the U.S.A. relating to something trimix scuba divers of today, over 70 years later, are quite familiar with:

DIVERS USE HELIUM
INSTEAD OF NITROGEN
IN THEIR OPERATIONS

Washington, D.C., Nov. 20---Helium, that rare gas which floats airships, is now being put to the novel use of aiding deep sea divers in their struggles at ocean bottoms.

Experiments by the bureau of mines
indicate that helium's utility will be as great
in the depths as it is in the heights, and
considerably more work-a-day in practical
value. With its assistance, new low levels
may be attained safely by the salvage worker
under water.

Divers who work with the usual equipment
suffer from what is known as "the bends"
when their stay and exertions under water are
prolonged. The cause of this sometimes fatal
ailment is the absorption by the diver's
tissue of nitrogen which causes bubbles in
the arteries. Helium, like nitrogen, is so
inert and transferable that it may be mixed
with oxygen, forming a synthetic
atmosphere compressible for supply to
divers and very nearly free of the tendency to
produce the internal bubbles for which
nitrogen is responsible. Many long
experiments were made by the miners' bureau
with animals and then the bureau's apparatus
invented for the divers was turned over to the
navy. Its first extensive utility was proven
in the raising of the submarine S-51 which
was sunk near Newport, Rhode Island.

However, using ordinary hardhat diving equipment, even at a relatively
shallow depth, proved fatal to a local man on one occasion in 1937. The
underwater world has not always proven to be a friendly place for visitors:

YOUTH DIES IN
A DIVING SUIT

T. H. Bickie of Toronto
Loses His Life at Gananoque

GANANOQUE, July 6---Thomas H. Bickie,
son of E.W. Bickie, prominent Toronto
stockbroker, died by asphyxiation at the
bottom of the St. Lawrence River near here
yesterday.

The tragedy occurred after the young
University of Toronto student had donned a
diving suit and gone down to the river
bottom in search of a lost outboard motor.

Bickie, together with three other young
men, was a guest of Col. Gerald Birks,

O.B.E. [Order of the British Empire], **Montreal, on board his large cruiser "Nomad."** Shortly before noon Monday the party was hailed by Thomas, Arthur and Leonard Goulett, of Syracuse, N.Y., who had lost the outboard motor from their boat near Jack Straw Lake, three miles from Gananoque.

Experienced Diver

An expert swimmer and experienced in diving, young Bickie offered to try and reclaim the lost motor for the United States trio who, for several seasons, have been summer visitors here. Diving equipment carried aboard the Nomad was donned by Bickie and he descended in 28 feet of water. When, after ten minutes, however, he had failed to signal other members of the party by pulling ropes attached to the diving helmet, alarm was felt for his safety.

The Goulett brothers dived down to see if Bickie was in trouble. Sensing something wrong, the signal was given and the young Toronto man immediately was brought to the surface.

Medical aid was obtained from Dr. Godfrey Bird and his father, Dr. C. H. Bird, both of Gananoque, who happened to be in a near-by boat at the time. The two doctors worked for more than an hour and a half at the waterfront in an unsuccessful attempt to revive the youth.[30]

Another topic guaranteed to make normal people wary of visiting the underwater realm is "sea serpents." Mythical creatures have frightened human beings throughout history, particularly if these terrifying creatures lived in the unknown depths of the environmentally-foreign underwater world.

If, however, you have turned green with envy at every mention of Scotland's Loch Ness monster, or of any of a variety of other aquatic creatures of unknown but dinosaur-like vintage, such as those sighted in Lake Champlain and in an Okanogan Valley lake in British Columbia, then read this next item from 1931 and be glad, for the Kingston area has its own unidentified sea monster!:

Main Ducks Reports Latest
Sea Serpent

According to the story told by one of the fishermen employed by Claude W. Cole, there is a sea serpent about three miles west of the Main Ducks.

The fisherman states that he was able to get but a fleeting glimpse of the sea serpent, or whatever it is, but to the best of his ability he describes it as having a length of about forty feet [12 metres], and a diameter of about a foot and a half [0.5 metre] in the largest part of its body. Its head seemed to be a cross between that of an angora goat with orchid colored whiskers, and a little nock clam. The body was shaped like that of a silk worm but was writhing and contorted as it dashed madly across the lake.

Just back of the monster's long goat-like ears, were two short arms sticking up into the air, the hands convulsively clutching at air.

The body of the serpent had large brilliant spots about the size of the one on any Japanese flag. The spots seemed to be of different colors and the main color of the creature was a good average between green and orange. From the upper jaw protruded two tusks of about half a foot [0.15 metre] in length, indicating that the owner might have ancestors among the walrus family.

One of the men in Captain Hinchley's dredging outfit also claims to have got a glimpse of the sea serpent.[31]

*   *   *   *   *   *   *   *

The Kingston area in eastern Lake Ontario has had active, colourful, and sometimes imaginative marine events in its relatively short history. More recent times have seen a winding down of some nautical activities, while others are actively on the rise.

The retirement in 1950 of the passenger vessel, *Kingston,* terminated 110 years of continuous service, started by the Royal Mail Line in 1840, between harbours on Lake Ontario and the St. Lawrence River. In 1968, the last shipyard in Kingston, which had begun operations in 1893, was officially closed,[32] ending another era in Kingston's colourful maritime history.

At about that time, our present epoch of marine archaeology and underwater exploration of the Kingston area commenced. The skeletal frames of old French vessels, long buried along the waterfront at Kingston, were excavated in 1953.[33] Scuba (short for "Self-Contained Underwater Breathing Apparatus"), invented during World War II, was becoming popular in sporadic areas of the Great Lakes, slowly but surely winning more adherents with each passing year. Important shipwreck discoveries in this area excited the public since the early 1960's, as subsequent chapters in this book will relate. Non-shipwreck, yet quite historic, underwater disclosures have been reported, such as that by the two scuba divers who, in late 1985, while doing routine maintenance on the 139-year-old walls of the Martello tower, located fifteen 32-pound (14.5-kilogram) cannonballs in Kingston's Confederation Basin. Parks Canada planned to "refurbish" these items for display at historic sites across the country.[34]

A new era in Kingston's marine heritage is here. Enjoy it.

---

[1]Richard Palmer. "Great Lakes Time Line, Lake Ontario." *Inland Seas,* Vol. 41, No. 4. Winter, 1985: 295.

[2]Cris Kohl, *Dive Ontario! The Guide to Shipwrecks and Scuba Diving,* Chatham, Ontario: self-published, 1990, rev. ed. 1995: 45.

[3]Palmer, op. cit.

[4]Cris Kohl, *Dive Ontario Two! More Ontario Shipwreck Stories,* Chatham, Ontario: self-published, 1994: 229-232.

[5]Palmer, op. cit.

[6]Many Loyalists were shipwrights, carpenters, blacksmiths, soapmakers, homemakers, child-raisers, farmers, and brewers (Anna Young, in her book, *Great Lakes Saga,* commented that "The Loyalists evidently brought their thirst for beer with them," because one of them set up the first brewery in Upper Canada at Ernesttown which, for many years, was the only tavern between Kingston and Toronto, then called York.)

[7]*Toronto Star,* October 23, 1996.

[8]Palmer, op. cit., 296.

[9]Bernard Grun, *The Timetables of History,* New York: Simon & Schuster/Touchstone, 1975 (third revised edition): 382.

[10]The Rush-Bagot Treaty, signed on April 28, 1817, limited each side's fleet to four vessels of not more than 100 tons each: one vessel each on Lake Champlain and Lake Ontario, and two vessels for the entire upper Great Lakes. Modifications have been made by mutual consent, particularly during the years of World War II, for the two countries to permit construction of larger vessels and allow naval training on the Great Lakes.

[11]Amiable politics have not eliminated nationalistic competitions, which readily surface when Canada wins the World Series in baseball, as it did in 1991 and 1992, or when the United States wins the World Hockey competition, as it did in 1996. Generally, however, Canada and the United States are among the strongest allies anywhere on this planet.

[12]The first steamship to travel on the fresh waters of the Lakes was the small, 40-ton, 85' (25.5-metre) long *Accommodation,* built at Montreal by John Molson, of brewery fame, in 1809. This vessel travelled between Montreal and Québec City, and was a financial setback to Mr. Molson, who was, however, determined to enter that business. In 1812, he built his second ship, the *Swiftsure,* whose engines came from England.

[13]Eric Heyl, *Early American Steamers, Vol. II,* Buffalo, New York: self-published, 1956: 89.

[14]Ibid., 181. The vast discrepancies between the "launching dates" and the "maiden voyage dates" compel the author to believe that both sides launched virtually bare hulls into the waters

(in their race to claim "first launching"), and then spent many months finishing the ship's construction! The important point here is that the competition was intense; which side was actually first is moot, akin to the 'large end-small end' of the egg opening argument.

[15]Ibid., 89. The steamer, *Ontario,* was named after the lake, not the present-day province which, at that time, was called "Upper Canada." Lake Ontario, the smallest (in surface area) and most eastern of the Great Lakes, is mutually-shared, with slightly more than half lying within Canadian boundaries. The word, "Ontario," is Iroquoian, meaning either "beautiful lake" or "rocks standing by the water," a possible reference to Niagara Falls.

[16]Ibid., 89, 181.

[17]J. B. Mansfield, ed., *History of the Great Lakes, Vol. I,* Chicago, J.H. Beers & Co., 1899, reprint ed., Cleveland: Freshwater Press, 1972: 862. Also mentioned in David Swayze's *Shipwreck!,* Boyne City, Michigan, Harbor House Publishers, 1992: 157.

[18]Ibid. (Swayze), 177.

[19]Donald Swainson, *A Shipping Empire, Garden Island,* Kingston, Marine Museum of the Great Lakes at Kingston, 1984: centrefold (pages not numbered.)

[20]*Hallowell Free Press,* December 16, 1833.

[21]*British Whig* (Kingston), November 8, 1882.

[22]Ibid., December 6, 1882.

[23]Ibid.

[24]Willis Metcalfe, *Canvas & Steam on Quinte Waters,* South Bay, Ontario, The South Marysburgh Marine Society, 1979: 152-153.

[25]Ibid., 107-108.

[26]*British Whig* (Kingston), December 22, 1902.

[27]Ibid., September 30, 1880.

[28]Ibid., December 9, 1918.

[29]*Daily British Whig* (Kingston), October 14, 1911.

[30]*Whig-Standard* (Kingston), July 6, 1937.

[31]*Picton Times,* July 30, 1931.

[32]Palmer, op. cit., 299.

[33]Dwight Boyer, *Great Stories of the Great Lakes,* New York, Dodd, Mead & Co., 1966: 228.

[34]*London* (Ontario) *Free Press,* November 29, 1985.

Chapter Two
The Early Losses (Pre-1870)

LE BLANC HENRI (1764?)

Had as much been documented as there has been gossiped about this French shipwreck, writing its story would require enormous work!

Certainly French vessels in the 18th century left proof that they sailed Lake Ontario; at least one distinctly French anchor has been found in the waters off Main Duck Island. However, no shipwreck has been located with it.

Available information on *Le Blanc Henri* is limited, secondary, hearsay-ish, and undocumented. No such vessel is mentioned in Mansfield's two-volume, 1899 *History of the Great Lakes.* Marine historian, Willis Metcalfe, wrote simply that this French vessel "is said to have been lost on a spit on Wolfe Island, near Kingston, with $100,000 in gold and silver bullion and specie."[35] He gave no date of the sinking. One sensationalistic publication from the early 1980's, objectively stated that, "The French frigate, *Le Blanc Henri,* foundered in a violent storm off Wolfe Island near Kingston, Ontario, on June 17, 1764. Numerous reports of $100,000 to $500,000 in gold coins and bullion in ship's strongbox."[36] With the passage of time and many repetitions of the tale, the value of the sunken treasure increases faster than a Canadian bank's profits!

One respected authority at the Marine Museum of the Great Lakes at Kingston emphatically stated that there was never such a ship. Unless primary documentation surfaces, the existence of this vessel will remain spurious.

PSYCHE (1814; abandoned 1830's)

This 32-gun, War of 1812 frigate, the frames of which were constructed at Britain's Chatham Dock Yard and transported in pieces to Kingston to establish British naval supremacy on the Great Lakes, was launched on Christmas Day, 1814.[37] Her length of keel was 121.1' (36.6 metres), and tonnage, 769.[38] The *Psyche,* however, arrived too late to participate in the war. The Treaty of Ghent had been signed on December 24, 1814, the day before the ship's launch.

After serving as short-distance convoy to British troops returning home, the *Psyche* returned to Kingston to be laid up, but began to decay within two years due to inferior fir construction and a hull planked with green wood. Unsold at auction, the ship was abandoned at the head of Deadman Bay. Reportedly, diver Eric Sharp of Ottawa identified the shipwreck remains in 12' (3.6 metres) in the early 1980's,[39] and Preserve Our Wrecks surveyed them in 1989.[40]

PRINCE REGENT   (1814; abandoned 1830's)

The British, two-decked, naval frigate, *Prince Regent,* was one of several vessels constructed by Sir James Yeo at Kingston to compete with another powerful fleet being built by American shipbuilders in New York state for supremacy over the lower Great Lakes.

Launched on April 14, 1814,[41] the *Prince Regent* sported 60 guns balanced throughout her keel length of 160'9" (48.2 metres) and beam of 43' (13 metres). Her draft measured 16'4" (5 metres). The *Prince Regent's* rounded, blunt bow consisted of a curved decoration, but minus an actual figurehead; the ship's rail was ornately carved to resemble a cable,[42] probably more for decoration than for utilitarian purposes.

For his attack on Fort Oswego on May 4, 1814, three weeks after his new vessel as launched, Yeo proudly made the *Prince Regent* his flagship. The entire invading fleet consisted of seven ships and eleven gunboats, and they succeeded in capturing the American fort. By the end of that year, however, both British and American forces were tired of fighting, and peace returned. Defeats and losses on both sides were about equally balanced, and the subsequent treaty restored the international boundary to exactly what it had been before the War of 1812.[43]

At war's end, the *Prince Regent* was kept in reserve with numerous other vessels at Kingston, finally sinking at Navy Bay after several years of inactivity. Raised and towed to Deadman Bay, the ship again sank, this time permanently.

Located in about 20 to 25 feet (6 to 7.5 metres) of water about 300 feet (90 metres) from the shore opposite Cartright Point, only the keel and ribs remain of this large warship. In the late 1980's, the marine conservation group named Preserve Our Wrecks measured, numbered, tagged, videotaped, and photographed these shipwreck remains.

H.M.S. Prince Regent, *left, attacking Fort Oswego.* PUBLIC ARCHIVES OF CANADA.

ST. LAWRENCE   (1814; abandoned 1830's)

The *St. Lawrence* was reputedly the mightiest sailing war vessel ever to sail the Great Lakes. Constructed at Kingston for use in the War of 1812, this vessel ironically took most of the war to construct. When she finally set sail across Lake Ontario to Niagara, no enemy ship was even sighted, let alone confronted!

The *St. Lawrence* was launched on September 10, 1814,[44] and, on October 15th, with Sir James Yeo (the man responsible for the fanatical British shipbuilding on Lake Ontario during this war) on board, sailed out into the lake with a small flotilla accompaniment, and, "for the remainder of the season, Sir James was Lord of the Lakes."[45] The mere presence of this massive vessel secured British control of the lake and hastened the call for a peace treaty.

With a length on keel of 171'6" (51.3 metres), a length on deck of 194' (58.2 metres), a beam of 52'5" (15.8 metres), a draft of 11'6" (3.5 metres), and a displacement of 2,304 tons, the mighty *St. Lawrence* was capable of carrying 112 cannon and nearly 1,000 men. [46] Although the vessel never faced a human enemy, she came close to destruction during her first voyage on Lake Ontario. Lightning violently struck one of this leviathan's tall masts, killing seven men and wounding 22 more, narrowly missing the cache of gunpowder on board.[47]

The *St. Lawrence* was stripped of her armament and masts, and towed to Morton's distillery, where her collapsed remains lie to this day in five to ten feet (1.5 to 3 metres) of water. This shipwreck is marked on Canadian Hydrographic Service chart #1459 as lying just east of the Kingston Penitentiary, at the foot of Morton Street. These remains were surveyed by P.O.W. in the late 1980's.

The largest sailing vessel of war ever to sail the Great Lakes, the St. Lawrence, *depicted in this C.H.J. Snider watercolour, ironically arrived too late to participate in the War of 1812 for which it was constructed.* METROPOLITAN TORONTO LIBRARY.

CAROLINE   (December 2, 1832)

The schooner, *Caroline,* loaded with drygoods, bound from Kingston to Ogdensburg, and mastered by Captain Tyler, succumbed to a frightening gale on December 2, 1832. One crewmember drowned during this late season storm on Lake Ontario. The captain and the remainder of the crew took to the yawlboat and succeeded in reaching the safety of Main Duck Island, from which they were removed by a passing vessel the next day.[48]

The *Caroline* had been launched at Kingston in 1825.[49]

BYTOWN   (October, 1837)

The paddlewheeler, *Bytown,* served the area between Ottawa and Kingston for only two seasons after her launch at the latter location in May, 1836.[50]

The Ottawa & Rideau Canal Forwarding Company, proud of its small fleet of vessels (namely the *Bytown,* the *Rideau,* and the *Margaret),* received this promotional write-up in the local press:

> ...It is worthy of remark, that particular preparations have been made by the Company for the convenience and comfort of travellers, to whom that route [between Kingston and Ottawa] must present many attractions, passing as it does through a great extent of country hitherto little known, and replete with interest and curiosity....[51]

The *Bytown* unfortunately was wrecked in October, 1837, at Kingston.

QUEEN CHARLOTTE   (1838)

Using leftover lumber and materials originally intended for the construction of the first Great Lakes steamer, the *Frontenac,* shipbuilders at Ernesttown, Ontario, built a second hull, the steamer, *Queen Charlotte,* which was launched on April 22, 1818. This shallower draft vessel (of 150 tons displacement, with a length of 130', or 39 metres, a beam of 18', or 5.4 metres, and a draft of eight feet, or 2.4 metres), was able to navigate river portions inaccessible to the larger Frontenac.[52] After many years of service among the ports of Kingston, Brockville, Prescott, and other communities, the *Queen Charlotte* was taken to Cataraqui Bay near Kingston and broken up,[53] with only her old hull left in place.

NEW YORK   (September 15, 1839)

The schooner, *New York,* of Oswego, became incapacited in a late summer storm on September 15, 1839, just off Marysburgh, Upper Canada, near Long Point. Severe gales forced the foundering vessel aground just offshore in seven feet (2.1 metres) of water. Of her crew of six, only two were seen alive as the ship grounded, and they, too, perished when waves knocked their vessel upside down. The masts, yards, blocks, rigging, part of the cargo of staves, and two bodies lashed to the shrouds were brought ashore later by local residents.[54]

CATARAQUI (April, 1840)

The paddlewheeler, *Cataraqui,* burned to a complete loss at Kingston in April, 1840.[55]

NAPANEE (June, 1840)

The paddlewheeler, *Wolfe,* was launched at Kingston in 1835. Renamed *Napanee* in 1837, this vessel, measuring 80' (24 metres) in length and 13' (3.9 metres) in beam, succumbed to a conflagration at Kingston in June, 1840.[56]

COMMODORE BARRIE (May, 1842)

This 144' (43-metre) paddlewheeler, launched at Kingston in 1835, sank in a collision in May, 1842, near Kingston. Sadly, this popular vessel was plagued with many repairs, for example, this description only a year after her launch:

> The beautiful steamer, *Com. Barrie,* has undergone expensive repairs and improvements. The boilers, &c. are new, and it is expected that the speed of this boat will be greatly increased. She is to be under the command of Capt. Patterson, formerly of the schooner *Union,* of Port Hope, and the travelling public have a right to expect much from the well known urbanity of his character.[57]

This vessel's short career spanned only seven years.

OTTAWA (September, 1851)

The paddlewheeler, *Ottawa,* measuring 82' by 19' (24.6 by 5.7 metres) and built at Trois Rivieres, Quebec, in 1840, was wrecked in a collision near Kingston in September, 1851.[58]

OCEAN WAVE (April 30, 1853)

Built in Montreal in 1852 by E. D. Merritt for the brewery baron, John Molson, and launched on May 22 of that year, the 241-ton *Ocean Wave* measured 174'2" (52.2 metres) in length, 26' (7.8 metres) in beam, and 11'6" (3.5 metres) in draft. The *Ocean Wave* joined six other steamers which ran the port-dotted route between Montreal, Quebec, and Hamilton, Ontario.[59]

Travelling between Hamilton, Ontario, and Ogdensburg, New York, on the evening of April 29, 1853, this fine (she had been completely reconditioned very recently), upper-cabin sidewheeler transported 26 passengers, a crew of 31, and a cargo of 1,500 barrels of flour, 200 kegs of butter, 80 barrels of ham and pork, 64 barrels of pearl ash, and miscellaneous freight.[60] Most of the human component on board, including Captain A. Wright of Prescott, Ontario, retired to bed early that night, and thus were startled from their sleep at 2:00 A.M. Fire had broken out, apparently having started from smokestack sparks which had alighted on the roof of a freshly repainted cabin.

One crewmember used an axe to chop an opening in the blazing cabin to free the passengers, but strong breezes whipped the flames into a frenzy, and the entire ship was soon enveloped. People desperately jumped overboard clinging to anything that would float, such as furniture or planks. The captain, upon awakening, evaluated the fire to be beyond control, so he promptly seized two flour barrels,[61] jumped overboard, and kicked towards shore; this behaviour was exonerated by the inquest.[62] The *Ocean Wave* sank at about 6:00 A.M., taking 28 lives (13 passengers and 15 crew) with her. One passenger, Mrs. Stevenson, tragically lost her three children, all under the age of six. Despite being hampered by the intense heat from the flaming steamer, the schooners, *Emblem* and *Georgianna,* assisted with rescues, as did a Point Traverse farmer who rowed out in his little boat. The first person he picked up was Captain Wright![63]

The Kingston inquest lasted several days, with the conclusion that, had a proper lookout been maintained, the fire could not have spread so quickly.[64]

The fire had broken out when the *Ocean Wave* was two miles from land near the Ducks, but the wind blew the vessel about six miles offshore. A team of divers, including Barbara Carson and Doug Pettingill, located this shipwreck in 1991 south of Point Traverse, upside-down in 153' (46 metres) of dark water.

The Canadian paddlewheel steamer, Ocean Wave. *(Based on a drawing by Heyl.)*

TINTO   (June, 1856)

The propeller-driven steamer, *Tinto,* built in 1855 at Sorel, Quebec, with a length of 135' (40.5 metres) and a beam of 25' (7.5 metres), burned to a complete loss near Kingston in June, 1856, only one year after her launch.[65]

LORD ELGIN   (December, 1856)

This steam-and-propeller-driven ship with the decidedly British name was launched in Oswego, New York, in 1845 as the *Syracuse*. The name change to *Lord Elgin* took place in 1852. This ship fell victim to a late season storm in

December, 1856, at Lake Ontario's Long Point west of Kingston. The *Lord Elgin* measured 116' (34.8 metres) in length, and 21' (6.3 metres) in beam.[66]

TRENTON   (March 2, 1858)

Launched at Montreal in 1854, the propeller-powered steamer, *Trenton,* measuring 134' (40.2 metres) in length and 23' (6.9 metres) in beam,[67] plied the waters of the St. Lawrence River and eastern Lake Ontario for only four years.

THE STEAMER

"TRENTON,"

(FOR THE REMAINDER OF THE SEASON,)

WILL make REGULAR WEEKLY TRIPS

FROM MONTREAL

TO THE

HEAD OF THE BAY OF QUINTE,

CALLING AT ALL THE PORTS.

UPWARDS:

Leave MONTREAL on Monday afternoons.
"   KINGSTON on Wednesday morn'gs,
and arrive in Belleville same
Afternoon.

This advertisement for the Trenton *appeared in the* Hastings Chronicle (Belleville) *on October 18, 1855, almost three years before the vessel's destruction at Picton.*

The local press described the vessel's demise:

BURNING OF THE STEAMER *TRENTON.*

This fine steamer was burned to the water's edge on the morning of Tuesday last. The fire was first perceived escaping from the opening near the machinery, about half past one o'clock.... ten hours before the fire was seen, some carpenters who were working on the boat say that everything was made safe at that hour, and all [work] fires were put out. Two hours before

> the fire broke several persons passed near the
> boat, and saw no light or any appearance of fire
> on board. When the fire was first seen it
> appeared to be confined to the upper saloon, as
> the glass windows surrounded the upper part of
> the boat illuminated both shores. The boat was
> moored about one hundred feet from the steam
> mill, at the entrance of the Picton Harbor, and
> was under the control of J.S. McQuaig, Esq. The
> *Trenton* was insured for eighteen thousand
> dollars, and valued, we believe, at thirty
> thousand dollars. About the cause of the fire
> people differ.[68]

The *Trenton's* boiler, fittings, etc. were auctioned off the next month at McFaul's wharf in Picton.[69]

WILLIAM IV   (April, 1858)

William IV, nicknamed "the British sailor king," ascended the throne in 1832, but was not likely aware that a vessel, launched on October 29 that same year at Gananoque, Canada West, had been named in his honour. Constructed under the supervision of New York builder, James Wood,[70] for a conglomerate of businessmen in Gananoque, the 118-ton sidewheeler, *William IV*, measured 135' (40.5 metres) in length and 25' (7.5 metres) in beam[71] and sported four smokestacks set in a rectangle near the bow, the only Great Lakes vessel with this unusual characteristic.

Serving primarily the ports of Prescott, Brockville, Gananoque, Kingston, Cobourg, Port Hope, Toronto, Hamilton, and Niagara,[72] the *William IV* experienced only one close call in her long career. On October 28, 1840, a violent storm pounded and battered her hull until she leaked. Finally, the captain purposely ran his vessel aground in South Bay, where everyone was evacuated to another ship. The *William IV* was raised two days later, restored, and returned to service. In April, 1858, her engine was removed at St. Catharines, and shortly thereafter, her hull was abandoned at Garden Island near Kingston. Reportedly her keel and frame timbers could still be seen underwater in 1933.[73]

R. H. RAE   (August 4, 1858)

The three-masted merchant bark of 344 tons and measuring 136.5' (41 metres) in length, the *R. H. Rae*, was launched on October 5, 1857, at the famous shipyard of Louis Shickluna at St. Catharines, Ontario. The vessel, however, was not built by him, but rather by Donaldson & Andrews, who had purchased the shipyard in late 1856 for $60,000 when Shickluna planned to retire; he changed his mind and re-acquired his yard for the same sum[74] in December, 1857, but not before the *R. H. Rae* was built and launched,[75] making her historically unique based solely on her background.

The *R. H. Rae* was the first Canadian ship to utilize a self-reefing topsail design, which avoided having to send sailors aloft to do this dangerous work. Demonstrated at her launch, one of her topsails was unfurled and reefed in three minutes with no men going aloft. Below deck, her "ceiling" was extended to the deck against the ribs, offering, along with her double bulkhead, solidity and extra strength. On deck, two strong iron bars were placed behind each mast, down through the keelson, thus creating stable braces at traditionally weak points. The *R. H. Rae* was "a piece of naval architecture...second to none on the lakes."[76]

The *R. H. Rae,* however, sank during her first full season of operation about two miles (three kilometres) south of Point Traverse, in a situation also considered quite unique. White squalls appear suddenly and forcefully on the Great Lakes, usually during summer months. It was just such a violent, unexpected blast of wind which capsized and sank the *R. H. Rae* at 11:30 A.M. on August 4, 1858, "in about 20 fathoms of water."[77] The crew, with great difficulty, saved themselves in their lifeboat. The swiftness was frightening: all this activity took place in only about three minutes![78]

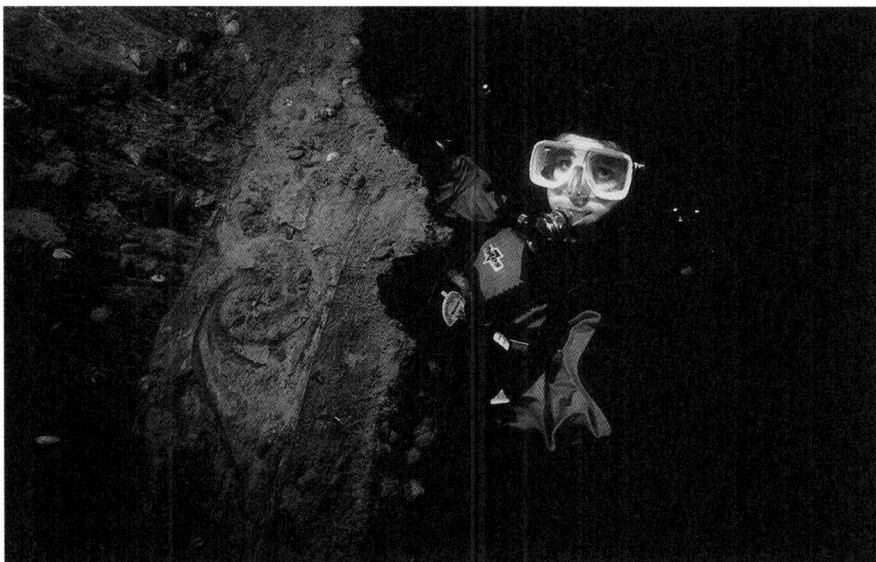

The carved bow stem of the barque, R. H. Rae, *sitting in 100' (30 metres) of water south of Point Traverse, is studied by diver Marcy McElmon.* PHOTO BY CRIS KOHL.

Confusion has long existed about the name of this vessel: was it the *R. H. Rae,* or the *John Rae?* Even contemporary accounts erred in their reports, once calling the *R. H. Rae* the *"John H. Rae."*[79] The *John Rae* was a totally different vessel, a two-masted schooner built at Kingston in 1853 and measuring only 111' 3" (33.4 metres) in length.[80] The *John Rae* was "in a bad condition" ashore at Timber Island on November 27, 1872.[81] Her final disposition is unknown.

Barbara Carson, longtime local marine historian, scuba diver, and shipwreck locater, found the *R. H. Rae* in 1976 and, because of her connection with the Marine Museum of the Great Lakes at Kingston, the exploration of this shipwreck was offered to Jacques Cousteau in 1980 on his only Great Lakes expedition. The Cousteau expedition removed many artifacts from the wreck for the museum, including the ship's wheel, found loose at the stern (was this an earlier, hardhat, almost-salvaged leftover?). Unfortunately, the *Rae* proved to be Cousteau's Great Lakes nemesis; he lost one of his divers at this site.[82] His subsequent films on this area, "Cries from the Deep" and "St. Lawrence: Stairway to the Sea," totally omitted any footage of the *R. H. Rae* and any mention of this unfortunate accident.[83] The wreck location returned to secrecy, known but to a few divers, until being relocated on July 25, 1996.[84]

The wreck of the *R. H. Rae* is well-settled, and settling more! The huge, wooden rudder rests on a twisted angle and most of the decking has collapsed, except at the bow, where penetration below deck is still possible. Items of interest include an ornately-carved bow stem, a huge windlass, copper cappings on the bow, samson, and windlass posts, a pump, a deck winch, blocks, deadeyes, and an 1857 toilet sitting in the open at the stern. A salvage attempt was made in the 1850's, but it doesn't look like the vessel was moved very far, if at all. Considering the depth of this shipwreck, hardhat divers of that era were probably satisfied with recovering the ship's anchors, and leaving it at that.

BRITTANIA (November, 1859)

The 278-ton sidewheeler, *Brittania,* constructed at St. Catharines, Ontario, in 1847, measured 135' (40.5 metres) in length and 23' (6.9 metres) in beam. This vessel reportedly fell victim to arson when it burned at Kingston in November, 1859.[85]

The NOVEMBER 27th, 1860, STORM:

MARY, COASTER, ENTERPRISE, RED ROVER, WELLAND, and WILD ROVER

This severe gale grounded numerous vessels in the Kingston area; some were damaged, but could be repaired and returned to service, while others became total losses. The schooner, *Mary,* of St. Catharines, ran ashore at Timber Island and "is likely to prove a total loss."[86] The propeller, *Coaster,* was wrecked at Glenora, then called Stone Mills.[87] The *Enterprise,* carrying 5,500 bushels of oats and 30 barrels of apples, landed on shore near the Point Petre lighthouse.[88] The schooner, *Red Rover,* was grounded and wrecked on Point Traverse's south shore, with commercial fishermen struggling hard to rescue the six crew-members.[89] The *Welland* and the schooner, *Wild Rover,* ended up ashore at South Bay.[90] This costly storm remained a topic of local conversation for years.

COMET   (May 14, 1861)

The elegant, graceful, 337-ton sidewheel steamer, *Comet,* first major project of shipbuilder George N. Ault of Portsmouth (Kingston), Ontario, in 1848, measured 174' 8" (52.4 metres) in length, 24' (7.2 metres) in beam (expanded to 45'. or 13.5 metres, if the sidewheels and their guards were included), and 10' (3 metres) in draft.[91] Twin, low-pressure engines, built in 1835 and removed from the small steamer, *Unicorn,* formerly *Shannon,* and capable of 45 horsepower each,[92] propelled the new vessel across Great Lakes waters.

However, the propulsion of ten miles per hour was not considered fast enough by crowds increasingly spoiled by Royal Mail Line vessels capable of 16 miles per hour, and the *Comet's* unfinished cabins on her brief maiden voyage failed to impress prospective travellers. Her penchant for bad luck gained momentum when she struck a shoal and sank in the St. Lawrence River after a few trips.[93] She was raised, repaired, and returned to service and more bad luck.

In early November, 1849, the *Comet,* about to enter Toronto harbour, burst a steam pipe, seriously injuring three Irish firemen, two of them fatally.[94] Then, in April 20, 1851, the *Comet's* boiler exploded as she was departing Oswego, New York, tragically killing eight people and ripping a huge hole in her hull. "Her boiler had been in use since 1834, but had been pronounced in good condition by one of the best engineers in Canada."[95] Eventually raised, the *Comet* was rebuilt at Montreal and, perhaps to lure good fortune, underwent a name change to *Mayflower.*[96]

The sidewheel steamer, Comet, *sank in 1861.* PHOTO COURTESY BILL HUMPHRIES.

However, more misfortune included the *Mayflower* running ashore at the Scarborough Bluff near Toronto on August 10, 1853 (she was pulled off the next day with no damage), being laid up at Portsmouth, Ontario during the financial panic of 1857, and receiving considerable damage when powerful winds on May

7, 1861, tore her from her moorings and slammed her against the Cataraqui Bridge.[97] A week later, the ship was fully repaired and restored to her original name, *Comet.* She left the safety of Kingston on her first voyage of the new season, only to encounter her final stroke of bad luck.

ART COURTESY OF THE METROPOLITAN TORONTO LIBRARY.

On May 14, 1861, Captain Francis Patterson commanded the *Comet,* amidst storm signals and rolling squalls, out of the safety of Kingston harbour. Simultaneously, the Cleveland schooner, *Exchange,* ran frantically before the storm in quest of a safe harbour. In the obscured visibility caused by the foul weather, the two ships experienced a close encounter:

> ...the steamer, Comet,...got involved among a large number of sailing vessels coming down the Lake, and struck a schooner on the side with her stem springing her own plank. The captain changed the steamer's course and bore after the schooner, they having hailed that they thought they were sinking and to keep close to bear a hand, but running past with the wind she got out of hailing distance.
>
> Meanwhile, the pumps were worked and the fires kept up for the purpose of making shore, the steamer at the time of collision being about ten miles above Nine Mile Point. The firemen waist deep in water, did not abandon their task until their fires were drowned and if the steamer had held out ten minutes longer, much would have been gained towards raising the steamer. During this time the life boat was swung out, with three lady passengers, one gentleman and the lady's maids, and brought round to leeward, and as many of the crew put into it as the Captain deemed consistent with safety.---These made for shore, but at the same time the large yawl was out towing astern and taking in water. Two hands, John Blake and John McCarthy, the former from the

neighborhood of Kingston Mills and the latter a salt-water boy from Dublin, Ireland, got out to bale her, but while about to do so she struck against the steamer's guard, thus throwing the men off their balance into the lake. Going down Blake cried out to his brother, a deck hand, "Good bye, Jim," and the "saltie" "Good bye boys," and thus they bade them farewell. The Captain at this time was busily engaged in the endeavor to run the steamer ashore, but finding it fruitless had the small yawl put out with thirteen men, and made for shore in the heavy sea....[98]

After striking the *Exchange,* the *Comet* travelled about eight miles (12 kilometres) before Captain Patterson abandoned ship. Passengers and remaining crew reached the safety of Simcoe Island, while the *Comet,* about 1.5 miles (2.2 kilometres) off the island, sank in approximately 90' (27 metres) of water. A public auction of the salvage rights to the *Comet* was set for June 10, 1861,[99] almost a month after the vessel sank. These auction results seem to have gone unrecorded.

There the *Comet* lay for over a hundred years, disturbed only by fish, algae, and diverse currents carrying variable quantities of silt.

THIS DAY.

UNDERWRITER'S SALE.

WILL BE SOLD by Public Auction on MONDAY NEXT, the 10th inst., at HOLCOMB, COWAN & Co's. wharf, foot of Gore Street,

THE STEAMER " COMET,"

lately sunk at the foot of Lake Ontario, about two miles S.W. of Nine Mile Point, with all the Materials and Furniture which may be found.

Terms Cash immediately at close of sale. Sale at 2 o'clock p.m.

JAMES LINTON,
Auctioneer.

Kingston, June 3, 1861.
(*Whig to copy*)

The *Daily News* (Kingston), June 3, 1861.

There had been talk of salvaging the vessel in 1861, but the ship's history of misfortune, her age, and the limited technology of that era worked against a recovery project.

On September 9, 1967, Kingston scuba divers Jim McCready and Dr. Robert McCaldon, inspired by an earlier maritime article about the *Comet* in the Kingston *Whig-Standard,* successfully dragged with two reels of line, sinkers, two boats and a depth recorder for this shipwreck. It had taken them almost five years of part-time searching to locate the *Comet.* The media reported that other members of the team included Ronald Hough, Donald Brierley, Tom Palmer, and Wayne Jackson, and that the discovery had been reported to the Receiver of Wrecks in Ottawa. Significant items recovered (or, in pre-conservation-era parlance, "skindivers have been quietly salvaging trophies"[100]) included a brass door latch, brass wine barrel spigot, handmade silver spatulas, English ironstone pitchers, wash basins, cups, saucers, bowls, and tureens, plus handblown glass goblets and several bottles of wine, "not very pleasing to the taste."[101]

In 1983, talk of raising the *Comet* surfaced. Maurice Smith, director of the Marine Museum at Kingston, was quoted as saying, "It [raising the *Comet*] would be a marvellous project for an active museum." Marine Museum exhibits already included numerous artifacts recovered from the *Comet*.[102] By late 1983, raising the *Comet* had become a ten-year plan, commencing with photographing and gathering of information. Data was gathered, but a proposed deal made in March, 1983 with a local marine services company to do a photographic survey of the shipwreck for $400.00 was voided in the late fall of that year after both parties agreed to cancel the arrangement.[103] There was also talk of maintaining the *Comet,* "perhaps as an underwater provincial park like those at Tobermory and elsewhere."[104] No underwater park has been created here to date, but, with the ongoing promotional, educational, and practical work undertaken by the Kingston marine conservation group named Preserve Our Wrecks (P.O.W.), underwater park status has not been a pressing concern.

The shipwreck itself is worthy of several visits by experienced divers. The *Comet's* bow and stern have collapsed, but her distinctive paddlewheels are still intact and tower about 25' (7.5 metres) above the lake floor. The rocker arms and walking beams are also clearly visible. Portions of her railings, doors, and smokestacks rest along the east side; remnants of her farm implements cargo lie scattered around the wreck. For trained and experienced divers, penetration below deck is possible at the stern to view the engines and twin boilers. Due to the zebra mussel invasion of the Great Lakes, water visibility has improved, but multi-layers of these pests now camouflage distinctive shipwreck details. The impressive view of the upright paddlewheels will surely take your breath away!

BANSHEE   (August 21, 1861)

The narrow, 400-ton, propeller-driven steamer, *Banshee,* launched at Portsmouth, Ontario, in 1852, measured 119' (35.7 metres) in length and 18' (5.4 metres) in beam. In 1860, for one season only, *Banshee* was renamed *Hero* before returning to the name *Banshee* in the year of her demise.[105]

On August 21, 1861, this vessel became the victim of a severe storm on Lake Ontario when her machinery broke down near Timber Island off Point Traverse. Becoming unmanageable, the *Banshee* slipped into a trough of the sea, possibly struck bottom, definitely ran onto the rocks in the shallows of Gull Shoal, and broke up.

FOR MONTREAL & INTERMEDIATE PORTS.

THE STEAMER

BANSHEE

CAPT. D. SINCLAIR,

WILL leave the St. Lawrence Wharf, for Montreal, on Tuesday morning, at six o'clock, calling at intermediate ports.

The *Daily News* (Kingston), June 10, 1861.

Of the 18 people on board, only one, a printer named John Nagle, drowned. Ten successfully reached shore in a small lifeboat, while the remaining seven clung to wreckage which eventually took them to shore. The vessel was a total loss, as was her cargo of 6,000 bushels of wheat, 250 barrels of flour, and 300 kegs of butter. A Mr. Rose of St. Thomas owned the *Banshee*.[106]

In the autumn of 1967, Dennis Kent and other Quinte Aqua Divers members from Belleville, located this badly broken up shipwreck in about 18' (5.4 m.).[107]

OSHAWA and CHARLES MOFFAT   (September 27, 1861)

One severe early-autumn storm in 1861 destroyed two steamers by impaling them on rocks and pounding them to pieces.

The propeller-driven ship, *Oshawa,* built at Laprairie, Quebec in 1854 and measuring 128' (38.4 metres) in length and 23' (6.9 metres) in beam,[108] called Brockville, Ontario, her home port. The ship sprang a leak near the Main Duck Islands and retreated into the relatively calm waters of South Bay where, after considerable time, she was purposely grounded about 2.5 miles (4 kilometres) from the extreme end of Long Point. A few days later, the hull was "in a ruinous and worthless condition. She lies wrenched out of shape, and large openings were distinctly visible underwater."[109]

The bow faced the lake and the ship rested in 10 feet (3 metres) of water about sixty feet (18 metres) from the actual shoreline. About 27 stoves and much of the flour cargo was lost overboard during the lurching of the vessel; some flour and three stoves were salvaged after the ship grounded, but most of the flour became a complete loss. Salvagers did not give up easily: "The grappling for stoves was quite amusing, but the loss of so many fine ones is to be regretted, as nearly all are broken, and but few will be at all saleable."[110] The *Oshawa* was considered one of the finest propellers of the Beaver Line; her loss was not total for her owners, since she was insured.

Violent winds and seas drove another propeller, the *Charles Moffatt,* ashore seven miles (11 kilometres) from Long Point. The steamer had broken part of her machinery but, with the aid of sails, succeeded in approaching South Bay. However, she could not reach that harbour's safety before being driven ashore. Her cargo of peas, becoming wet and swelling in the hold of the vessel, completely wrecked her.[111] Fortunately, no lives were lost in these marine incidents.

ECHO   (October 11, 1861)

The Canadian schooner, *Echo,* enroute from Toronto to Oswego with a load of 2,042 of barley for the firm of Young & McFaul, Oswego, ran ashore one-half mile (0.8 kilometre) off Gull Bar near False Duck Island on Friday, October 11, 1861. The local press reported that "It is supposed that the vessel will be a total wreck, and the cargo a complete loss."[112] No lives were lost. Members of the Quinte Aqua Divers, of Belleville, Ontario, located the wreck of the *Echo* in about 22 feet (6.6 metres) of water on September 17, 1967.[113]

MOIRA   (October 9, 1862)

The propeller-driven steamer, *Moira*, 123' (36.9 metres) in length and 25' (7.5 metres) in beam, slid down the launchramp at Belleville, Ontario, in 1855,[114] her owners excited about their fine vessel's future, running the Belleville, Picton, and Oswego route.

For seven years, all went well for the ship and her owners, with the *Moira* establishing a solid reputation as a reliable vessel.

These advertisements for the popular steamer, *Moira*, appeared in the following newspapers: *Hastings Chronicle* (Belleville), August 28, 1856 and August 25, 1858, and the *Picton Gazette*, April 13, 1860 and October 18, 1861.

Captain Thomas McIntosh took command of the *Moira* at the beginning of the 1858 season. The high esteem with which business people held him is seen in a letter published in local newspapers at that time:

CAPT. McINTOSH OF THE *MOIRA*.

The Oswego Daily *Times* of the 6th inst. [May 6, 1858] offers a flattering testimonial to Capt. McIntosh, signed as it will be seen, by most of the leading business men in Oswego,---thus proving that in assuming the command of the *Moira,* the right man is filling the right place. The following is the testimonial:---

Oswego, May 1, 1858.

Capt. Thomas McIntosh:

Dear Sir---The undersigned are each plaeased to see you in command of the propeller Moira, again upon the old route between Oswego and Belleville, and intermediate ports on the Bay of Quinte.

Our long acquaintance with you, and knowledge of the prompt and efficient manner in which you transacted all of your business while master of the schooner Schuyler, running to the same ports, is a guarantee that we should not err in bestowing all the patronage in our power upon the popular propeller, now in your charge. We will use our best endeavors to encourage and increase the business of your boat, and wish you and her owners a prosperous season.

Penffeld, Lyon & Co., Ames & Sloan, Thos. A. Mott, S. H. Lathrop, Mollison & Hastings [plus ten more firms].[115]

Unfortunately, a mechanical failure ultimately caused the *Moira* to sink.

The *Moira* left Oswego, New York, on the night of Wednesday, October 8th, 1862, bound for Picton-Belleville. A heavy sea ran when the *Moira,* passing to the south of Main Duck Island at three o'clock in the morning, encountered a leak in the boxing around her propeller shaft. Several attempts to stop the leak proved fruitless and, with the steamer filling more and more with water, the passengers and crew took to the lifeboat and the yawl.

The lifeboat headed right for Long Point on the mainland of Ontario, but the yawlboat, with 14 people in it and only a single oar (the four good oars had been taken in the lifeboat), bobbed for several hours before rescue arrived in the form of the schooner, *Mary Ann,* also from Belleville. The rescuing vessel decided not to change course after picking up the shipwreck victims, opting instead to take them to the *Mary Ann's* original destination, Oswego.[116]

One of the *Moira's* crew wrote, in a style alternating between factual and melodramatic, praiseworthy and sexist (by today's standards), an anonymous firsthand account which the press published:

To   the   Editor   of   the   Intelligencer.

LOSS OF THE MOIRA

Belleville,   Oct.   15,   1862.

Sir,---On the morning of Thursday, the 9th inst. about three o'clock, we found ourselves in a very unpleasant and also extremely dangerous situation, caused by part of the machinery giving way. In order that some information may be laid before the public respecting the accident, I propose to give you the particulars, which may be of interest to your readers.

At the hour above mentioned, the packing box through which the shaft which turns the screw works, was discovered to have become displaced, causing a serious leak---the water rushing into the opening thus created, with great violence, baffling all attempts made to prevent its entrance, although every exertion was made by the engineer and fireman, assisted by the crew. Finding, at length, it was impossible to stop the leak, Captain McIntosh, anxious to save the lives of all on board, gave orders to have all the boats got ready for launching, which was done properly---no excitement other than a little uneasiness, which is not unusual, and which is quite pardon- able---was manifested on the occasion, with the exception of the women on board, for whom due allowance is to be made. The first boat launched was the life-boat, which was passed from its position on the larboard bow, to the after larboard gangway, into which went two of the crew to steady and assist to row the boat: all the women on board (five in number), two male passengers, the engineer, the mate, and the Captain---in all twelve souls. The Captain's intention on leaving the boat was to reach the shore as soon as possible and then return immediately, in order to relieve the other boat, but on his way back he discovered a propeller, which was supposed to be the *Indian*, which he endeavored to reach to obtain assistance, which would have been of great service to him, but which, alas! he failed in reaching---they turning a deaf ear to his entreaties. Consequently he was unable to return as soon as he anticipated.

Meanwhile, the other boat had been launched and after all those remaining on board had got themselves safely in her, the crew put to sea, deeming it unsafe to remain any longer on board the ill-fated steamer taking with them a number of water pails, with which to bail out the boat; their propelling apparatus consisting of two cedar life buoys, and a damaged oar, which was manned admirably though carefully by the purser and one of the firemen, one of the wheel-men being stationed in the bow of the boat to watch the direction of the running sea and give directions for steering the frail craft, (containing fourteen souls) which threatened every minute to swamp and usher those clinging to it for their lives, into eternity. They continued in this state for the space of four hours and a half, when they were picked up by the schooner *Mary Ann*, Captain Hunter, who in conjunction with her crew, gave us a hearty welcome and treated us very kindly, setting a good example worthy of being imitated by all who traverse river, bay, lake or ocean.

Yours respectfully,

ONE OF THE CREW.[117]

The captain and his party were picked up from the mainland shore and taken to Kingston. The initial hope that the *Moira* did not sink was due to the fact that, after she was abandoned, she was still in sight for several hours, and, because of the large quantity of wood between her decks, there could be sufficient buoyancy to counterbalance the weight of her boiler and machinery, and that the water in the hold had levelled off. However, at a time and place unknown, the *Moira* did sink. One newspaper later reported that "The propeller *Moira,* it is now ascertained, sank in fifty feet of water, about one and a half miles S. S. E. of the Main Ducks...."[118]

The *Moira's* importance was summarized thusly: "Her loss will prove a serious inconvenience to the traveling and business public, as most of the trade between this port [Oswego] and the Bay of Quinte was transacted through her."[119]

Two steam tugs from Oswego, hearing of the loss, searched the area in hopes of finding the *Moira* still afloat and salvaging her. The *Moira's* saloon, or cabin, however, had broken loose and was seen floating, but the rest of the vessel had disappeared. The tugs "ascertained that she had sunk in about 70 feet of water."[120] The *Moira* has not yet been located to ascertain her true depth.

The *Moira's* cargo consisted of about 20 tons of coal, some general merchandise, and a horse. In addition, all of the *Moira's* "books, papers, and money were lost."[121] The passengers' and crew's personal belongings all remained with the *Moira.* B. Flint, Esq., of Belleville, owned the lost vessel, which was valued at $18,000. He carried no insurance on her.

EMPRESS   (March 18, 1868)

The steamer, *Empress,* was about 20 years old when she burned to a total loss at Kingston on March 18, 1868.

Built at Kingston in 1848 and launched as the *New Era,* the 170-foot (51-metre) *Empress* received that name either in 1862[122] after a major rebuild, or in 1864 when she changed routes.[123] Kingston was the transfer point for passengers and freight changing from "river boats" (travelling up the St. Lawrence River from Montreal) to "lake boats" (for ventures across and beyond Lake Ontario.) The *New Era/Empress* laboured between Montreal and Kingston from 1848 until 1864. Since, by 1850, there were only 66 miles (about 100 kilometres) of railroad in all of Canada,[124] these St. Lawrence River/Great Lakes ships were of vital economic importance.

The tragic loss of the popular steamer, *Empress,* described in detail by the local press, reveals several facets of the mechanical operations and failures, and community reaction and involvement, during a winter emergency in those old days when the nation called Canada was less than a year old:

STEAMER EMPRESS BURNED.

LOSS $15,000

At a few moments after two o'clock this morning (Wednesday) an alarm of fire was rung out by the bell in the city clock tower. A bright light was seen reflected from the harbour between Princess and Queen streets, and it was soon ascertained that the steamer Empress, which was lying in the slip at Mr. Gildersleeve's wharf, was on fire and burning furiously. The vessel was burning aft, which portion was first consumed, the flames spreading rapidly forward until she was in a general blaze. [Fire] Engines Nos. 1 and 3 were brought down as soon after the alarm was given as they could be conveniently got out; the former being stationed on Gildersleeve's wharf at the foot of Queen street, the other on Chaffey's wharf, opposite the burning vessel. It was some time, however, before the steam from either engine could be brought to bear on the burning mass. No. 3, which was worked slowly by a few men, with no more to replace them at the brakes when they were worn out, poured a feeble stream upon the fire, which eventually had the effect of keeping down the blaze, and preventing the fire from spreading to the wharf and vessels in the vicinity; but No. 1 refused to suck the water from the hole which had been cut in the ice seven or eight feet below the level of the engine, and consequently could not be worked at all. An attempt to supply this engine through a hose attached to the hydrant at the corner of King and Brock streets, also failed, and there it lay perfectly useless in the hands of the men at the brakes. In the meantime, a quantity of cordwood belonging to Mr. Gildersleeve, piled on the edge of the wharf nearest the burning vessel, took fire and threatened to connect the flames with the wharf and the vessels lying between this wharf and Berry's.... There was still a chance of the fire spreading, when Alderman Henry Cunningham, seeing that there was no hope of immediate assistance from No. 1 Engine, went to the quarters of the Commandant of the Garrison, Colonel Gibbon, and procured from that officer---who is always ready and willing to assist in any emergency---an order for a Company of the 17th Regiment and one of the Royal Canadian Rifles, who were speedily marched to the scene of the fire. With this reinforcement engine No. 1 was thoroughly worked and kept going until all danger was past. Previous to this the suction difficulty had been overcome by Mr. McNeil, and the engine did good service in preventing the fire in the wood piles from spreading, a portion of the principal pile having been previously removed by men hired for the purpose by Mr. Gildersleeve. About twenty cords of wood were burned. Towards the close the steamer consumed slowly, and it was sometime before the mast fell to which the bell was attached, and the walking beam, which was supported by a heavy framework of wood. The steamer eventually burned to the water's edge and settled in the slip, the heat melting the ice round about her sufficiently to let her down.

A few planks and beams will replace the injury done to Mr. Gildersleeve's wharf, the damage not being very great.

The Empress was formerly the New Era, and was sold to Mr. Owen Lynch, of Beauharnois, for $15,000 in April, 1865. A brother of the owner has been in charge of the vessel during the winter, and the owner himself was here a few days ago making arrangements to prepare her for the opening of navigation. There is said to be an insurance of $15,000 on the vessel, probably in Montreal, as there does not appear to have been any insurance effected on her in this city. The wind was fortunately low; had this not been the case the damage to surrounding property must have been very great. One of Mr. Chaffey's tugs was in danger at one time, but by dint of watching and a good water supply it escaped. The origin of the fire is unknown.[125]

WATER WITCH   (October 24, 1869)

The Kingston-owned, 365-ton barque, *Water Witch,* loaded with 200 tons of scrap iron, left Kingston on the morning of Friday, October 22, 1869, and immediately strained through gale-tossed waters towards Cleveland. Off Long Point, the ship was obliged to run back to the shelter of South Bay, where she anchored for two days. Winds then abated, and the *Water Witch* proceded with all sails set, on course and in the company of the schooner, *E.P. Dorr.* [126]

There is a saying, which I have heard said about each of the Great Lakes as I visited them separately, that if you don't like the weather now, just wait ten minutes. It will change. The *Water Witch* encountered that situation in reverse.

A sudden squall threw the *Water Witch* on her beam ends, and she quickly began filling with water, particularly through some open hatches. Aware that the merciless waves and rushing water controlled the stability of their vessel, all on board, ten in number, evacuated their sinking ship on a lifeboat within two minutes. The *E.P. Dorr,* then about one and a half miles (2.4 kilometres) to windward, had been signalled, and she turned around, picked up the yawlboat, and towed it back to the safety of South Bay, landing the crew of the *Water Witch* there before continuing on her course. On its own, the small lifeboat would not have made shore in those towering seas. The next day, Monday, October 25, 1869, the crew sailed their yawlboat back to Kingston, arriving there at noon.

> The crew saw the last of the Water Witch before they left the scene of the wreck on the Dorr, as she plunged down in over 200 feet of water.... She was classed B1, valued at

> $3,000, and insured for two-thirds that
> amount in the Home Insurance Company. She
> was one of the fastest boats on the lake, but
> this year has been unfortunate, having on
> one occasion been occupied, through
> contrary winds, for forty days on one trip.[127]

The entire crew of the *Water Witch* survived, thanks to help from the captain and crew of the schooner, *E.P. Dorr.* The *Water Witch,* with its scrap iron cargo, sits in deep water, awaiting discovery by modern technical divers.

[35]Metcalfe, op. cit., 91-92.

[36]*Treasure Ships of the Great Lakes.* Detroit: Maritime Research & Publishing Co., 1981: 60.

[37]*Psyche.* Ship Information and Data Record, Runge Collection, Milwaukee Public Library.

[38]Robert Malcomson. "HMS *Psyche*" *Seaways' Ships in Scale,* Vol. IV, No. 6, November/December, 1993: 19.

[39]Ibid., 19-20.

[40]"P.O.W. Kingston 1812 Freshwater Fleet Research Project." *Save Ontario Shipwrecks Newsletter,* Summer, 1989: 30-32.

[41]James P. Barry. *Ships of the Great Lakes, 300 Years of Navigation.* Berkeley, California: Howell-North Books, 1973: 35.

[42]*Prince Regent.* Ship Information and Data Record, Runge Collection, Milwaukee Public Library.

[43]Barry, op. cit., 35-37.

[44]Bruce Wishart. "Sir James Yeo and the S*t. Lawrence,* 'A Remarkable Fine Ship'." *The Beaver,* February-March, 1992, 17.

[45]Mansfield, op. cit., 178.

[46]*St. Lawrence.* Ship Information and Data Record, Runge Collection, Milwaukee Public Library.

[47]Robert Malcomson. "HMS *St. Lawrence.*" *Seaways' Ships in Scale,* Vol. V, No. 1, January/February, 1994: 46.

[48]Metcalfe, op. cit., 50-51, from a story which appeared in the *Hallowell Free Press.*

[49]John M. Mills. *Canadian Coastal and Inland Steam Vessels, 1809-1930.* Providence, Rhode Island: The Steamship Historical Society of America, Inc., 1979: 22.

[50]Ibid., 18.

[51]*Hallowell Traveller,* May 6, 1836.

[52]Heyl, op. cit., 211.

[53]Mills, op. cit., 97.

[54]*Chronicle and Gazette* (Kingston), September 23, 1839, and the *Oswego Palladium,* September 25, 1839.

[55]Mills, op. cit., 23.

[56] Ibid., Supplement Two.

[57]*Hallowell Traveller* (Picton), May 6, 1836.

[58]Mills, op. cit., 89.

[59]Heyl, op. cit., 175.

[60]Roy F. Fleming. "The Burning of the *Ocean Wave.*" *Inland Seas,* Vol. 13, No. 3, Fall, 1957, 226.

[61]*Daily British Whig* (Kingston), May 27, 1853.

[62]Ibid.

[63]Willis Metcalfe. *Marine Memories.* Picton, Ontario: The Picton Gazette, 1975: 12.

[64]The *Daily British Whig* (Kingston), reported extensively the testimony and results of this inquest in its issues of May 13, 14, 16, 20, 21, 27, and June 1, 1853

[65]Mills, op. cit., Supplement Two.

[66]Ibid., Supplement One.

[67]Ibid., 118.

[68]*Hastings Chronicle* (Belleville), Wed., March 10, 1858, quoting the *Picton Times.*

[69]*Picton Gazette,* April 23, 1858.

[70]Heyl, op. cit., Vol. VI, 335.

[71]Mills, op. cit., Supplement Two.

[72]*Chronicle & Gazette and Kingston Commercial Advertiser,* July 16, 1836.

[73]Heyl, op. cit., Vol. VI, 337.

[74]Peter D. A. Warwick. "Pioneer Shipbuilder of the Great Lakes." *Canadian Geographical Journal,* Vol. 94, No. 3, June/July, 1978: 28.

[75]Richard Palmer. "Great Canadian Shipbuilder: Louis Shickluna." *Inland Seas,* Vol. 41, No. 1, Spring, 1985: 17.

[76]*St. Catharines Journal,* Thursday, October 8, 1857.

[77]*Weekly British Whig* (Kingston), August 4, 1858, and *Daily British Whig* (Kingston), August 5, 1858.

[78]Ibid.

[79]*Daily British Whig* (Kingston), August 13, 1858.

[80]*John Rae.* Computer printout, Marine Museum of the Great Lakes, Kingston, Ontario.

[81]*Daily News* (Kingston), November 27 and December 2, 1872.

[82]*Whig-Standard* (Kingston), September 4, 5, and 10, 1980.

[83]*Whig-Standard* (Kingston), February 8, 1983.

[84]The *R. H. Rae* was picked up on sidescan sonar, while searching for another shipwreck, by Jim and Pat Stayer and Cris Kohl, working under the latter's provincial government archaeological license.

[85]Mills, op. cit., Supplement Two.

[86]*Daily British Whig* (Kingston), November 27, 1860.

[87]Metcalfe. *Canvas & Steam on Quinte Waters,* op. cit., 54.

[88]*Picton Gazette,* November 30, 1860.

[89]Metcalfe. *Canvas & Steam on Quinte Waters,* op. cit., 121.

[90]*Picton Gazette,* November 30, 1860.

[91]*Mayflower* (Canadian). Ship Information and Data Record, Runge Collection, Milwaukee Public Library.

92Walter Lewis. "The *Comet/Mayflower." Inland Seas*, Vol. 41, Number 2, Summer, 1985: 112-113.

93Ibid., 113.

94*British Whig* (Kingston), Nov. 8, 1849, quoting the Toronto *Globe,* and Nov. 10, 1849, quoting the Toronto *British Colonist.*

95*Syracuse* (New York) *Standard,* April 24, 1851.

96Heyl, op. cit., Volume V, 70.

97Ibid., 70-71.

98*Picton Gazette,* May 24, 1861.

99*Daily News* (Kingston), June 3, 1861.

100*Globe and Mail* (Toronto), undated article entitled "Skindivers find steamer sunk in 1861," circa October, 1967. On file at the Marine Museum of the Great Lakes at Kingston, *Comet* file.

101Ibid.

102*Whig-Standard* (Kingston), August 8, 1983.

103Marine Museum of the Great Lakes at Kingston, copy of letter , dated March 22, 1983 and voided in writing at a later date, in the *Comet* file.

104*Whig-Standard* (Kingston), October 1, 1983.

105Mills, op. cit., 12 and Supplement Two.

106*Picton Gazette,* August 30, 1861.

107Metcalfe, *Canvas & Steam on Quinte Waters,* op. cit., 43.

108Mills, op. cit., Supplement Two.

109*Picton Gazette,* October 4, 1861.

110Ibid.

111Ibid.

112*Picton Gazette,* October 18, 1861.

113Metcalfe. *Canvas & Steam on Quinte Waters,* op. cit., 59.

114Mills, op. cit., Supplement Two.

115*Hasting Chronicle* (Belleville), May 12, 1858, quoting the *Oswego Daily Times* of May 6, 1858.

116*Picton Gazette,* October 17, 1862.

117*Belleville Intelligencer,* October 17, 1862.

118*Belleville Intelligencer,* October 17, 1862, quoting the *Oswego Times* of October 10, 1862.

119Ibid., quoting the *Oswego Times,* October 9, 1862.

120*Picton Gazette,* October 17, 1862.

121Ibid.

122Mills, op. cit., Supplement Two. Heyl (Vol. III, 247) lists the launch year as 1849.

123Heyl, op. cit., Vol. III, 248.

124Ibid., 247.

125*Daily News* (Kingston), March 18, 1868.

126*Daily British Whig* (Kingston), Thursday, October 28, 1869.

127Ibid.

Chapter Three
The 1870's

JESSIE (October 31, 1871)

The loss of the two-masted, Port Stanley schooner, *Jessie,* with all hands prompted the Canadian government to construct the lighthouse at Salmon Point (earlier named "Wicked Point" due to its notorious danger to navigation; see the drawing of the Salmon Point lighthouse on page 11 of this book) and establish the first lifeboat, or lifesaving station, on the Canadian side of Lake Ontario, and probably in the entire Great Lakes system.[128]

Heavily loaded with 13,000 bushels of wheat, the *Jessie* sought shelter from the storm on Lake Ontario and somehow successfully sailed across the shallow bar into Sandy Bay near Salmon Point. She dropped her anchors and headsails (or jibs), and left her lower sails in place. The wind, however, shifted from the southeast to the west, and the *Jessie* was unable to exit the bay,[129] a place which now became her nemesis rather than her protector.

> ...The Captain could not have been up to business, else he would have known that the prevailing wind at this time of year comes from the west, nor could he have calculated his chances of escape from his retreat in such an event, as all who know the locality are well aware that it would be impossible, unless the vessel could ride out the storm at anchor, which is a dangerous experiment....[130]

The schooner "dragged her anchors and struck bottom about 30 rods [a distance of 495 feet, or 148.5 metres, since a rod is 5.5 yards, or 16.5 feet] from shore."[131] The relentless fury of the wind and the waves gradually tore apart the *Jessie,* with her crewmembers clinging to the ship's rigging or the main boom in hopes of imminent rescue from the terror-stricken spectators gathering helplessly along the shore. A small, open boat soon appeared in the shore crowd, but the pounding waves repulsed any attempts to launch it.

> ...At about ten o'clock in the forenoon all hopes and all doubts were suddenly brought to an end. The vessel seemed to break asunder in the centre, the huge spars fell in different directions, the sea washed over the crumbling ruins and eight human beings were enveloped by the angry waters! Shrieks from the assembled crowd of witnesses mingled with the howling of the winds to constitute the funeral

dirge of the poor creatures so suddenly plunged into watery graves....[132]

Two or three of the sailors kept themselves above the waves for a few minutes, but all lost their struggles for life. One powerful man, apparently an expert swimmer, was carried parallel to the beach by the current in his attempt to reach shore, but disappeared just before he attained the halfway point to land. His body washed ashore a short time later, while another male body, presumably from this crew, was located a month later.[133] The other seven crewmembers were never found, presumably taken by the undercurrent into deep water off Salmon Point.

The nine men (not eight, as initially reported) lost on the *Jessie* were Captain John Sheolin from Belleville, Mate Daniel Ryan from Kingston, Second Mate Harry Dupont from Belleville, seaman Michael Burke from Kingston, seaman Andrew Stephens from Kingston, seaman Thomas Patrick from Kingston, "Scottie" from Quebec, Martin Ryan from St. Catharines, and an unknown man who shipped aboard at the Welland Canal. Fragments of the ill-fated vessel littered the beach for about half a mile; "nearly every timber seemed to be completely rotten---in fact we scarcely saw a fragment amongst the tens of thousands that we could not pound to pieces and pulverize with a small mallet."[134] The *Jessie* was built in 1854-55 by famous St. Catharines shipwright, Louis Shickluna, at Port Robinson, and she measured 121' 6" (37.5 metres) in length, 23' (6.9 metres) in beam, and 10' (3 metres) in draft.[135]

JOHN GREENWAY   (October, 1871)

The small, 45-ton sidewheeler, *John Greenway,* burned to a total loss at Picton, Ontario, in October, 1871. This former U.S. vessel, launched in 1863 at Geneva, New York, and under Canadian registry (#51676) at the time of loss, measured 82' (24.6 metres) in length and 17' (5.1 metres) in beam.[136]

HERCULES   (December 9, 1871)

Shipbuilder Henry Roney constructed the 331-ton wooden sidewheel steamer, *Hercules,* at Garden Island near Kingston in 1858,[137] and fire destroyed this vessel at the same location on December 9, 1871.[138] The ship had measured 122.2' by 25.8' by 11.5' (36.6 by 7.7 by 3.5 metres).

HIGHLANDER   (December, 1871)

The 300-ton sidewheeler, *Highlander,* burned to a total loss at Garden Island, Ontario, in December, 1871. Launched at Montreal in 1850, this long, narrow ship measured 173' (51.9 metres) in length and 24' (7.2 metres) in beam.[139]

KINGSTON   (June 11, 1872)

The iron-hulled, 344-ton, sidewheel steamer, *Kingston,* laden with about 100 passengers, left Brockville, Ontario, shortly after one o'clock on the afternoon of Tuesday, June 11, 1872, bound for Kingston. As she approached Grenadier Island, about 18 miles (25 kilometres) above Brockville, someone on board shouted "Fire," and the passengers and crew scrambled in hasty confusion. The flames, which had sprouted from a stateroom above the engineroom, filled the passenger saloon with smoke within moments. Captain Carmichael, acting quickly "with the most praiseworthy coolness and prudence,"[140] immediately attempted to run his vessel ashore to ease safe evacuation, but the ship grounded in shallow water about 600 feet (180 metres) from land; the passengers had to reach shore as best they could, using lifejackets or whatever would float to assist them. The widow of Kingston's Dr. Thomas Jones, "a lady of sterling worth,"[141] attempting to descend from the hurricane deck to the main deck to escape the quickly-spreading flames, fell into the water and drowned.

The passing propeller, *Dominion,* took the crew and passengers from the beach and returned them to Brockville by eight o'clock that Tuesday night. A boy working on the steamer was also missing and presumed drowned.[142] The earthly remains of Mrs. Jones were conveyed to a Brockville hotel, a coroner was summoned on Wednesday, an inquest was held on Thursday with the verdict of "Accidental Death" rendered that same day, and the body was returned to Kingston and interred on Friday; frontier action was swift and only slightly delayed by bureaucracy. Today, that process would take weeks!

The 176' (52.8-metre)-long *Kingston,* built at Montreal in 1855[143] and insured for $32,000.00 in 1872, burned to the bare hull, completely destroying the cargo and baggage. The local newspaper reported that, upon the steamer's previous trip, the crew had gone on strike for an increase in wages, and were discharged as a result. Suspicion of the fire's cause fell upon the inexperience of the hastily-hired new crew.[144]

The *Kingston's* iron hull was rebuilt after this destruction and renamed the *Bavarian.* Unfortunately, the new ship tragically burned to the hull the following year, in November, 1873. Again rebuilt, the vessel received yet another new name, the *Algerian,* under which she laboured for over thirty years before being renamed the *Cornwall* in 1904. After 75 years of service to the Kingston area, the *Cornwall* was scuttled in Lake Ontario (see chapter 9).

CHINA   (October, 1872)

Launched at Kingston early in 1872, the 130-foot (39-metre), 333-ton, propeller-driven steamer, *China,* carrying a load of pig iron and general merchandise, burned to a total loss in the Kingston area later that same year in

October. The vessel was insured for $24,000,[145] and her master, Captain Patterson, was not long without a new ship to command.[146]

The *China* rests in about 120 feet (36 metres) of water east of False Duck Island towards Nine Mile Point. Scuba divers searching for the schooner, *Annie Falconer,* in the 1970's accidentally located this shipwreck. Although badly burned and sitting in deep, dark waters, the *China's* remains include her steeple compound engine, boiler and four-bladed propeller.[147]

MEDBURY   (November 5, 1872)

The schooner, *Medbury,* sank in a collision with the schooner, *Hercules,* at 10:30 P.M., Tuesday, November 5, 1872, off Four Mile Point, Lake Ontario, with no loss of life. The *Hercules,* bound from Kingston to Hamilton with a load of railroad iron, encountered unfavourable weather, came about, and headed back to Kingston when she sighted the *Medbury,* loaded with salt for Chicago. Although both vessels displayed the proper lights that night, neither captain accurately judged their proximity, and the ships struck violently. The *Hercules,* severely bow damaged, remained afloat; the *Medbury* was stove in and sank.[148]

Days later, the *Medbury* was still a problem:

> ...The master of a schooner, which arrived grain laden in port last night, reports having nearly passed over the wreck [of the schooner, Medbury] in the impenetrable darkness of the night. He says she lies off the south of the Point (Four Mile), and a craft deviating from a straight line down the lake is almost sure to come in close proximity, if not in contact, with the barrier which the Medbery [sic] has become --- a worthless loss. Steps should be taken therefore to have her moved around the point, and obviate the extreme probability of a collision.[149]

Any action taken upon the lost *Medbury* was not reported.

QUAIL   (March 17, 1873)

The petite steamer, *Quail,* which usually plied the waters between Kingston, Napanee, and Belleville, was waiting out winter quarters at Northport when she caught fire and burned to a total loss on March 17, 1873.[150] Insured for $2,500, the 15-ton *Quail,* measuring 53' (15.9 metres) in length and 13' (3.9 metres) in beam, had been built only five years earlier at Chatham, Ontario.[151]

NEW YORK (1878)

The small (129-ton), wooden sidewheeler, *New York,* built at Ogdensburg, New York, in 1861 and measuring 96' (28.8 metres) in length and 17' (5.1 metres) in beam, passed into Canadian ownership in 1877, but was never used. The ship burned to a complete loss at Deseronto, Ontario, in 1878.[152]

---

[128]Metcalfe, *Marine Memories, op. cit.,* 68.

[129]Metcalfe, *Canvas & Steam on Quinte Waters, op. cit.,* 88.

[130]*Daily British Whig* (Kingston), November 7, 1870.

[131]Ibid.

[132]Ibid.

[133]Metcalfe, *Marine Memories, op. cit.,* 69.

[134]*Daily British Whig* (Kingston), November 7, 1870.

[135]Metcalfe, *Canvas & Steam on Quinte Waters, op. cit.,* 89.

[136]Mills, *op. cit.,* 63.

[137]Donald Swainson. *A Shipping Empire: Garden Island.* Kingston: Marine Museum of the Great Lakes, 1984: centre chart (pages not numbered).

[138]Mills, *op. cit.,* Supplement One.

[139]Ibid., 55.

[140]*Daily News* (Kingston), Friday, June 14, 1872.

[141]Ibid.

[142]*Daily News* (Kingston), Wednesday, June 12, 1872.

[143]Mills, *op. cit.,* 66.

[144]*Daily News* (Kingston), Wednesday, June 12, 1872.

[145]*Daily News* (Kingston), October 16, 1872.

[146]*Daily News* (Kingston), November 22, 1872.

[147]Kohl, *Dive Ontario Two! More Ontario Shipwreck Stories, op. cit.,* 30.

[148]*Daily News* (Kingston), November 6, 1872.

[149]*Daily News* (Kingston), November 12, 1872.

[150]*Daily News* (Kingston), March 18, 1873.

[151]Mills, *op. cit.,* 97.

[152]Ibid., Supplement Two.

Chapter Four
The 1880's

TRANSIT   (May 7, 1880)

Launched at Toronto in 1856, the 109-ton sidewheel steamer, *Transit,* burned to a complete loss at Belleville, Ontario, on May 7, 1880. The ship's measurements were 115' (34.5 metres) in length and 17' (5.1 metres) in beam.[153]

OLIVE BRANCH   (September 30, 1880)

A mystery vessel sank between the Ducks Islands on September 30, 1880. The Belleville newspaper, in its "Marine Notes" column, reported that

> We mentioned yesterday that a vessel had been lost near the Ducks, and that her name and other circumstances were unknown. The [Kingston] Whig furnishes further particulars: ---The masters of the Huron, Fitzhugh and Augusta all brought the information to port that en route hither they saw a schooner in the distance ahead of them, that about noon she suddenly disappeared, and that they all concluded a disaster had occurred. Their impression is confirmed by the captain of the schr. Dudley, who saw the topmast of a vessel above water as he sailed down the lake for Kingston in the afternoon. Various have been the surmises, but up to the time of writing no reliable clue has been obtained respecting the name of the missing schr. or the crew, who are generally supposed to have perished. They did not seem to have had an opportunity to prepare for the emergency, and were without anything to assist in buoying them up for any considerable length of time. The case is at present shrouded in mystery, an explanation of which will only be forthcoming when the water gives up its dead after the lapse of a few days, or when some other evidence is supplied to place the question of identity beyond a doubt. In the meantime the accident is a matter of much speculation, and the friends of Kingston sailors must suffer not a little from suspense.[154]

Initial suspicions held the unfortunate vessel to be either the schooner, *Ocean Wave,* the schooner, *Olive Branch,* or the schooner, *Great Western,* but local sailors, gloomily shaking their heads, considered it to be the *Olive Branch* "that may have went down."[155]

By October 4th, two days later, the safety of the schooners, *Great Western* and *Ocean Wave,* had been ascertained, so presumptions about the *Olive Branch's* fate were made. The captain of the schooner, *H. P. Murray,* daringly cruised through immense waves past the topmast sticking out of the water at the wreck site, and his description of the vessel's fly (a small flag used to tell wind direction) corresponded with that of the *Olive Branch.*[156] The strong winds continued the next day, and "vessels from Kingston have been unable to get out to the sunken craft on account of the heavy sea outside."[157]

On October 4th, the steamer, *Edith,* from Sackets Harbor, retrieved an unmarked cabin stool and a plank floating near the Ducks, and fishermen on Grenadier Island thought the lost ship could be the schooner, *Volunteer.*[158]

On October 7th, the Kingston press reported that "Mrs. Capt. McKee, of the schr. *Richardson,* made the fly for the schr. *Olive Branch.* If it could be secured and brought to the city the identity of the vessel might be established beyond a doubt. Mrs. McKee would know the fly."[159]

A crewmember's single shoe on the deck of the shipwreck acts as a grim reminder of the tragic loss of the schooner, Olive Branch. PHOTO BY CRIS KOHL.

The wind and the waves refused to subside, but a daring captain and his crew ventured to solve the mystery of the sunken craft:

> Captain Dix, of the "White Oak," en route to Kingston, lowered a boat and approached the mast of the sunken vessel at the Ducks. The fly was secured and brought to this city, and submitted to the inspection of Mrs. Capt. McKee, who made it. She believes it belongs to the "Olive Branch." Suspicions have thus been confirmed almost beyond a doubt. Capt. Dix says the vessel lies about two miles from Timber Island, in about seventy feet of water. Her bow is about

eight or ten feet higher than her stern. She is on a sloping shoal. Had she sailed a mile nearer the city, she would have survived the storm, or at least the crew would have been saved. All hands must have been on deck at the time of the disaster and their bodies will probably rise to-day or to-morrow.

Rev. John Aull, of Ratho, a brother of the unfortunate Captain, has written to a citizen asking for particulars of the accident. The captain has four sisters and two brothers.

It is hardly probable that the vessel will be raised. Some vessel coming down the lake in the night will break off the spars, and that will be the end of her.[160]

Operating mostly as a barley carrier, the *Olive Branch* was loaded with coal when she left Oswego bound for Kingston, and sank off False Duck Island near one of the Pennicons. All on board were lost: Captain Aull of Kingston, the cook, Mrs. Minnie Jarvis of Belleville, plus two French and one Oswego sailor. One account names an additional sailor, William Rose of South Bay, Ontario.[161]

This uninsured (her insurance had expired on September 15th, two weeks before her loss!) two-masted schooner, *Olive Branch,* measuring 92' (27.6 metres) in length, 22' (6.6 metres) in beam, and 8' (2.4 metres) in draft, was built in Picton, Ontario, in 1871 by Messrs. Redman. She was painted white above and green below. The *Olive Branch* was rated B1, with a value of $3,000. A hardhat diver, inspecting the wreck when calmer weather prevailed, noted that the vessel's garboard strake, the plank next to the keel, was sprung for a length of several feet. The ship could have struck a reef, and it was likely that her crew frantically pumped the vessel while the captain unsuccessfully attempted to run her onto False Duck Island.[162]

In about 1961, local marine historian Willis Metcalfe met a Kingston scuba diver named Guenter Wernthaler and, with charts in hand, discussed the probable resting place of the schooner, *Olive Branch.* A dot was pencilled onto the chart, and Mr. Wernthaler, with his depthsounder-equipped boat, excitedly proceeded to the spot and found the shipwreck within a half hour of searching.[163]

The *Olive Branch* is intact, sitting upright at the base of a shoal down which she seems to have slid (the original accounts placed the wreck in about 70 feet, or 21 metres, or water, but she now rests in 98 feet, or almost 30 metres). A sidescan sonar image of the steep slope just off the wreck's stern suggests a possible skid mark left by the vessel. Most of her original artifacts remain on board, including a windlass, the ship's wheel, deadeyes, blocks, a standing capstan near midship, a pump near the bow, hinged catheads (the starboard one still holding a steel-stock fluke anchor), a Quebec stove in an open hold near midship, a fallen mast, complete with a crosstree and wire rigging, lying on the vessel's starboard side, and a collapsed bowsprit.[164]

Thus the physical remains of a terrible tragedy from the past continue to fascinate visiting scuba divers today.

CARRIE & CORA   (November 10, 1882)

Hundreds of barrels, marked with the letters "J." and "M. T." and filled with apples and potatoes, came ashore between Point Petre and South Bay Point during a nasty November storm in 1882. Mr. John Palmatier of Long Point personally rescued 850 of the apple barrels. A large amount of wreckage, including a vessel's stern and cabin, plus furniture and fixtures, washed ashore; the schooner, *Carrie & Cora,* had succumbed to the violent waves.[165]

HENRY FOLGER   (November 30, 1882)

The three-masted, 326-ton bulk freight schooner, *Henry Folger,* was pounded to pieces after stranding on Salmon Point reef on November 30, 1882, with tragic loss of life.

The *Henry Folger,* "one of the staunchest vessels sailing on the lakes,"[166] had had a brush with disaster just a week earlier on Lake Erie, when she encountered seas that made a clean breach over her deck and prohibited the crew's movements from forward to aft. She had also lost her yawl boat, fore jibs and foresail. Her seams had opened, her bulwarks were stove in, and she carried only tattered remnants of sails. By some miracle, she reached Buffalo, and enough repairs were made to continue through the Welland Canal and into Lake Ontario in a mad dash to reach home port. With all the damage the vessel had sustained, the delivery of her load of 695 tons of coal bound from Cleveland to Brockville for P. D. Conger and the Grand Trunk Railway Company[167] would be the ship's last load of the season. The *Folger* was attempting that final run across the lake to deliver her cargo and then head home, to Clayton, New York, for winter lay-up, when she and her crew encountered calamity.

The rocks, wind, and waves that violently destroyed the wooden ship at Salmon Point dealt equally savage blows to the bodies of the nine men on board the *Henry Folger.*

...The bodies that came ashore were badly mangled by being beaten on the rocks by the surf. They were at once coffined and buried....

The Henry Folger was first observed by the lighthouse keeper half a mile off Salmon Point at daylight on Friday morning. Two men could be seen lashed to the rigging. An unsuccessful attempt was made to launch a boat to rescue them. The schooner went to pieces about 11 o'clock and two bodies were washed ashore, which have been identified as those of Capt. McDonald, of Clayton, and First Mate Wiley, of the same place. Only the two bodies have thus far been recovered. They were buried at Cherry Valley on Saturday, but the friends arrived to-day and they have been disinterred and

taken away. It is supposed that the schooner struck the shoal during the night, the lighthouse being obscured by the snow storm. About thirty tons of coal came ashore and is lying in piles on the beach....

The schooner Henry Folger when first seen was about three-quarters of a mile from shore. Her mizzen mast was gone and her stern had the appearance of being stove in. A volunteer crew consisting of D. Hudger, Jonathon Bowerman, Peter Pickman, H. Huff and S. Manning, launched a staunch fishing boat, and made an attempt to reach the ill-fated vessel, but although making almost superhuman efforts failed to reach the wreck, the gale and breakers proving too much for their strength. About 9 o'clock the mainmast went down, and the timbers could be seen to heave, and the seas washing through her. A few minutes later the foremast toppled over, and nothing was left of what was a few hours before a fine schooner, commanded by a brave captain, and manned by a fine crew of eight men....[168]

Several days later, two more bodies from the wreck of the *Folger* drifted ashore at Salmon Point and were conveyed to Picton. By that time, reportedly all that was left of the vessel were her anchors and chains.[169]

The press immediately berated the political powers-that-be for having, just a few months earlier, relocated two metallic lifeboats from Salmon Point. "A lifeboat station is needed on this point, thoroughly equipped, and in charge of a trained lifeboat crew. The men on the *Folger* could have been saved if the necessary boats, thoroughly equipped, could have been obtained."[170] Lifesaving stations were set up on the shores of Prince Edward County the next year.

ELIZA QUINLAN   (December 4, 1882)

The 131-gross-ton Canadian schooner, *Eliza Quinlan,* was built in 1870 at Port Hope, Ontario,[171] and measured 97' 3" (29 metres) in length, 18' 8" (5.5 metres) in beam, and 9' (2.7 metres) in draft.[172] On December 4, 1882, the *Quinlan* was loaded with coal from Oswego to Napanee, when wind drove this unfortunate vessel aground just offshore at Poplar Point, three miles (4.6 kilometres) west of the Point Traverse light. Her crew endured several hours of terror before succor arrived through the gallant efforts of Jackson Bongard of Long Point. He and several men heroically guided a fishing boat to effect the rescue of the distressed crew. At first, the uninsured *Eliza Quinlan,* when the tug, *McArthur,* failed to release her, was considered "damaged beyond the possibility of repair,"[173] but when salvage efforts were postponed until the following spring, it was "hoped to save her, and that she will not suffer much damage in the meantime."[174] In the spring of 1883, however, the *Eliza Quinlan* still refused to yield from her stubborn roost, and she was abandoned. For several years, her hull remained in place until finally destroyed by the elements of nature.[175]

EDITH SEWELL   (July 30, 1883)

The little steamer, *Edith Sewell,* loaded with boxes of fish from Georgian Bay, sank, stern foremost, in about 60' (18 metres) of water off Long Point between Long Island and Pigeon Light while running between Kingston and Sackets Harbor. The crew, consisting of Capt. Bailey, Engineer Bailey, and Steward McKee, were saved. A reporter who was picnicking on Horse Shoe Island observed the sinking:

> ...she gave a lurch and her whole bottom and one side were seen. Some fish boxes rolled off...noticed a change in the tug's course. She headed for Long Point but had only gone about 200 yards when she gave a plunge on the crest of a wave and went into the trough of the sea. She mounted a second wave, went backward and disappeared stern first. From the time the vessel gave the first lurch until she went down she vigorously blew her whistle. The sound could not be heard but the escaping steam could be distinctly seen. The crew clung to the wreckage and fishermen shortly afterwards pick (sic) them up and landed them safely....[176]

The powerful, little tug, *Edith Sewell,* built in 1875, had a value of $3,000 at the time of her sinking. Unfortunately, she carried no insurance.[177]

MILWAUKEE   (November 10, 1883)

The Kingston headline screamed PROBABLE CALAMITY![178] when the coal barge, *Milwaukee,* sank in the gales of November 10th, 1883. The tug, *D. G. Thompson,* was towing the barges, *Senator* and *Milwaukee*, both laden with Montréal-destined coal, from Charlotte towards Kingston. Off Main Duck and Galloo Island, the *Milwaukee,* last in the line, had her steering gear disabled and, becoming unmanagable, swung around into the trough of the sea and her hawser (towline) snapped. In these stormy conditions, the tug and remaining tow were powerless to turn around and retrieve the *Milwaukee,* and the captain of the *Senator* thought he heard, above the sighing of the wind, the agonizing wail, "We are sinking." The *Milwaukee's* master, Capt. Langevin, from Valleyfield, Quebec, left behind a wife and six children. Most of the other four crewmembers also hailed from there, probably because the *Milwaukee* was owned by the Montreal Transportation Company.[179] The conclusion was that the violent storm "was death-dealing to the little crew, and that they sank in the waters which in a few minutes had been lashed into a perfect fury."[180]

EUREKA   (November 26, 1883)

The Lake Ontario seas of late November, 1883, rolled over the lee rail of the 152-ton schooner, *Eureka,* as she laboured heavily on her trip carrying 270 tons of coal from Oswego to Kingston. The ship and crew had left Oswego at 12:30. Captain Chambers, half-owner of his command, had to jibe his vessel when the strong winds shifted to south-southwest. He knew they were in trouble. Approaching Main Duck Island, the *Eureka* sprang a leak and, goaded by desperation, the crew strained energetically at the pumps.

Captain Chambers regularly checked the condition below deck and, returning above, stalwartly ordered his three-man crew to keep pumping. He mentioned nothing of the rising waters in the ship's hold.

By 6:00 P.M., as the sinking schooner bore southwest off Pigeon Island light, Captain Chambers decided to beach his vessel on that tiny haven of solid land. He ordered a man aloft to unfurl the gaff topsail in an effort to increase their speed, but with the winds howling increasingly, the sailor could not climb to that point. The captain knew they would not reach land. He summoned his crew to the stern.

"Boys," he stated matter-of-factly, "we must leave the vessel."

He then made two passes with his knife at one of the ropes holding up the schooner's yawl boat; a crewmember quickly slashed the other end, and they all jumped into the freed vessel.

There was no time to go below and collect personal effects. Capt. Chambers momentarily cursed the loss of his brand new suit of clothing, the vest pocket of which contained $30.00 in cash. The towering seas, raging gales, and freezing waters quickly returned him to reality. He was no stranger to shipwrecks, having been on the bark, *British Lyon,* when that vessel was wrecked off Long Point in 1875, and he sailed on board the *George Thurston* when that ship was wrecked in Georgian Bay in late 1882. However, he had never seen such threatening conditions of nature as those in which he now found himself.

Desperation makes an excellent teacher; the four men, Captain Chambers, Mate Stephen Tyo, George Belcher, and James Shughrue, became persistent, bravehearted machines, set upon survival, as the daunting winds and dreadful seas tried to intimidate them by controlling the course of their little yawl boat.

At about 9:00 that evening, their yawl boat hit the shallow rocks of Simcoe Island. The men hastily struggled through the breakers and, weak and almost helpless from their cold, wet ordeal, staggered to the nearest residence and knocked on the door. It was the home of Mr. Horne and his family, who immediately offered assistance to the unfortunate shipwreck victims.

The next day, the scow, *Minnie,* transported the four men from Simcoe Island to Kingston. They had survived a tumultuous experience.

The schooner, *Eureka,* did not fare as well. The ship sank shortly after being abandoned, never to be recovered. Classed B2, she was insured for $1,800 of her $2,500 value.[181]

NORMAN   (November 30, 1883)

The 153-ton steambarge, *Norman,* while sheltered at MacDonald's Cove in the Bay of Quinte, caught fire and burned to the water's edge on the night of November 30-December 1, 1883, a total loss. She was light (containing no cargo), having just returned from delivering a load of barley to Richardson & Sons in Oswego. Insurance company policies were such that insurance on hulls expired at noon on November 30th, so, as fate would have it, the *Norman* was newly-uninsured when she was destroyed.[182] Launched in 1872 at Opinicon Lake, Ontario, this 98' (29.4 metre)-long vessel worked mostly on the Rideau Canal. Capt. Collins, Prince Edward County, owned the *Norman* at the time of loss.[183]

PRINCE EDWARD   (June, 1884)

The 72-ton sidewheeler, *Prince Edward*, launched at St. Catharines, Ontario, in 1868, burned to a total loss at Belleville in June, 1884. This small, beamy steamer measured 81' (24.3 metres) in length and 36' (10.8 metres) in beam.[184]

INDIAN   (October 26, 1885)

The propeller-driven steamer, *Indian,* claimed a tumultuous early name-history. Launched at Buffalo in 1853 as the U.S. vessel, *Cincinnati,* her name was changed to *City of Hamilton* when she was sold to Canadian interests in 1855. For the year 1857, she sailed by the name, *Alps,* until, finally, in 1858, she was renamed *Indian.* This 452-ton vessel, measuring 141' (42.3 metres) in length and 26' (7.8 metres) in beam, was rebuilt early in 1880.[185] That year was not particularly good for the *Indian:*

> The Indian, recently converted from a propeller into a steambarge, ran into this harbor [Kingston] yesterday for refuge. Her siphon pipe having been broken during the gale, there was three feet of water in her hold when she reached Gunn's wharf. She was laden with 150,000 feet of lumber, consigned from Trenton to Oswego. She should have had her bottom caulked here, but could not be drawn out laden. A dry dock is an absolute necessity.[186]

A few days later, at Oswego, more misfortune befell her:

> While the steambarge Indian was backing up in Oswego harbor the bell-cord broke, severing communication between the captain and engineer, and the Indian backed against the schooner E. K. Hart, carrying away her jib-boom. The Indian is docked to be caulked.[187]

The *Indian's* immediate troubles were soon solved. However, in October, 1885, she burned to a complete loss at Kingston on the west side of Belle Island.[188] Her remains were later used as firewood by local residents.

GLENORA or GLENDORA   (November 19, 1887)

Confusion reigns supreme among secondary sources of information about the vessels named the *Glenora* and the *Glendora*. (See chapter 8 for an unidentified vessel nicknamed the *Glendora*). The spelling of that name, with and without the letter "d" in the middle, has invariably been interchanged.

This *Glendora* was likely a local vessel, either a sloop or a small schooner, which reportedly sank 2.5 miles (4 kilometres) southwest of Amherst Island on November 19, 1887.[189] The rumour of her carrying $60,000 (a more modest source states $25,000)[190] in gold and silver is likely just that---a rumour. If anyone can prove otherwise, my telephone number is (519) 351-1966.

JULIA   (November 25, 1887)

The Canadian schooner, *Julia,* sank in a storm off the Point Petre light on November 25, 1887. She was valued at $5,000.[191]

QUINTE   (October 23, 1889)

The tragic loss of the 331-ton wooden steamer, *Quinte,* occurred on the evening of October 23, 1889. Launched as the *Beauharnois* at Quebec City in 1871, she measured 128' (38.4 metres) in length with a beam of 23' (6.9 metres). Her name change took place in 1882 after a rebuild.[192]

The Deseronto Navigation Company had purchased the *Beauharnois* from her Quebec owners in 1882; besides refitting the vessel for local traffic, this company was the one which changed the ship's name to *Quinte.*[193]

The catastrophe which claimed several lives is summarized in this newspaper account:

BURNED TO THE WATER'S EDGE.

The Steamer Quinte Destroyed by Fire
Near Deseronto, Ont.---Four Lives
Supposed to Have Been Lost.

DESERONTO, ONT., October 23---The steamer Quinte was burned to the water's edge about three miles from Deseronto on the way to Picton, about 6 o'clock this evening. Four lives are supposed to be lost---Capt. Christie's mother and young brother Charles, the ladies' maid and young son named Davern, of Trenton. As far as can be ascertained the passengers were all saved. Three or four have severe

> burns, but the doctors report none seriously. Many
> were chilled by being in the water. All the survivors
> have been brought to Deseronto and are being
> properly cared for. The fire, it is supposed, started
> in the furnace room and spread quickly to the whole
> boat. The captain ran her ashore only a short
> distance away, where she lies almost entirely
> destroyed. All freight and baggage was lost.[194]

Many people were seriously burned before rescuers arrived (this may account for an eventual fifth fatality, mentioned in some sources). The nearby steamers, *Ripple* and *Deseronto,* raced to the scene and picked up survivors. Some passengers, clinging to the paddlewheels, were rescued by people in rowboats. Because of the deaths, a Department of Marine court of inquiry was ordered.[195]

The sidewheeler, Quinte, *with a full load of passengers. She carried only 24 passengers the day she caught fire and was destroyed.* PUBLIC ARCHIVES OF CANADA.

---

[153]Mills, op. cit., 118.

[154]*Daily Intelligencer* (Belleville), Friday, October 1, 1880.

[155]*British Whig* (Kingston), Saturday, October 2, 1880.

[156]*British Whig* (Kingston), Monday, October 4, 1880.

[157]*British Whig* (Kingston), Tuesday, October 5, 1880.

[158]*British Whig* (Kingston), Wednesday, October 6, 1880.

[159]*British Whig* (Kingston), Thursday, October 7, 1880.

[160]*British Whig* (Kingston), Friday, October 8, 1880.

[161]Metcalfe, *Canvas & Steam on Quinte Waters,* op. cit., 105.

[162]Ibid.

[163]Interview with Mr. Guenter Wernthaler by the author on July 23, 1996.

[164]Kohl, *Dive Ontario! The Guide to Shipwrecks and Scuba Diving,* op. cit., 78-81.

[165]*British Whig* (Kingston), Monday, November 13, 1882.

[166]*British Whig* (Kingston), Saturday, December 2, 1882.

[167]*British Whig* (Kingston), Monday, December 4, 1882.

[168]Ibid.

[169]*British Whig* (Kingston), Friday, December 8, 1882.

[170]*British Whig* (Kingston), Monday, December 4, 1882.

[171]Mansfield, op. cit., 876.

[172]Metcalfe, *Canvas & Steam on Quinte Waters,* op. cit., 62.

[173]*British Whig* (Kingston), Saturday, December 9, 1882.

[174]*British Whig* (Kingston), Monday, December 11, 1882.

[175]Metcalfe, *Canvas & Steam on Quinte Waters,* op. cit.

[176]*Weekly British Whig* (Kingston), August 2, 1883.

[177]Ibid.

[178]*British Whig* (Kingston), Thursday, November 15, 1883.

[179]Ibid.

[180]*British Whig* (Kingston), Friday, November 16, 1883.

[181]*British Whig* (Kingston), Tuesday, November 27, 1883.

[182]*British Whig* (Kingston), Saturday, December 1, 1883.

[183]Ibid.

[184]Mills, op. cit., 94.

[185]Ibid., Supplement Two.

[186]*Daily British Whig* (Kingston), Monday, May 31, 1880.

[187]*Daily British Whig* (Kingston), Thursday, June 3, 1880.

[188]Mills, op. cit.

[189]Metcalfe, *Canvas & Steam on Quinte Waters,* op. cit., 75.

[190]Karl E. Heden. *Directory of Shipwrecks of the Great Lakes.* Boston: Bruce Humphries Publishers, 1966: 85.

[191]Ibid., 87. This information also appears on Paul Ackerman's "Lake Ontario Dive Chart," published by the Midwest Explorers League, Chicago, 1990.

[192]*Beauharnois.* Master Sheet. Institute for Great Lakes Research, Bowling Green State University, Ohio.

[193]Metcalfe, *Canvas & Steam on Quinte Waters,* op. cit., 119.

[194]*Detroit Free Press,* October 24, 1889.

[195]Metcalfe, *Canvas & Steam on Quinte Waters,* op. cit.

Chapter Five
The 1890's

McARTHUR   (April, 1890)

The propeller-driven steamship, *McArthur,* burned to a total loss at Collins Bay, Ontario, near Kingston, in April, 1890. This 169-ton ship, measuring 103' (30.9 metres) in length and 25' (7.5 metres) in beam, slid down a launchramp in nearby Portsmouth in 1877. She was rebuilt just three years before her demise.[196]

MUNSON   (April 30, 1890)

In early April, 1890, the Belleville-headquartered dredge, *Munson,* used for maintaining adequate water depth at harbour entrances or similar work, received several contracts, the most important of which was to ensure that the Montreal Transportation Company's immense new schooner-barge, the *Minnedosa,* would have adequate launch depth at Kingston on Saturday, April 26, 1890.

This connection with the four-masted *Minnedosa,* the largest Canadian sailing vessel ever built on the Great Lakes (she measured an incredible 250', or 75 metres, in length),[197] proved to be of lasting historical significance to the *Munson.* That the *Minnedosa* turned people's heads even in the United States, is seen in this newspaper article which appeared about a month after the ship's launch:

> **When the schr. Minnedosa came into** (Cleveland) **port she probably attracted more attention than any vessel that has been here for many a day and she deserved it all the more, too, even if she was from Canada. She is a four master with as finely modelled lines as any sailor would care to look upon, and taken altogether is as clean and trim a looking craft as was ever seen on the lakes. She was built at Kingston last winter and is on her first trip coming from Kingston. Her dimensions are larger than are usually found in sailing vessels being 250 feet keel and 36 feet beam. She rides the water like a swan, and, after seeing her, vessel men felt disposed to take back many of the hard things they had said about the ability of Canadians to build a good-looking vessel.[198]**

The Kingston press added that

> Marine men think the M(ontreal) T(ransportation) company should have registered the Minnedosa in Kingston instead of in Montreal. A boat as well modelled and staunchly built has never been built in the Montreal district.[199]

Thus, the launch of the leviathan, *Minnedosa,* again guaranteed Kingston a place in the Great Lakes maritime records books. The *Minnedosa* launch project, the little dredge *Munson's* most important job, also turned out to be her last.

This working dredge from the early part of the twentieth century is similar to the Munson. *Extracting* Munson *documentation is difficult because dredges were not required to be registered.* AUTHOR'S COLLECTION.

On Wednesday, April 30, 1890, her job at Kingston completed, the *Munson* was taken in tow of the tug, *Emma Munson,* along with two scows, and hauled westward to resume construction work on the new Bay of Quinte bridge at the town of Rossmore. A few miles west of Kingston, just off Lemoine Point near the Brothers Islands, the dredge appeared to be leaning to one side.

> ...She had been leaking before leaving [Kingston], but it was thought that it would not amount to much. When opposite Lemoine's Point, and when the crew least expected it, she sank to the bottom, in about one hundred feet of water. The tow lines were cut in order to save the tugs. The dredge went down beam ends first. The cook, in the kitchen at the time making preparations for dinner, was told to come up,

but before he had [time] to run to the stairway, the
vessel was under water. The fellow went down, but
soon came up and was rescued by the crew in an
exhausted state. He stated afterwards that the suction
of the dredge going down kept him from coming to
the surface. He had to wait until the dredge had
reached the bottom. A lot of timber on her deck came
up after she sank.[200]

A later newspaper account fleshed out the details, including that the *Munson*
sank within four minutes of her tilt first being noticed, that soundings showed
she lay in 130 feet (39 metres) of water, that William Green, the cook, was
taken 30 feet (nine metres) underwater when the dredge sank, that the men lost
everything, that the vessel was valued at about $15,000, and that the sinking
likely occurred "by the springing of a plank on the bottom of the craft"[201]

In 1981, scuba divers retrieved many of the artifacts on board the *Munson,*
including hundreds of plain, functional porcelain and enamel tin utensils which
Bill Green had possibly counted among his favourite kitchen items. In the spring
of 1991, 180 of these artifacts were donated to the Hastings County Museum in
Belleville, Ontario, thus heralding the beginning of that institution's Marine
Heritage section.[202]

The *Munson,* sitting in 110' (33 metres) of water, is today a popular scuba
dive site, offering exploration of her basic, skeletal layout and views of her
distinctive crane and bucket features and numerous artifacts displayed on deck.[203]

Dozens of the Munson's *artifacts remain on the shipwreck site, particularly this
arrangement of bottles, china, and other kitchen utensils.* PHOTO BY CRIS KOHL.

OCEAN WAVE   (November 9, 1890)

An unfair proportion of maritime accidents seems to have befallen vessels on their last trips of the sailing season. It is doubly (no, triply!) lamentable when the captain and the mate of the lost vessel had also planned to make this their final voyage before retiring.

Captain Brokenshire and Mate Martin did not worry about the leaks in their schooner's yawl boat. They planned to load their vessel, the *Ocean Wave* (this schooner is not to be confused with the steamer of the same name; see Chapter Two), with a load of lumber for delivery to Oswego, where they would pick up a cargo of coal, head home to Cobourg, Ontario, with it, and "settle down ashore for the rest of our lives."[204]

This, however, was the last earthly voyage this ship and crew were to make.

LOSS OF THE OCEAN WAVE.

Those of the Crew Who Are Known to Have Sailed Her.

The schr. Ocean Wave, found capsized near Oswego, was owned by the captain and mate and had been in the employ of the Downey Co., of Belleville, off and on for years. She left Belleville port on Thursday last for Trenton after having discharged her second cargo of coal for Capt. Eccles. At Trenton she took on a heavy deck load of lumber, lath and heading and put out for Oswego on Friday. On the way down the bay she put into Belleville and shipped Joseph Wells, which completed her crew. The schooner was found about fifteen miles off Oswego, bearing north, lying on her side, with spars in water and stern washing out. There was no one aboard. It will be difficult to tow her to port in her present condition. She was a light, draught vessel and of the small class. Her capacity was not more than 100,000 feet of lumber.

The storm on the lakes on Sunday night [the night the *Ocean Wave* disappeared] was the most terrific ever experienced by the oldest mariners. Wells, the victim from Belleville, was from Quebec,...He was unmarried and eighteen years of age....[205]

The heavy deckload of lumber on the small schooner likely altered her centre of gravity detrimentally when she faced the storm's onslaught. The *Ocean Wave* was built by William Redmond of Picton, Ontario, and launched in 1868.[206]

B. W. FOLGER   (November 24, 1894)

Fire was the worst and most dreaded enemy of wooden boats. Early steamers, deriving their propulsion from a fire source, were particularly susceptible to this deadly danger. Boilers exploded regularly with tragic loss of life; satisfactorily distancing and insulating a firebox from the rest of a wooden boat was often unsuccessful. On occasion, schooners also became fire victims.

The explosion of a liquid fuel lamp started a fire on board the wooden schooner, *B. W. Folger,* near Amherst Island on November 24, 1894. Laden with lumber, the ship burned to the water's edge.[207] No lives were lost.

Insurance companies bear reluctance to pay claims resulting from human error. Although the *Folger* was insured for $2,000, with a valuation of $3,000, the Mercantile Insurance Company offered to pay only $1,350 for her loss.[208]

The *B. W. Folger,* a versatile vessel in the course of her career, carried a variety of cargoes locally, e.g. "The schr. *B. W. Folger,* from Fair Haven, arrived yesterday. She carried 250 tons coal for J. Smith. She made the run from Fairhaven to this city in seven hours":[209] "The schr. *B. W. Folger* loads telegraph poles for Oswego at 15¢ each":[210] and "The *B. W. Folger* has been in the ice business since the 9th of March. She took the last cargo of 2,000 tons at Baker's Island, near Trenton, on Saturday. She also loaded lath for Charlotte."[211]

JULIA   (February 25, 1895)

The 108-ton schooner, *Julia,* burned to a complete loss at Wolfe Island, near Kingston, on February 25, 1895.[212] Once again, the insurance company which covered her bargained in their settlement with the owners; the Commercial Union company settled the loss for a mere $1,350.[213]

NED HANLAN   (October 9, 1895)

The small schooner, *Ned Hanlan,* named in honour of Canada's great oarsman, burned to the water's edge in Belleville on the morning of Wednesday, October 9, 1895. The ship had been out of commission for several months and sat idle on the harbour bottom due to low water conditions. Unable to be moved, the *Ned Hanlan* was a sitting duck waiting for bored vandals to destroy her. The local press observed that the fire "was doubtless the work of an incendiary."[214]

Constructed at Jacob Harris' shipyard at Dog Lake, near Kingston, and launched as the *Mary Fox of Bath,* she measured 81.4' (24.2 metres) in length, 20' (6 metres) in beam, and 7.6' (2,2 metres) in draft. Her name change to *Ned Hanlan* occurred after a rebuild in 1880.[215]

HIRAM A. CALVIN   (December, 1895)

Home is the sailor: the old paddlewheel tug, *Hiram A. Calvin,* built at Garden Island, Ontario, in 1868 by Henry Roney,[216] burned to a total loss at the shipyards at Garden Island, Ontario, in December, 1895. This 309-ton ship measured 134' by 43' (43.2 by 12.9 metres).[217]

ALBERTA   (July 21, 1899)

The flat barge, *Alberta,* is not to be confused with the wooden steamer, *Alberta,* which burned to a total loss at Trenton, Ontario, on October 8, 1902.[218] This *Alberta,* a 62-ton, 65' (19.5 metre)-long paddlewheeler, built at Deseronto, Ontario, in 1888,[219] sank on July 21, 1899 opposite Prinyer's Cove on the Bay of Quinte. Her remains lie upside-down in 105' (31.5 metres) of dark water.[220]

---

[196]Mills, op. cit., 78.

[197]John O. Greenwood. *Namesakes, 1900-1909.* Cleveland: Freshwater Press, Inc., 1987: 340. The name, *Minnedosa,* is a Sioux First Nation word meaning "waters of the rapids."

[198]*Daily British Whig* (Kingston), Friday, May 23, 1890, quoting the *Cleveland Press.*

[199]*Daily British Whig* (Kingston), Friday, May 23, 1890.

[200]*Daily British Whig* (Kingston), April 30, 1890.

[201]*Daily British Whig* (Kingston), May 1, 1890.

[202]*Quinte Weekly News,* Wednesday, May 22, 1991.

[203]Kohl, *Dive Ontario Two! More Ontario Shipwreck Stories,* op. cit., 45-47.

[204]Metcalfe, *Canvas & Steam on Quinte Waters,* op. cit., 102.

[205]*Daily British Whig* (Kingston), Wednesday, November 12, 1890.

[206]Metcalfe, *Canvas & Steam on Quinte Waters,* op. cit.

[207]*Detroit Free Press,* November 25, 1894.

[208]*British Whig* (Kingston), March 4, 1895.

[209]*British Whig* (Kingston), Monday, May 31, 1880.

[210]*British Whig* (Kingston), Tuesday, June 1, 1880.

[211]*British Whig* (Kingston), Tuesday, May 25, 1880.

[212]Heden, op. cit., 87.

[213]*British Whig* (Kingston), March 4, 1895.

[214]*Daily British Whig* (Kingston), Wednesday, October 9, 1895.

[215]Metcalfe, *Canvas & Steam on Quinte Waters,* op. cit., 60 and 98.

[216]Swainson, op. cit., centre pages (pages not numbered).

[217]Mills, op. cit., 55.

[218]Greenwood, op. cit., 464.

[219]Mansfield, op. cit., 789.

[220]Kohl, *Dive Ontario Two! More Ontario Shipwreck Stories,* op. cit., 30.

Chapter Six
The 1900's, First Decade

FABIOLA   (October 21, 1900)

The old workhorse schooner, *Fabiola,* foundered about a quarter of a mile (almost half a kilometre) to the southeast of False Duck Island at two o'clock in the morning of Sunday, October 21, 1900.

The weather was fine when Capt. Daniel Bates, the *Fabiola's* owner and master, commanded the vessel, loaded with 250 tons of soft coal for Swift & Company in Kingston, to depart Charlotte at four o'clock on Saturday afternoon. By eight o'clock, when the schooner reached Long Point light, heavy seas and strong winds arose. By the time False Duck light was made, the ship leaked badly. Capt. Bates hoped that his three-man crew, pumping nonstop, could keep the *Fabiola* afloat until she reached smooth water in the lee of False Duck, or, if necessary, until he could beach her on the island, but the sinking ship lurched badly in the mountainous seas. The captain sensed the end, so he ordered the lifeboat lowered, and just in time. The *Fabiola* took a final lurch and disappeared beneath the waves. Sailor Michael McMahon manned the bow pump too long and just barely escaped the sinking ship by throwing himself into the freed lifeboat with the others.[221]

Although bobbing close to False Duck Island lighthouse, the men had lost one of their oars. They drifted at the mercy of the wind for six hours, constantly bailing out their endangered, little lifeboat with their caps and boots, before landing, exhausted, at Indian Point, where a farmer provided food and shelter,[222] 12 miles (18 kilometres) from the scene of the sinking. Proceding to the town of Bath, home of mate Roy Osleton, they procured a horsedrawn rig and drove to Kingston by four o'clock in the afternoon of the day they lost their ship. Capt. Bates praised his crew, "who behaved so cooly in such danger."[223]

The *Fabiola* was valued at $1,000, while her coal cargo was appraised at $800. Neither was insured. Lloyds rated the *Fabiola* in class B1½, essentially too old and worn to procure insurance coverage.[224] This two-masted ship, measuring 95' by 22' 4" by 9' (28.5 by 6.7 by 2.7 metres), slid down the launchramp at Oakville, Ontario, in 1852 as the *Red Oak*.[225] Twice rebuilt, the vessel's name changed to *Fabiola* in 1876.

For 61 years, the *Fabiola* lay undisturbed. A newspaper article by Willis Metcalfe in the summer of 1961 detailed the shipwreck's discovery:

...Last week, all sorts of interesting things were brought to the surface of the lake by skin divers from the sunken hulk of an unidentified two-masted sailing schooner off the False Ducks.

Discovered quite by accident, by Mel and Raymond McIntosh, with the use of their 45 ft. fishing craft, the ill-fated vessel was located sitting upright on the mud bottom in 65 feet of water, with a full cargo of coal.

Iron stone china dishes, jugs from the ship's galley were retrieved by skin divers. A caulking hammer, axe head, large clamp and deadeye was found on the vessel's oaken deck and kindly donated by the McIntosh Bros. to the writer for the collection of marine relics.

The vessel is some 100 ft. in length with a 24 foot beam and according to her size has a registered tonnage of from 125 to 175 tons, according to systems of measurements. The ship's anchors are nearby, the iron capstan and steering wheel base have been found. Her cabin has been washed away, one of her masts is broken in half, but her wooden rudder is still intact. The bowsprit is missing.

...It could be the Maggie Hunter....It could be the Eliza Quinlan....[226]

One local mariner conjectured that this shipwreck could be the remains of the *Katie Eccles*.[227]

With time, during the period when many of the artifacts, big and small, were removed (as was customary then among scuba divers, but is unethical and illegal today), it was determined that she was, indeed, the *Fabiola*.

Picton diver Doug Pettingill examines the Fabiola's *windlass, a cylindrical, horizontal, chain-hauling, ratchet device used to raise anchors.* PHOTO BY CRIS KOHL.

HERO   (June 14, 1901)

The passenger-and-freight combination steamer, *Hero,* built at Sorel, Quebec, by the Marcel Girard Shipyard in 1878, measured 138' (41.4 metres) in length, 29' (8.7 metres) in beam, and 7' (2.1 metres) in draft.[228] In spite of her relatively short length, the *Hero* was licensed to convey the huge number of 475 passengers and several railway carloads of package freight, and boasted beautiful staterooms and excellent dining room service.[229]

Fortunately, no passengers were on board when the *Hero* burned at her Belleville dock early on the morning of Friday, June 14, 1901. They had all disembarked by midnight the previous evening when the ship returned from Picton. The captain and his 12 crewmembers retired, but were soon roused by fire on board, and quickly fled the burning vessel. A young deckhand named Canning, finding the gangway below deck blocked by flames, groped his way through the pantry, jumped out of the port into the water, and swam to shore.

The fire alarm was rung at 1:47 A.M. By the time the local fire brigade arrived, the *Hero's* cabins had burned and she was floating with her stern at Queen Victoria Park and her bow pointing at the nearby Rathbun dock. A reporter later praised the good work of the firefighters, who had ensured that the buildings and vessels in close proximity to the floating inferno remained undamaged. A severe electrical storm had begun after midnight, and the captain, among many others, felt that the *Hero* was struck by lightning (although one rumour, unproven, had a lamp exploding below deck.) The *Hero,* valued at $25,000, was insured for $15,000. The crew carried no insurance on their personal effects.[230]

The loss of this ship to the local communities was great: "...No finer vessel for her size than the *Hero* ran on the blue waters of the Bay of Quinte, and her place will be hard to fill...." The steamer, *Aletha,* replaced her the next day.[231]

The "big, little boat," Hero, burned at Belleville, Ontario. AUTHOR'S COLLECTION.

D. FREEMAN   (1902)

The Canadian schooner, *D. Freeman*, of 182 net tons, was constructed at Port Burwell in 1875[232] and measured 120' (36 metres) in length, 24' (7.2 metres) in beam, and 9'8" (2.9 metres) in draft. Commissioned by and named after Ohio entrepreneur, Downey Freeman (1824-1899), this ship was built across Lake Erie in Canada by David Foster because Ohio shipwrights were temporarily unavailable.[233] The *D. Freeman's* value at the time of her launch was $4,000.[234]

The wooden-hulled *D. Freeman* plied Great Lakes waters for only five years before requiring a rebuild, which was carried out at Kingston in the summer of 1880.[235]

By the turn of the century, the *D. Freeman* was no longer in a trustworthy condition for use on the open lake, so she was retired at Kingston as a floating storage hull for grain. It is generally believed that her remains were abandoned in place.

The schooner, D. Freeman, *was 27 years old when she was retired from active duty and used as a floating grain bin at Kingston.* AUTHOR'S COLLECTION.

OWEN   (October 12, 1902)

Built at Prairie Siding, Ontario, along the shores of the Thames River in Kent County in 1884,[236] the 103-ton, propeller-driven steambarge, *Owen,* had travelled far from her original home when, eighteen years later, she went to pieces on Gull Shoal a few miles east of Point Petre on the Prince Edward County shoreline.[237]

The date of the loss was October 12, 1902. Loaded with 5,000 bushels of wheat and rye bound from Wellington, Ontario, to Richardson's grain elevator at Kingston, the *Owen's* stokestack suddenly toppled over in the rough seas off Long Point and broke the steampipe, leaving the ship powerless. Anchors failed to snag a hold on the lake bottom, and the *Owen* gradually drifted onto the shoal where she grounded firmly. No lives were lost. The Donnelly Wrecking Company of Kingston raced to the scene the next day, and installed a pump in the *Owen's* hull. The steambarge, *John Milne,* had earlier removed about 600 bushels of the *Owen's* cargo, which was not insured. However, the vessel broke to pieces and became a total loss right when her salvage was attempted. The *Owen* was valued at $5,000, but carried only fire insurance.[238]

JOHN E. HALL and JOHN R. NOYES   (December 13, 1902)

> **The morning of December 13, [1902], two steamers had cleared Charlotte [Rochester, New York] with coal for Canada. Each had a barge in tow. The Canadian steamer *Resolute* was towing the full rigged schooner *Abbie L. Andrews*. The *John E. Hall* was towing the schooner *John R. Noyes*. Captain Timothy Donovan of Oswego commanded the *Hall,* and his son commanded the *Noyes*.[239]**

It was the final voyage for the latter two vessels; father and son were separated forever when the entire crew of one ship survived, while the total crew of the other perished.

The schooner, John R. Noyes, *left, worked as a lighter for the* Arthur Orr *in 1898.*
GREAT LAKES MARINE COLLECTION OF THE MILWAUKEE PUBLIC LIBRARY.

A mid-December crossing of Lake Ontario has always been a risky prospect. Perhaps that was why those four vessels attempted a flotilla-style traversal, for in numbers lies safety.

However, when the gales blew relentlessly and the snow flew blindingly, it became a case of every man for himself. Making headway became impossible, so both steamers cast off their tows. The *Andrews* hoisted her sails and cruised the entire length of Lake Ontario to the shelter of Port Dalhousie.

The *Noyes* carried no sails. For the next day, the four men and the mate's wife, who worked as cook, bobbed aimlessly on board in the freezing waters of the lake at the mercy of the wind and waves. They were first reported in distress at 5:30 P.M. on December 14, 1902, three miles (4.5 kilometres) off the New York shoreline. The Charlotte Lifesaving crew, enduring enormous hardship, finally reached the northward-blown schooner and rescued the crew at about noon the next day. The *Noyes* had drifted 20 miles (32 kilometres) to the middle of Lake Ontario. The wind eventually swept the abandoned hull onto the Canadian shoreline near Salmon Point,[240] where it broke up. The *John R. Noyes* had been a fast vessel: "The schr. *J. R. Noyes* arrived this morning [at Kingston] from Chicago with 19,000 bushels of corn. The *Noyes* made a quick trip, seven days."[241] This schooner was valued at $10,000, and her cargo of coal, $1,400.[242]

The 300-ton schooner, *John R. Noyes,* built in 1872 by James Navash at Algonac, Michigan, measured 137' by 25' by 12' (41.1 by 7.5 by 3.6 metres).[243]

The empty steamer, John E. Hall, *washed ashore in Canada; her crew was never seen again.* GREAT LAKES MARINE COLLECTION OF THE MILWAUKEE PUBLIC LIBRARY.

The steamer, *John E. Hall,* succumbed to the storm:

> **Capt. Thomas Donnelly has received a message from the lighthouse keeper at Salmon Point, that a steambarge is ashore and a total wreck on the south side of the Main Ducks, and that there is no sign of the crew. This is likely the steamer Hall.**[244]

About a week after the *Hall* went missing with her entire crew, wreckage washed ashore at Stony Point, New York, and hopes for the crew's survival faded further. A few days later, on Christmas Eve day, a newspaper article reflected the despairing mood:

ALL HOPE IS GONE.

The Steambarge Hall and Its Crew Lost.

> **An Oswego paper says: "There is no further doubt but that the steambarge John E, Hall and her crew of eleven were lost in the vicinity of the Ducks sometime during the gale of Saturday, December 13,....**
>
> **Capt. Charles Ferris and the tug Ferris arrived here Saturday night with a cupboard from the galley of the steamer, which Capt. George Donovan identified as belonging to his father's steamer, and other wreckage. The wreckage was found on the south side of the Main Ducks. The Hall's small boat and fenders have since been found, washed ashore. In all the Catholic churches of this city Sunday references were made to the late marine disasters on Lake Ontario and prayers were offered for the repose of the souls of the unfortunate dead.**[245]

Also loaded with coal from Charlotte to Deseronto on her last trip, the *John E. Hall,* valued at $15,000, measured 139' (41.7 metres) in length, 28' 6" (8.5 metres) in beam, and 10'9" (3.2 metres) in draft.[246] This ship was built at Manitowoc, Wisconsin, in 1889 by Hanson & Scove. Her high pressure, non-condensing engine came from the Grand Haven Iron Works, Grand Haven, Michigan, while the boiler's fire box was built by the Johnston Brothers in Ferrysburg, Michigan.[247]

EMPIRE STATE   (June 5, 1903)

The wooden sidewheel passenger steamer named the *Empire State* was a "saltie" (her copper hull helped repulse corrosive and/or damaging saltwater elements) that made the transition to the Great Lakes. Built by Thomas Collyer and Company at Athens, New York in 1863 and launched as the *Sylvan Stream,* this 379-ton ship's purpose was to run on the East River between New York City and Harlem as a passenger or excursion steamer. With her 25-foot (7.5-

metre) paddlewheels containing 22 buckets each, she cruised at 17.5 miles (28 kilometres) per hour, developing a reputation as a fast vessel. She was sold for service on the St. Lawrence River in 1887, but her owner, the Thousand Island Steamboat Company, did not rename her the *Empire State* until 1893. She measured 157' 2" (47.2 metres) in length, 26' 6" (7.9 metres) in beam, and 8' 4" (2.5 metres) in draft.[248]

After the 1901 navigation season, the *Empire State* was laid up at the Canadian Pacific Railway dock in Kingston for badly-needed hull and engine repairs. Unfortunately, repairs were never carried out, and the ship burned at that dock on June 25, 1903. Her remains were towed to nearby Collins Bay and abandoned.[249]

The regal paddlewheeler, Empire State, *proudly cruised the St. Lawrence River area for about the last 15 years of her life before burning at Kingston.* AUTHOR"S COLLECTION.

ANNIE FALCONER   (November 12, 1904)

The two-masted schooner, *Annie Falconer,* carried a variety of cargoes during her long life on the Great Lakes: lumber, ice, coal, shingles, staves, stone, salt, and grain. Built at Kingston by George Thurston,[250] this ship was launched on May 22, 1867, five weeks before Canada became a country. Mr. Daniel Falconer named this vessel in memory of his late wife, Kingston-born-and-raised Mary Ann ("Annie") Falconer, nee Baker, (1832-1860), seven years after her death.[251] What a strong and memorable love theirs must have been! The ship was christened by their young daughter, also named Annie, who, according to reports, swung the christening bottle, but missed! The vessel glided down the launchramp anyway. Some pessimists viewed this as an ill omen, but the ship enjoyed a long and virtually problem-free life.[252]

The *Annie Falconer's* maiden voyage was to Toronto with a load of stone, accomplished without any noteworthy incidents, as were most of her travels in her long life. Once, in 1887, the *Falconer,* having departed Oswego, was caught in a severe gale which sank another ship; the *Falconer* sustained only minor damage to her rigging.[253] She did, however, run aground on Saturday, October 14, 1893,[254] at Weller's Bay, Ontario, and spent the winter there high and dry[255] before being pulled off the shore on April 21st the following spring.[256]

The fore-and-aft schooner, Annie Falconer, *from a painting by Gibbons.*

Measuring 108' (32.4 metres) in length, 24' (7.2 metres) in beam, and 9' (2.7 metres) in draft, the *Annie Falconer* was valued at only $8,000 in 1875, $6,000 in 1882, and $4,500 by 1890. At the time of her loss in 1904, the aging *Annie* had an estimated value of only $1,000, while her coal cargo, at $1,500, was worth considerably more.[257]

This vessel foundered in a violent storm off South Bay Point about 1.5 miles (2.4 kilometres) north of False Duck Island, near Timber Island, on November 12, 1904,[258] while underway with a cargo of soft coal for A. W. Hepburn bound from Sodus Point, New York, to Picton, Ontario. The crew of seven reached Amherst Island in the ship's yawl boat, but the first mate, James Sullivan, died of exposure shortly thereafter when he wandered away from the rest of the crew.[259] The survivors found shelter in a nearby farmhouse and, the next day, proceeded to the village of Emerald, where the captain telephoned the results of the disaster to his wife and to the late mate's friends in Picton. The steam yacht, *Madge,* operated by the Hepburn boys, raced to Amherst Island and conveyed the remains of the crew and the deceased to Picton.[260] The *Annie Falconer* was owned and sailed by Capt. Murray Ackerman, of Picton, Ontario, which was the home town of the entire crew.

Captain Ackerman gave a detailed account of the tragedy:

> "We left Big Sodus at nine o'clock Saturday morning, loaded with coal, and the prospects were never finer for a nice run across the lake. The wind was but an ordinary sailing breeze, but as we got farther in the lake, it became fresher and when about half way across had raised to almost a gale. Everything went well, however, until about ten miles off False Duck Island when it was discovered the vessel had begun to leak. The pumps were immediately manned, but we soon discovered that the water was gaining on us and I then determined to try and beach her at the foot of Timber Island. In this efort we almost succeeded, having got about midway between the two islands when she went down about two o'clock in the afternoon. W had to make a hasty flight to the yawl boat, not having time to secure anything except what was on our backs. We could do nothing but go directly before the wind and saw that we would land somewhere upon Amherst Island, providing the little craft could live to get us there. We had no dish or pail of any kind with us and the men were forced to use their hats in order to bail the water from the boat. However, we all struggled bravely for existence, and at about 7:30 in the evening we landed at the foot of Amherst Island, a distance of about 22 miles, completely exhausted from the cold and hunger.
>
> "Phil Sullivan, the mate, the most exhausted of any, was helped from the boat to shore, and while the rest of us were trying to make secure the boat, he became lost to us in the darkness. After searching for him and calling his name, without response, it was thought he had wandered on in search of a farmhouse. We all struck out then in search of shelter, and after a tramp of about three miles through brush, woods, marshy places, and barbed wire entanglements, we came to a farm residence, where dry clothing, food, and stimulants were administered.
>
> "A further search was then made with lanterns for Sullivan, but no trace of him could be found. At daybreak the search was again resumed and after a short time, he was found dead only about 200 feet from where we had landed."[261]

The aging *Annie Falconer* had prompted concerns about her abilities among local shippers. The cargo she carried at the time of her demise was intended for A. W. Hepburn, but her previous two loads of coal had gone to another agent who refused to hire the vessel for yet another crossing of the lake:

> The Annie Faulkner (sic) had brought two
> loads of coal, 400 tons each time, to Mr. C.
> C. Leavens, of this city [Belleville], and her
> owners were anxious to bring another, but
> Mr. Leavens was afraid of the fall storms and
> secured another vessel. To-day he is
> congratulating himself on the fact that his
> caution has saved him the loss of 400 tons of
> coal.[262]

Port quarter view of the schooner, Annie Falconer, *at Oshawa.* AUTHOR'S COLLECTION.

The wreck of the *Annie Falconer* was located by Barbara Carson, Audrey Rushbrook, and Doug Pettingill in 1975. Many of the ship's artifacts were raised and donated to the local marine museum at South Bay, where they are on exhibit.

The *Annie Falconer* sits upright in about 80' (24 metres) of water, on a bottom of combined rock and mud. She is uniquely well-preserved, with deadeyes, anchors, ship's wheel, blocks, and chain still in place. Her stern has broken off, but it lies within visibile range, usually, at an angle to the main hull.[263] The bowsprit has collapsed in recent years, and the hull is splitting open gradually. In the summer of 1996, the port anchor, which had been hanging precariously on the edge of the bow rail by the ball on one end of its crossarm, fell to the lake bottom.[264] The starboard bow anchor hangs by the tip of a fluke.

In late 1982, the Kingston-based marine conservation group named Preserve Our Wrecks (P. O. W.), along with the Deep Six Scuba Club of Picton, decided to organize a survey project on the *Annie Falconer*. The actual underwater work lasted from May 13 until September 25, 1983, and members of the two groups, with assistance from the Marine Heritage Program of Ontario's Ministry of Culture and Communications, formed the Quinte chapter of Save Ontario Shipwrecks, which produced a published report of their detailed findings.[265] This was one of the first underwater archaeological surveys done by amateurs in Ontario. A stone heritage plaque measuring two by four feet (0.6 to 1.2 metres), donated by Campbell Monuments of Belleville, Ontario, and inscribed with the vessel's history, was placed on the hard lake bottom immediately under the *Falconer's* bowsprit.[266]   On-going work by Ken Mullings of P. O. W., studying the *Annie Falconer's* natural disintegration, has proved to be unique and invaluable.[267]

The ship's wheel is the usual focal point of any shipwreck. The absence of a silty patina on the wooden handles of the Falconer's *wheel indicates that many visiting scuba divers have taken turns "steering the* Annie." PHOTO BY CRIS KOHL.

C. HICKOX   (December 2, 1906)

Early December, 1906, witnessed some levity at the city's yacht club dock involving Kingston's colourful mayor, as the local newspaper reported:

> **Mayor Mowat and J. C. Stewart again dived off the yacht club wharf this morning, with the thermometer registering ten degrees below zero. Two dips were taken in the waters of the harbor. His worship, when interviewed later in the day, stated that the water was not much colder than it was yesterday. He said that he would continue to enjoy his early morning bath in the harbor until the ice prevented him from**

getting into the water. His friends are threatening that they will ask the Humane Society to act if he doesn't cease his gambols in this wintry weather.[268]

It is not known precisely how the Humane Society would have controlled the mayor's frolics. His friends seem to have shared his sense of humour.

Meanwhile, off Main Duck Island, a serious matter was taking place. Sailors on a sinking vessel, unlike Kingston's mayor, were trying their hardest to avoid contact with the freezing waters of Lake Ontario.

The 314-ton steamer, C. Hickox, *in winter lay-up.* AUTHOR'S COLLECTION

A feeling that something had gone wrong with the steamer, *Hickox*, was reported in the local press:

> A despatch from Belleville, Ont. says: Grave fears are felt here that the steambarge Hickox, owned and commanded by Capt. [Henry] Smith of this city, has been lost, on Lake Ontario. The vessel left Oswego on Sunday, loaded with coal for Belleville, and has not yet turned up. A steamer which left after her has arrived safely at Picton. It is hoped that the Hickox may be ice-bound somewhere, but the worst is feared. She had a crew of five Belleville people.[269]

The steamer, *C. Hickox,* had indeed left Oswego at about noon on Sunday, December 2, 1906, Belleville-bound with about 350 tons of coal, but after a few hours, the vessel encountered a heavy snowstorm with strong gales. Just before ten o'clock that evening, after making slow progress against powerful headwinds, the steamer caught on fire. Every crewmember fought the advancing flames, but the fire gained headway. Capt. Smith witnessed them losing the battle, and headed his ship to the nearest land, Main Duck Island, a few miles away. The ship was beached just offshore, and the captain and crew launched the yawl boat and rowed to the safety of shore, from which they were soon rescued.[270]

>   **Captain Smith says that the fire was likely caused by spontaneous combustion. He has been very unfortunate in losing vessels by fire, having had several burned in former years. There is insurance against fire of $2,000 on the vessel and an insurance of $1,500 on the coal.[271]**

Black Creek, Ohio, was the building port of the steamer, *C. Hickox,* in 1873. The Henry D. Root Shipyard was the builder. This American vessel, measuring 131' (39.3 metres) in length and 25' (7.5 metres) in beam, was purchased by Canadian interests in early 1906, and failed to survive her first season under her new owner.[272]

This vessel was, for some strange reason, shunted from owner to owner. In 1875, her owner was Calkins & Company of Cleveland, Ohio, and her value was listed as $27,000. The Kelley Island Line Company of Cleveland owned the *Hickox* in 1879, when she was valued at $18,000. In 1884, Mann & Company of Muskegon, Michigan, owned the ship, which was then appraised at $14,000. By 1893, her owner was the Foerster lumber Company of Milwaukee, Wisconsin. In 1905, when she was 32 years old, her owner was Belknep & Phillips, of St. Clair, Michigan, and she was valued at a mere $6,000.[273]

This namesake of this ship was Mr. Charles Hickox (1810-1890), a Cleveland entrepreneur who was president of an iron company, major owner of a railroad, and founder of a flour mill company, along with investments in iron ore mines in the Lake Superior area.[274]

The ship's large, fire-box-type boiler in the shallow water on the southwest side of Main Duck Island is all that remains of the steamer, *C. Hickox,* today.

FLEETWING (1909)

Along an obscure shore lined with dense underbrush at South Bay, Ontario, partially out of the water, rest the broken up remains of a two-masted schooner named the *Fleetwing.* A sign, supposedly made from a plank from that ship and mounted on the fence along the main roadway, reads "Fleetwing," attempting to guide rare visitors to the water's edge. But so badly disintegrated are these last timbers of her bow stem, keel, and ribs, that they will soon be unrecognizable as having belonged to a vessel that plied these local waters.

The 218-ton *Fleetwing* was built by D. McNott at Wilson, New York, for the Brighton, Ontario, company named Dearborn and Quick, in 1863.[275]

One tragic event early in the *Fleetwing's* career was commemorated in a brief, 1883 newspaper article:

> **Eighteen years ago the schooner Fleetwing capsized off Cobourg, drowning the Captain's wife and child. On Wednesday she** [the *Fleetwing*] **reappeared in the harbor for the first time since the catastrophe. She had a cargo of lumber from Toledo for the Car Works, Cobourg.**[276]

Another sad loss occurred on April 21, 1893, while the *Fleetwing,* sailing from Oswego to Kingston with 350 tons of coal, attempted to navigate through some late-season ice shrouded in dense fog near Nine Mile Point. One of her crew, H. Lester McCrimmon, fell overboard and cried for help. Two of the remaining crew (on board were Capt. Shaw, four sailors, and the captain's wife and daughter) sprang into action and launched the lifeboat, but were unable to locate the lost man. A few days later, his body was recovered, and his remains lie in the South Bay cemetery, quite near what is left of the schooner, *Fleetwing.*[277]

The schooner, Fleetwing, *at dock near the end of her long career on the Great Lakes.*
GREAT LAKES MARINE COLLECTION OF THE MILWAUKEE PUBLIC LIBRARY.

Not all of the significant moments in the *Fleetwing's* career were tragic. On at least one occasion, in late 1890, the vessel indirectly helped save a life:

> **Hugh McLaren, keeper of Knapp's Point light house, got into trouble in the harbor yesterday. About 4:30 o'clock he**

left the city in a sailing skiff for home. He carried a good deal
of canvas, perhaps too much, and was unable to manage the
boat after he got into the channel. The wind was blowing
pretty free and the waves rolled high. When Mr. McLaren got
opposite Point Frederick he found it impossible to keep his
skiff free from water. She dipped every moment and was soon
sinking. Mr. McLaren sat at the stern while the boat was
filling with water. His dangerous condition was seen by
persons on the shore. The alarm was raised that a man was
drowning, and in a short time two yawl boats were pushing out
to rescue Mr. McLaren. A sailor of the schr. Fleetwing reached
him first, dragged him into a yawl boat and brought him to
shore. He was very much exhausted and his clothes were
soaking wet. On landing he went to the Union hotel where he
was fitted out with a dry suit of clothes. He said to a reporter
that he had been sailing up and down the lakes for many years
but never had such a narrow escape from drowning. He
attributed his misfortune to carrying too much sail.[278]

After a full, active life on the Great Lakes, the schooner, *Fleetwing,* stripped
of anything useful, was abandoned along South Bay's shoreline.

TRADE WIND   (April 15, 1909)

The old, two-masted schooner, *Trade Wind,* built by Michael Lummeree at
Port Colborne, Ontario, in 1853,[279] was active into her 52nd year of service on
the Great Lakes. Fire destroyed this retired vessel in Kingston harbour on April
5, 1909. She measured 106' by 21' 1" by 9' (31.8 by 6.3 by 2.7 metres).[280]

The schooner, Trade Wind, *burned at Kingston at the age of 56.* AUTHOR'S COLLECTION.

[221] *Weekly British Whig* (Kingston), Wednesday, October 24, 1900.

[222] *Daily Intelligencer* (Belleville), Monday, October 22, 1900.

[223] *Weekly British Whig* (Kingston), Wednesday, October 24, 1900.

[224] *Daily Whig* (Kingston), Tuesday, October 23, 1900.

[225] Metcalfe, *Canvas & Steam on Quinte Waters,* op. cit., 64-65.

[226] *Picton Gazette,* Wednesday, July 19, 1961.

[227] *Kingston Whig-Standard,* Friday, July 21, 1961.

[228] Greenwood, op. cit., 175.

[229] Metcalfe, *Canvas & Steam on Quinte Waters,* op. cit., 81.

[230] *Daily Intelligencer* (Belleville), Friday, June 14, 1901.

[231] Ibid.

[232] Mansfield, op. cit., 827.

[233] Greenwood, op. cit., 5.

[234] Metcalfe, *Canvas & Steam on Quinte Waters,* op. cit., 58.

[235] *Daily British Whig* (Kingston), Thursday, June 3, 1880.

[236] Mills, op. cit., 90.

[237] *Daily British Whig,* Monday, October 13, 1902.

[238] *Daily British Whig* (Kingston), Monday, October 13, 1902.

[239] Quoted in Richard F. Palmer, "The Longest Pull." *Inland Seas,* Vol. 40, Number 3, Fall, 1984: 200-204. This article consists of an exciting recollection of the Charlotte, New York, Lifesaving crew's hardships while rescuing those on board the *Noyes.*

[240] Metcalfe, *Canvas & Steam on Quinte Waters,* op. cit., 76.

[241] *British Whig* (Kingston), Friday, October 1, 1880.

[242] *John R. Noyes.* Ship Information and Data Record, Runge Collection, Milwaukee Public Library.

[243] *John R. Noyes.* Master Sheet, Institute for Great Lakes Research, Bowling Green State University, Ohio.

[244] *Daily Whig* (Kingston), Wednesday, December 17, 1902.

[245] *Daily Whig* (Kingston), Wednesday, December 24, 1902.

[246] *John E. Hall.* Ship Information and Data Record, Runge Collection, Milwaukee Public Library.

[247] *John E. Hall.* Master Sheet, Institute for Great Lakes Research, Bowling Green State University, Ohio.

[248] *Empire State.* Ship Information and Data Record, Runge Collection, Milwaukee Public Library.

[249] Greenwood, op. cit., 490.

[250] *Annie Falconer.* Ship Information and Data Record, Runge Collection, Milwaukee Public `Library.

[251] Greenwood, op. cit., 396.

[252]Reportedly a Scotsman lunged for the intact bottle after it failed to hit its intended mark, pulled the cork, and took a swig, only to discover, to his enormous disgust, that the alcohol had been replaced by water. Apparently another Scotsman had downed the original elixir an hour before the launch and replaced it with the unsatisfying substitute!

[253]*Daily Whig* (Kingston), Wednesday, October 26, 1887.

[254]*Daily British Whig* (Kingston), Monday, october 16, 1893.

[255]V. Pat Ryan, "Beloved Shipwreck." *Canadian Diving Journal,* Summer, 1983, 10-11. Article also printed in *Save Ontario Shipwrecks Newsletter,* Spring and Summer, 1983.

[256]*Daily British Whig* (Kingston), Saturday, April 21, 1894.

[257]*Annie Falconer,* Runge Collection, op. cit.

[258]*Annie Falconer.* Master Sheet, Institute for Great Lakes Research, Bowling Green State University, Ohio.

[259]*British Whig* (Kingston), Monday, November 14, 1904.

[260]*Picton Gazette,* Tuesday, November 15, 1904.

[261]Ibid.

[262]*Daily Intelligencer* (Belleville), Monday, November 14, 1904.

[263]Kohl, *Dive Ontario! The Guide to Shipwrecks and Scuba Diving,* op. cit., 70.

[264]The author explored the *Annie Falconer* twice in the summer of 1996, on July 26th and August 24th. The port bow anchor crashed to the lake bottom from the ship's railing some time between those dates. He swears he didn't touch it!

[265]Robert Harvey and Ken Mullings, "Report from S. O. S. Quinte," *Save Ontario Shipwrecks Newsletter,* Winter, 1984, 17-18.

[266]Ken Mullings, "Quinte's Favourite Dive Site," *Save Ontario Shipwrecks Newsletter,* Spring/Summer, 1988, 20.

[267]Ken Mullings. "Monitoring the Falconer, An Archaeological Site Update of the Fore-and-Aft Schooner 'Annie Falconer.'" Preserve Our Wrecks, Kingston, January, 1992. Plus updates for 1993, 1994, and 1995.

[268]*Daily British Whig* (Kingston), Tuesday, December 4, 1906.

[269]Ibid.

[270]*Daily British Whig* (Kingston), Thursday, December 6, 1906.

[271]Ibid.

[272]Mills, op. cit., 19.

[273]*C. Hickox.* Ship Information and Data Record, Runge Collection, Milwaukee Public Library.

[274]Greenwood, op. cit., 22.

[275]Metcalfe, *Canvas & Steam on Quinte Waters,* op. cit., 69-70.

[276]*Weekly British Whig* (Kingston), Thursday, August 2, 1883.

[277]Metcalfe, *Canvas & Steam on Quinte Waters,* op. cit.

[278]*British Daily Whig* (Kingston), Wednesday, November 26, 1890.

[279]Metcalfe, *Canvas & Steam on Quinte Waters,* op. cit., 133.

[280]Greenwood, op. cit., 367.

Chapter Seven
The 1910's

D. D. CALVIN   (April 11, 1910)

Garden Island vessels seemed to be plagued with incendiary problems. The 750-ton wooden steamer, *D. D. Calvin,* built at Garden Island, Ontario, (near Kingston) in 1883,[281] burned to a complete loss on April 11, 1910, and sank in place.

Named after Mr. Dileno Dexter Calvin (1798-1884), the American timber entrepreneur who moved his business operations to Garden Island in 1836, this bulk freighter had her engine installed at Cleveland and worked for the Calvin Company for most of her life. Sold to the Carlow and Smith Company in early 1910, the ship was awaiting outfitting when fire caused her demise.[282]

The *D. D. Calvin* measured 166' (49.8 metres) in length and 32' (9.6 metres) in beam.[283]

Other ships that ended their careers by fire at Garden Island, where they had been constructed, were the sidewheel steamer, *Hercules,* destroyed on December 8, 1871, and the paddlewheel tug, *Hiram A. Calvin,* in December, 1895.

The wooden bulk freighter, D. D. Calvin, *built at the Henry Roney Shipyard at Garden Island, Ontario in 1883, seemed to instinctively return home at the end of her life. She burned at that place on April 11, 1910.* AUTHOR'S COLLECTION.

H. B.   (October 16, 1912)

Built at Montreal, Quebec, by W. & G. H. Tate Company in 1890, the workhorse schooner-barge named the *H. B.* (the initials of her Winnipeg financier, Mr. Herbert Beck, who lived from 1852 until 1932) measured 176' 3" (52.9 metres) in length , 33' 8" (10.3 metres) in beam, and 13' (3.9 meters) in draft. On October 16, 1912, the *H. B.*, coal-laden and bound from Oswego to Montreal, became a complete loss when a storm drove her ashore.[284]

The schooner-barge, *H. B.,* succumbed to a Lake Ontario storm. AUTHOR'S COLLECTION.

GRANTHAM   (July 6, 1913)

The summer of 1913 was an interesting one. The *Montreal Herald* reported that another survivor of the famous Charge of the Light Brigade (1854) at Balaclava had just died, "thus bringing up the total number of alleged survivors of the noble six hundred to fifteen hundred and sixty-seven."[285] Meanwhile, in Toronto, workmen excavating for the street railway company found fifty pieces of solid silverware, marked "Royal Canadian Rifles," buried at the foot of Frederick Street. The press speculated that "it is possible that the treasure was the booty of some thief nearly a hundred years ago," and that "the silverware is to be divided amongst the workmen who unearthed it."[286]

That summer also saw the demise of the oak-built schooner-barge named the *Grantham,* owned by the Donnelly Wrecking Company of Kingston and used for salvage operations. This vessel sank while assisting the coal-carrying steamer, *A. E. Ames,* near Salmon Point, on July 6, 1913.[287] The *Ames* was salvaged.

Built by Julian Abbey at Port Robinson (St. Catharines), Ontario, in 1873, the *Grantham* measured 146' 6" by 23' 7" by 11' 7" (43.9 by 7 by 3.5 metres).[288]

NAVAJO   (December 6, 1914)

Robert Davis constructed this wooden, propeller-driven steamer at Kingston in 1895. The local press responded with glee to the February 16th launch:

LAUNCHED A VESSEL.

A Winter Sight at Davis' Shipyard This Morning

Daily Whig, 16th.

It is quite an unusual thing to see a launch in the winter and consequently quite a large number of mariners gathered about Davis' shipyard this morning to witness the sliding off of Capt. Ira Folger's new steambarge. The boat was built on ways next to the railway track in a horizontal position. Little execution was necessary to start her. It was indeed a beautiful sight, the vessel plowing through the snow-covered ice until coming in contact with a snow bank she eased up with a graceful lurch. Capts. Saunders and James Dix had seen many a launch during their experience as sailors but this was the gem of them all. The reason she was let down now is on account of the low water in the bay in the spring. As soon as the ice gives she will be floating out of the nook.

The new barge will be named "King Ben," and it is not an unbecoming title. When Capt. Folger purchased the steambarge Freemason last fall it was intended to rebuild her but on further consideration a comparative new boat was decided on. The Freemason's boiler and engine will be used, as they are as good as new and very powerful. This is about the only portion of the old boat that has been reserved. King Ben is 111 ft. long, 22 ft. beam, 8 ft. 6 in. hold, and 160 tonnage. She can carry over 200 tons

> dead weight. The owner will take charge of
> the barge himself next season and intends
> running her between Oswego, Kingston and
> Ottawa. She is a beautiful model and good
> speed is looked for.[289]

Launched as the *King Ben,* she was renamed the *Navajo* in 1904.[290]

On December 6, 1914, while carrying grain bound for Kingston, the *Navajo* attempted to free the grounded wheat-laden towbarge, *Ceylon,* stranded on Main Duck Island, but ran aground herself and broke up in place. All 21 people on the *Navajo* were saved by local fishermen.[291] The *Ceylon* was salvaged, only to be abandoned on saltwater in 1943.[292] The *Navajo's* Fitzgibbon-type boiler, built in 1912 by John Inglis & Company of Toronto, sits in shallow water on the west shore of Main Duck Island.

The steamer, Navajo, *was 19 years old when she broke up.* AUTHOR'S COLLECTION.

CITY OF SHEBOYGAN   (September 25, 1915)

By the summer of 1915, World War One (1914-1918) had been going on for a year and, even though most people had incorrectly thought "the boys" would be home from war by Christmas, 1914, spirits remained high. The population of Kingston had actually increased by 64 between 1914 and 1915 (from 21,261 to 21,325), notwithstanding the fact that over 1,000 men from that city had gone overseas in the war. Kingston boasted having 6,005 children of school age, 778 men paying statute labor tax, and 739 dogs and 93 bitches.[293]

ont sense.

It was a time of change. Sarah Bernhardt, "the world's greatest actress," gave up stage performances "after a single performance here [in Paris] for the movies" and retired to her home in Bordeaux, France,[294] and the Kingston newspaper was contemplating the question, "Why Not a Father's Day?"[295] Kingston's Grand Opera House still offered vaudeville performances every afternoon and evening, but motion pictures were quickly replacing them. Actress Lillian Gish starred in "Lord Tennyson's Masterpiece, 'Enoch Arden,' ...produced by the world's foremost picture artist, D. W. Griffith," at the grand opening of Kingston's Strand Theatre which offered four performances daily with a full orchestra in a fireproof building, at a cost of five cents for matinees and ten cents for evenings, and Charlie Chaplin starred "in a Roaring Comedy entitled 'His Musical Career'" at the Wonderland Theatre, "where you get quality and quantity."[296]

Flying in the face of this optimism, the loss of the schooner, *City of Sheboygan,* off Amherst Island became the first tragic shipping incident of the decade.

Built by Fred Hamilton at Sheboygan, Wisconsin (not to be confused with Cheboygan, Michigan, after which another vessel was named), as a three-masted lumber schooner, and launched on July 5, 1871 (with her documentation enrolled at Milwaukee on that same date),[297] this 261-gross-ton ship enjoyed a career which spanned almost 45 years on the Great Lakes.

The schooner at left is the City of Sheboygan, *docked at Collingwood, Ontario, supposedly in 1871, her first season afloat.* AUTHOR'S COLLECTION.

Her original dimensions of 135' 3" (40.6 metres) by 25' 8" (7.6 metres) by 10' 4" (3.1 metres) were widened to 30' 1" (9 metres) when she was rebuilt in 1882. Prior to that, she was a canal schooner, but after 1882, she was too wide for that category of vessel. J. S. Dunham of Chicago owned the *City of Sheboygan* from 1894 to 1897, and Winand Schlosser of Milwaukee was her owner from 1900 until 1915.[298]

The schooner, *"City of Sheboygan,"* which sank at Detour, Michigan, on Lake Huron, in the autumn of 1886, but was raised in June of the following year "with her masts, rigging, and hull in good shape,"[299] was likely not the same *City of Sheboygan* that ended her career near Kingston years later. Contemporary newspaper accounts, unfortunately, did not seem too concerned about whether the correct spelling of this vessel's name began with the letter "S" or the letter "C."

The City of Sheboygan. INSTITUTE FOR GREAT LAKES RESEARCH, BOWLING GREEN, OHIO

Until the spring of 1915, the *City of Sheboygan* was engaged in the lumber-carrying business on Lake Michigan; at that time, however, Capt. Edward M. McDonald of Toronto purchased the vessel for use on Lake Ontario in the mineral feldspar trade. The *City of Sheboygan* "was one of many idle American vessels bought cheap in 1915...."[300]

The marine column in Kingston's newspaper briefly and unsuspectingly announced the preparations for the *City of Sheboygan's,* and her crew's, final voyage into eternity:

> The schooner City of Cheyboygan [sic] will
> load feldspar at Richardson's wharf for
> Buffalo.[301]

After she was loaded with 500 tons of feldspar mined near Verona, north of Kingston,[302] the old schooner, *City of Sheboygan,* arranged for a tug to tow her a fair distance out of Kingston before releasing her under her own sail power. One of the tug's crew later recalled that

> Upon completion of the loading of her
> cargo, we got a line aboard the vessel and
> towed her out to Nine Mile Point. They got as
> far as Point Petre, when she encountered a
> storm and ran for the foot of the Lake. Five
> days later she was lost off Nut Island, south
> of Amherst Island. She was heavily
> overloaded.[303]

The storm that sank the *City of Sheboygan* on Sunday, September 25, 1915, blasted so violently that the Kingston ferry, *Wolfe Islander,* unable to make her usual landing at Kingston, was forced to return to Wolfe Island.[304] "The wind blew a regular hurricane" which also ran the steamer, *Arabian,* aground a few miles west of Niagara at the other end of Lake Ontario.[305]

Joseph Bray, a resident of Amherst Island, was among those safely on shore observing the loss of the vessel, incapable of offering any assistance to the drowning crew. He was the one who hastened to the nearby town of Bath to telephone local authorities, including newspapers, about this sinking.[306] Capt. McDonald, fearing a bad gale that his vessel could not handle, had attempted to run into the lee, or protected side, of Amherst Island. He lost the race.

> On Sunday morning about 11 o'clock the
> schooner City of Cheyboygan [sic]...sank in
> full view of Joseph Bray, a fisherman of
> Amherst Island. During the terrible storm of
> Sunday Mr. Bray beheld the three-masted
> schooner founder and disappear one and a
> half miles south of Nut Island, a small island
> south of Amherst Island.

> The Cheyboygan [sic] carried a crew of
> five men [author's note--it was really four men and a
> woman]. It left here Saturday morning with her
> bulwarks no more than three feet above the
> surface of the water. She was caught in the
> heavy seas that raged. Mr. Bray called others
> to witness the sinking, but to try and rescue
> the crew was impossible. The hull of the boat
> quickly disappeared....

> All Sunday Mr. Bray watched along the
> shore to see if he could notice any of the

victims struggling in the water, with the view of seeing them if they were washed ashore. His efforts were in vain, and the search was given up when night came.

....Several times Capt. McDonald got into trouble by running aground, twice at Nine Mile Point. his wife was cook on the schooner.

The other members of the crew were "Jerry" Lavis, Cobourg; Robert Milne, Port Hope, and W. Joyner, who signed up just before the vessel sailed Saturday morning. The latter was at one time employed by the Street Railway Company and left its employ a few weeks ago.

The Cheyboygan [sic] had more than her share of trouble this year. Early in the season the schooner was out in a terrible gale, was missing for several days, and was given up for lost. However, Capt. McDonald managed to get into shelter in a cove where there was no telegraph communication. The schooner at this time was on her way from Oswego to Toronto with coal. On two occasions the vessel ran aground in the vicinity of Nine Mile Point and was regarded as a "hoodoo" among marine men.

Capt. McDonald, his wife and members of the crew were all well known in Kingston, and there was much regret expressed over the sad affair when the news spread around the city....[307]

The *City of Sheboygan* had been listed as missing on Lake Erie,[308] but turned up safe a few days later, just a few weeks before her actual demise.

After the storm, only a small portion of the tops of the masts remained above the water[309] as silent sentinels marking the site of the tragedy. The first body to be located was that of the captain's wife, Mrs. McDonald, the ship's cook, on Wednesday, October 6, 1915, ten days after the sinking,

...found floating in the lake five miles out from Long Point by...fishermen. The body was badly decomposed.... The body was identified by Capt. James Oliver of the schooner Abbie L. Andrews, Kingston. Relatives of the deceased in Toronto, were notified and an uncle is expected to arrive at Bath to take the body back to Toronto....[310]

The two, white Pomeranian dogs which Mrs. McDonald had on board were not located. The other body that surfaced was one of the sailors:

> **Lake Ontario has given up another of its dead,...in the finding on Saturday afternoon of the body of Robert Milne, of Port Hope....The body was found about 5 o'clock about a mile and a half from the scene of the wreck...by two fishermen....**
>
> **The body was identified by a medal worn by the deceased with the initials, "P. H. C. C.," awarded to him by the Port Hope Curling Club. Papers were also found in his clothing which established his identity.**
>
> **The late Mr. Milne was about thirty-five years of age, and had a wife and family. He was well-known in Kingston and other lake ports, and held in high esteem by all his friends....**[311]

Several factors besides the nefarious weather conditions must be taken into account for the cause of the sinking. Capt. McDonald, about 45 years of age, had sailed only on steamers, most recently in and out of Kingston on board the *John Rolph,* and had no experience mastering a schooner.[312] The schooner itself had just recently left Davis' Dry Dock, where she was undergoing repairs to her hull,[313] indicating a need to maintain the integrity of this 44-year-old vessel. That the ship was overloaded with feldspar was witnessed by several people the day she sailed, observing that "her main rail was only three feet above water."[314]

Two years after the schooner sank, an example of how the passage of time can change facts into something a bit more sensational appeared in a local newspaper: the *City of Sheboygan* supposedly "went down two years ago, with all on board, when enroute from Oswego, with a cargo of coal for the penitentiary."[315] In two short years, that journalist had twisted the fact that this ship was really on a routine run from Kingston to Buffalo loaded with feldspar.

In the early summer of 1963, three scuba divers named Lloyd Shales, Barbara Carson, and John Birtwhistle, with assistance from James McRady, Peter Ottenhof, and Ronald Hughes, located the remains of the schooner, *City of Sheboygan.*

> **"...Miss Carson did most of the research work which located the general area of the wreck. The sounding equipment then came into use and resulted in the divers finding the wreck lying on bottom during their first dive....**
>
> **"It's getting a little risky at that depth," Mr. Shales noted. The divers have been**

working from an 18-foot outboard. At least one, Mr. Shales, has used a decompression meter to check saturation of his blood with nitrogen.

During early operations visibility was up to 25 feet and lighting similar to that of a full moon. The divers now report that the water is cloudy and visibility more limited....

Divers have also found the work uncomfortable because of the frigid waters. Several have used dry suits with up to four suits of underwear beneath the suits....[316]

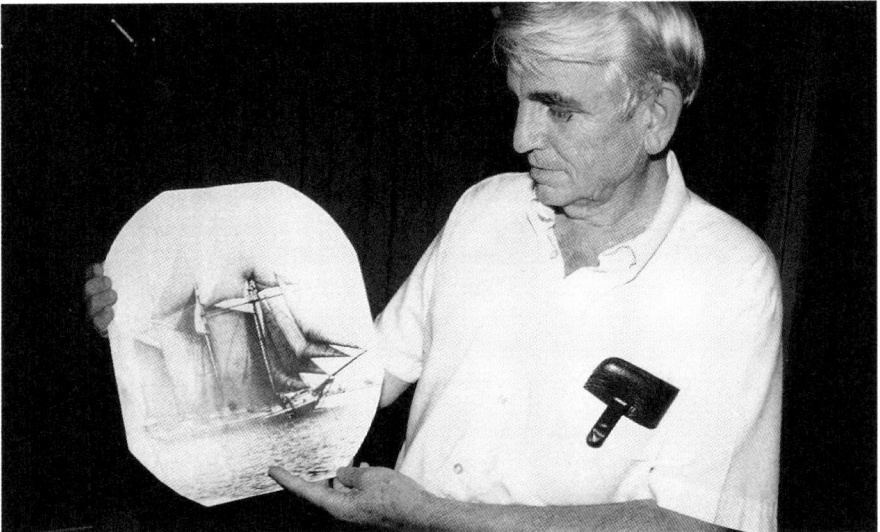

Lloyd Shales, one of the original locaters of the City of Sheboygan, *studies a photo of a similar vessel, the schooner,* Ford River, *in August, 1995.* PHOTO BY CRIS KOHL.

The wreck is deep, about 100 feet (30 metres), and hence well-preserved. Much of her rigging and most other shipboard items, including deadeyes, are intact on the wreck, with her masts broken, but identifiable.[317] The ship's wheel and an anchor are at the nearby Marine Museum at South Bay, having been donated to that institution by Lloyd Shales and Barbara Carson.[318] Anyone can view and appreciate the remains of the tragic ship named the *City of Sheboygan.*

FRANK C. BARNES   (November 2, 1915)

In November, 1915, North America enthusiastically viewed the new D. W. Griffith epic film, "The Birth of a Nation." Kingston's Grand Theatre billed it as the "8th Wonder of the World, 18,000 People, 3,000 Horses, Car Load of

Electric and Scenic Effects, Symphony Orchestra of 30" and charged the unheard-of top prices of $1.00 for a matinee and $1.50 for an evening showing.[319]

While people raved about "The Birth of a Nation," some mourned the death of a tugboat crew.

Only a few weeks after the tragic sinking of the *City of Sheboygan,* a wooden tugboat of the Canada Steamship Lines, the *Frank C. Barnes,* foundered with the loss of all hands while enroute from Port Dalhousie to Montreal. Young (he was merely 30) Captain Bert LaRush planned this as his last run of the 1915 season, but instead it "proved to be his last venture in this world."[320]

The stout tug, Frank C. Barnes, *sank with all hands in 1915.* AUTHOR'S COLLECTION.

A resident of Point Traverse, Dorland Dulmage, wrote a letter to Capt. John Donnelly, of the famous Kingston wrecking company, relating an eyewitness account of the *Barnes'* sinking on Tuesday, November 2, 1915:

> ...Then I drove in to Gull Pond and I found a man by the name of Frost who gave me more information.
>
> He told me he saw this boat on Tuesday, 2nd November. He said when he first saw her, he picked her up about three miles below Point Petre right opposite to Gull Pond, and when he first saw her she was going very slow with but little steam and a gale of wind....This was about ten or half past ten in the morning. Then he turned round and looked at her again and she had disappeared

> altogether. I think she is located as well as
> you can ever locate her. Now she is about
> three miles southeast of Gull Pond....[321]

Captain Donnelly took his wrecking vessel, the *Cornwall,* out on the lake in search of the missing tugboat on Sunday, November 7, 1915, but found no trace of the *Barnes.*[322]

A week later, on Sunday, Nov. 14, 1915, the unidentifiable body of a man wearing a "Frank C. Barnes" lifebelt washed ashore at Consecon, Ontario; this body, which remained unidentified, was sent to Toronto and buried at the Metropolis.[323] On Nov. 15, 1915, a portion of the pilot house of the *Frank C. Barnes* was found ashore near Oswego, on the other side of the lake.[324]

Another body from the tug, *Barnes,* was found off Salmon Point on Sunday, November 21, 1915. Local resident, B. E. Dunham, was looking after his boats early that morning when he noticed a body floating in the water. With assistance from some neightbours, he retrieved the corpse and sent it to Picton, where Captain Bongard identified the body as that of Archibald MacGregor Cummings. Cummings had left Captain Bongard's steamer, *Terbinia,* as Second Engineer when that ship was laid up, to become First Engineer on the fateful tug, *Barnes.* His body was sent to Toronto to the only surviving relative, a sister.[325]

The body of the Japanese cook, Harry Yips, aged about 35 years, was found on the lakeshore at Cressy, Ontario, on November 28, 1915, "in a good state of preservation" with "a small amount of money and a gold chain, with a $10 gold piece as a charm." No one claimed the body, so it was buried in Glenwood Cemetery (which likely kept his valuables as payment for interment). The man who had found Yips' body had seen another floating in the high seas near shore, but could not recover it.[326]

The five people lost when the tug, *Frank C. Barnes,* sank off Salmon Point were Captain LaRush of Toronto, Mate J. E. Houghton of Collingwood, First Engineer A. M. Cummings of Hamilton, Second Engineer E. Watters of Toronto, and Cook Harry Yips, from Barrie.[327]

The 46-ton *Frank C. Barnes,* built in 1892 at Manistee, Michigan, and sold to Canadian interests in 1906, measured 66' 7" (19.9 metres) in length, 16' 3" (4.7 metres) in beam, and 7' 2" (2.1 metres) in draft.[328]

HOBOKEN (1916)

The schooner-barge, *Hoboken,* built for the lumber trade, carried mostly coal on eastern Lake Ontario in the latter years of her career. Built by Simon Barker at Clayton, New York, in 1868, this vessel measured 145' (43.5 metres) in length, 26' (7.8 metres) in beam, and 11' (3.3 metres) in draft. The *Hoboken* last operated in her 44th year (1912), lay idle at Kingston's Middle Ground for four years, and was finally abandoned in 1916.[329]

GEORGE A. MARSH   (August 8, 1917)

"Hello. My name is Greta Smith, and I am twelve years old. At least, that's how old I was when I died.

"My dear father, Captain John Wesley Smith, was half owner of the beautiful schooner, *George A. Marsh*. His partner, Mr. Jonathon J. B. Flint, who also lived in our home town of Belleville, Ontario, had purchased this sturdy ship in Chicago four years earlier, in 1913. Fortunately for him and his family, Mr. Flint was not with us when our ship sank.

"My poor father had had his share of joys and tribulations in life. Born in Belleville, the Captain spent all his life, when he was not at sea, in that city where he was well known and much respected. As a sailor, he was reported lost many times, but always made port in safety. Hard work on the Great Lakes kept him so busy that he married my mother, Sarah, comparatively late in life. By the time he reached middle age, the Captain had a large and youthful family to feed.

"However, he felt far from resentful, for he found great contentment and peace with his growing family. He was especially anxious to have his children well-educated. But this pure happiness lasted for only a few years. Mother died just before Christmas, 1914.

"Mother's death was a truly sad time in our lives. I was only nine years old then; my younger siblings were Eva, who was five, Jack, who was three, and Clarence who was only one year old, while my older brother, Horace, was 13 and my sister, Margaret, was 12. For all of us children, it was truly the saddest Christmas we ever had.

"When Mother died, the shaken Captain, who had never considered the possibility of something this tragic happening so soon in his life, immediately purchased a cluster of six cemetery plots in the Belleville Cemetery, not far from the waterfront and labelled collectively "N 15 25." Mother was the first to be buried in the Smith plots. The date was December 21, 1914. I had no idea that I would occupy another of the plots in less than three years' time!

"It was bad enough that a Great War had just begun in Europe, the Greatest War that mankind had ever known, so we were told. Thousands of soldiers and innocent civilians were dying every week, but to us children, Europe was far, far away. Mother's death was right in our own home, and her passing left an enormous gap in each of our young lives.

"But I think my father, the Captain, suffered more than any of us. To find himself suddenly a widower at the age of 45, with six children between the ages of one and thirteen in his sole care, was a sad and direful situation.

"Less than a year after our mother's death, the Captain surprised everyone when he successfully wooed and married 20-year-old Gertrude Manning of

Demorestville in neighbouring Prince Edward County. Her love of children and sympathy for the Captain's situation were quite evident, and our initial surprise soon changed to joy; the younger children were happy to have a wonderful new mother, and I felt like I suddenly had another older sister in whom I could confide!

"My new stepmother, Gertrude, and the Captain also got along quite well, and within a year, I had another sibling, a baby sister named Lorraine.

"The *Marsh* had been completely overhauled in the spring of 1917; my father had seen to it that the vessel was caulked and freshly painted before equipping her with new sails and lines. He was so proud of his ship!

"Four years earlier, he had sailed the *Marsh* from Chicago all the way home to Belleville, where he had the ship completely overhauled. He always maintained her in excellent, seaworthy condition. Yes, my father, the Captain, was truly proud of this vessel.

"The Captain, a conscientious man, had been kept busy working hard during most of the spring and early summer of 1917 to provide for his still-growing family.

"My father had seen to it that the vessel was caulked and freshly painted before equipping her with new sails and lines. He was so proud of his ship!" GREAT LAKES MARINE COLLECTION OF THE MILWAUKEE PUBLIC LIBRARY.

"Normally, my loving, careful, and competent father conducted his business of hauling cargoes of coal across eastern Lake Ontario without the presence of his family on board. Many times, I had offered to help sail the *Marsh,* but the

Captain, in his polite yet playful way, told me I was too skinny and weak to perform the hard work of a sailor.

"By July, 1917, he suspected that we could all use a brief, pleasant change in our lives. He prevailed upon friends and family members to go sailing on Lake Ontario for a few days, even though Gertrude was more interested in furnishing the new house she and the Captain had just built. However, for the sake of family togetherness in an activity that normally precluded most of us, she complied.

"We sailed the graceful, three-masted schooner, *George A. Marsh* (named after an 1800's Chicago lumber baron; the Captain knew that changing a ship's name brings bad luck!), out of Belleville harbour on Thursday, July 26, 1917, in perfect picnic weather. On board were my father, Captain Smith, my stepmother and confidante, Gertrude, eight-year-old Eva, six-year-old Jack, four-year-old Clarence, 18-month-old Lorraine, and myself, Greta; the mate, Mr. William J. Watkins, 66 years of age, who was also the landlord of the Ferry Hotel in Belleville; sailors and deck hands, George Cousins, a relative by marriage who was 59 years old, Neil MacLellan (who brought along his wife and their seven-month-old son, Douglas MacLellan, and a four-year-old nephew visiting his aunt from Toronto, George Greaves), and my uncle, William Smith, the Captain's older brother who was about 50 years old.

"Four years earlier, he had sailed the Marsh *from Chicago all the way home....He always maintained her in excellent, seaworthy condition. He was so proud of his ship!"* GREAT LAKES MARINE COLLECTION OF THE MILWAUKEE PUBLIC LIBRARY.

"Horace and Margaret, my older siblings, fortunately did not go on this trip; Horace had stayed behind to procure a job in the mill of the Steel Company of Canada. These two became the only family members left alive after the *George A. Marsh* sank.

"Mr. Watkins, Mr. Cousins, Mr. Maclellan, and, of course, my Uncle Bill, were much more than hired help on board the *George A. Marsh;* they numbered among my father's dearest friends, and had sailed with him for many years.

The outline of the schooner, George A. Marsh, *appears ghostly in this photograph taken one foggy morning at Racine, Wisconsin, while the steamer behind it, the* William H. Wolf, *seems even more spectral. Four years after the* Marsh's *loss, the* Wolf *burned and sank in the St. Clair River with two lives lost.* GREAT LAKES MARINE COLLECTION OF THE MILWAUKEE PUBLIC LIBRARY.

"Combining business with pleasure, the *George A. Marsh*, on that same trip, planned to pick up a cargo of coal at Oswego, New York, across the lake, for the Downey Company of Belleville. However, this coal could not be secured, so the *Marsh* instead would load 450 tons of coal consigned to the Sewards Coal Company for the Rockwood Hospital in nearby Kingston, Ontario.

"The voyage across the lake had been pleasant and uneventful. After several days of casual lingering at Oswego, we watched as dock workers loaded the coal cargo, and left, sailing straight into a strong gale that swept Lake Ontario for about 24 hours. Winds reached 40 miles an hour (marine men felt that the velocity of the wind was remarkable for a summer month!), and the fierce rain beat down steadily in the darkness of that frightening night.

"The next day, before news of our deaths reached shore, the Kingston newspaper warned its readers that 'A heavy gale swept over the lake on Tuesday night. It was accompanied by rain at times, and the waves, which had been lashed to a pitch of fury, tore at the moorings of the vessels in port and caused anxiety to the masters on the lake.' The anxiety to the masters on the lake struck our ship several hours before that newspaper ran off the presses.

"Near midnight on Tuesday evening, August 7, 1917, crewmembers discovered that the *Marsh,* in all the pounding from the heavy seas, had sprung a leak and was rapidly taking on water. Besides a manual pump being used nonstop, the steam pump and siphons were made operational. Everyone aboard was roused and gathered on deck, just as a precaution in case we needed to abandon ship quickly.

"Our anxiety levels rose. At one point, when water washed over the increasingly submerged deck, I remember hearing Mr. MacLellan yelling to my uncle, 'Bill, I guess we've had it!' The Captain hoped to reach the Kingston dock, but, after a few hours, and realizing the improbability of that occurrence, would have settled for running the *Marsh* aground on the nearest land. However, we never reached shore.

"The truly horrifying event occurred at five o'clock in the morning: our ship suddenly sank from under us!

"Years later, a group of young musicians from England wrote a song that begins with the words, 'Wednesday morning at five o'clock as the day begins....' I think these musicians went under the strange name of the 'Beatles,' and the song was called 'She's Leaving Home.' Coincidentally, most of us on the *George A. Marsh* left this world at five o'clock as the day began on that Wednesday morning in August, 1917.

"We had been making good headway, and had we stayed afloat for about another twenty minutes, the Captain would have beached the *Marsh* on shore and we would have had better chances of survival. The rain still poured and the wind still howled when our ship took the final plunge about two miles off Pigeon Island in about 85 feet of water.

"The seas were running so high that it was impossible to launch the lifeboats. The crew and passengers, however, did take refuge in the lifeboats, overcrowding them due to our large number, and, as the *Marsh* sank, the boats intended to save lives capsized, and most of the people therein were lost by drowning. My father had also equipped the *Marsh* with a large motorboat besides the usual lifeboats, but the storm thundered with such vehemence that no small boat could survive in it.

"When the *Marsh* sank, Mr. MacLellan dived in an attempt to rescue his wife, but the waves swept her over the side, and she disappeared from view forever. Sailor George Cousins and one of the little boys (was it one of my poor brothers, Clarence or Jack, or little Georgy "Buster" Greaves? I am not certain) clung to the provisions box on deck. My struggling father surfaced momentarily, but then was yanked down by the swirling waters. I never saw him again.

"I did not die until about five hours after the *George A. Marsh* sank. I was, in fact, the last one of 12 people, from a total of 14 on board, to die.

"Uncle Bill, Mr. MacLellan, and I desperately held on to the smooth underside of one of the overturned lifeboats which the huge waves were attempting to destroy with all their might. For over five hours, I clung to this lifeboat's slippery underbelly, hoping against hope that we would be rescued or washed up on shore where we could reach safety. The two men encouraged me to hang on as long as possible, and they themselves held me up for as long as they were physically able. Their own courage was fortified by liberal chaws from a plug of chewing tobacco which Uncle Bill had managed to snatch out of the forecastle just prior to the sinking, but their physical strengths diminished greatly after several hours of constant struggling.

"At about 10:30 A.M., I finally succumbed to the long exposure. Even though it was early August, my skinny and frail body found the lake water to be intolerably cold, and I could no longer maintain my tiring struggle for life against wind and waves. My body ached from Nature's pounding; over my left forehead was a large bruise, while a nasty cut marred my right eyebrow. My arms and legs were scraped and bruised from constant pounding against the sides of the yawlboat. Above all, I felt an increasing numbness. Finally, I released my grip on the lifeboat and was immediately swept away by the massive waves. I vaguely remember feeling an all-encompassing aura of peace and a glow of tranquility overcome me, relief supplied by the soothing supernatural as I entered the Hereafter....

"The gale had blown the overturned lifeboat about eight miles towards Amherst Island, where two commercial fishermen named Hugh McCaugherty and Benjamin Wemp rescued Uncle Bill and Mr. MacLennan, lame and stiff from their trying experiences, about an hour after I died. They became the sole survivors from the sinking of the *George A. Marsh*.

"Mr. Neil MacLellan, personally blessed with enormous luck, was said to bring nautical misfortune with him wherever he went. He was a sailor who had worked on the schooner, *Oliver Mowat,* but was not on board when that vessel sank four years later. He had survived an incident on board the *Sophia Minch* when that vessel was in a wreck, and he sailed on the *Scheobazer,* which foundered at almost the same spot where the *Marsh* sank; Captain MacDonald and his wife, of the *Scheobazer,* were drowned in that incident. He was aboard a vessel named the *Kitchen* when it sank outside the Eastern Gap, but a tug rescued him from that sinking ship. His great luck stayed with him when the *Marsh* sank.

"Four-year-old George Greaves, clinging to a plank, floated close to shore, but he did not survive. His body was still dressed in the Indian suit which his parents in Toronto had bought for him before he went away to visit his aunt in Belleville and which he had worn on board the *Marsh,* when his remains were discovered at Lemoine's Point, on the shore at Dr. Black's farm at noon on the day after the sinking.

"Four-year-old George Greaves, clinging to a plank, floated close to shore, but he did not survive...." Photo from DAILY BRITISH WHIG (KINGSTON), Wednesday, August 14, 1917.

"My lifeless body was recovered next, on the afternoon of the day after the sinking, near the Amherst Island shore about a mile beyond where Georgy Greaves had been located, and close to where I was swept off the overturned lifeboat. The men who found me marvelled that, as they put it, 'in the sweet sleep of death, no signs of her horrible experience can be traced on her peaceful face.'

"The body of Mr. George Cousins, a captain in his own right who had volunteered to work as part of the crew on the *Marsh,* was recovered off Amherst Island on Sunday afternoon, August 12, 1917; he had clung to wreckage until about a mile from shore, when he was seen to disappear in the waves. The Kingston newspaper provided details to the public:

ANOTHER BODY IS FOUND

THREE KINGSTON MEN DISCOV-
ERED REMAINS OF G. COUSINS

They Were Taking Pictures of the
Wreck --- Found the Decomposed
Body in Three Feet of Water.

About two o'clock on Sunday afternoon three local young men, William Poulter, 133 Clergy street, John McGeethy and Frank Wilson unexpectedly discovered the body of George Cousins, one of the victims of the foundering of the schooner George A. Marsh on Wednesday morning last.

The young men left early on Sunday morning for a row up the lake in a small skiff with the intention of taking pictures of the ill-fated schooner. About noon, after two hours of hard rowing, they arrived at the wreck and for some time they took snaps of the boat. One of them climbed on the middle mast, which is about ten feet out of water, had his picture taken, and when taken into the boat again he brought a piece of the halyard rope with him. His explanation of this was that they might come across one of the bodies and they would have a piece of rope with which to tow.

Mr. Poulter had been looking on the shore line at this time with a pair of binoculars and suddenly he espied on a shoal running from The Brothers, a group of islands, a large box. He suggested rowing to the spot. When they arrived there they found that it was a large refrigerator box. The shoal is in very shallow water and they landed on it to conduct an examination.

On the other side they made the gruesome discovery of the body of the late George Cousins in about three feet of water, and in a position where it must have been washed over the shoal. The body was in a very decomposed state although it had been in the water only a few days. This is thought to have been caused by the heat of the sun and by the heavy waves which would keep the body on the tops of the crests and troughs.

The young men immediately rowed over to Amherst Island and had a telephone message sent to S. S. Corbett, undertaker, to despatch a rig for the body. They returned to the place where the drowned man lay and, notwithstanding the disagreeableness of their task, tied the rope which had been brought by a happy fore-thought around the dead man's waist. In this way they towed him to the shore line across the lake to Grass' farm where they were met by S. S. Corbett who transferred the remains to the city.

The body was in a very decomposed and discolored state but was recognized from the descriptions that have been given. In the pockets were found a carpenter's pencil, a red handkerchief and a gold filled watch which had stopped at 6:45.

Efforts were made by the young men to get in touch with Neil MacLennan, one of the survivors, at Amherst Island whence he had gone from Kingston on Friday afternoon, but they ascertained that he had left for Bath.

The late Captain George Cousins was one of the wrecked mariners who made a great fight for life. In the tragic moments before the vessel foundered by the mighty power of the elements he had stood by his post---true to the traditions of marine life---but when the vessel lurched before its last great plunge he was swept clear and managed to get inside the refrigerator box which was found near his body. He was seen in the box by some people on Amherst Island at five o'clock in the morning and he seems to have made the grim fight against death for an hour and a half at least against the mountainous waves which swept his little craft hither and thither on the darkened lake.

The deceased was born in England fifty-nine years ago, but when only a lad of sixteen he came to Canada and has been a resident of Belleville since that time. Practically all his life he sailed on the great lakes [sic] where he was well and favorably known. He is survived by his wife who resides at the corner of Wharf and Church streets, Belleville, one son, Arthur George of Sarnia, a sailor on the great lakes [sic], and two daughters, Mrs. J. A. Vanderwater, Napanee, and Mrs. Frank Keegan, Belleville.

J. A. Vanderwater of Napanee, a son-in-law of the deceased, arrived in the city on Sunday evening and made the funeral arrangements. The remains were transferred to Belleville at two o'clock on Monday afternoon for interment....

"My family and the Cousins family were related by ties of marriage. It seems indeed a remarkable fatality that the disaster should have occurred on this, the one and only trip which the wives and children and friends took together!

"Another corpse was located 12 days after our ship sank. The body of a woman, thought to be either my stepmother, Gertrude, or Mrs. MacLellan, was found floating in several feet of water shortly after 8:00 A.M. on Monday, August 20th. A man named Louis Smith, no relation to my family, but ironically an employee of the Rockwood Hospital to which our cargo of coal was destined when the *Marsh* sank, was walking along the shore past Lake Ontario Park near 'Sandy Bottom' when he espied the body of a woman in the water some little distance from shore. He called another man for assistance, and together they brought the body to shore.

"This body, considerably bloated, was discolored slightly from exposure in the water. It appeared to have been a woman about 40 years of age, although my stepmother was only 22, and Mrs. MacLellan, only 25.

"The next day, my older sister, Margaret, identified the body as that of our stepmother, Gertrude, wife of the Captain. She was wearing her wedding ring and a ring set with an opal stone (Mrs. MacLennan wore a wedding ring with a diamond ring at the time of her death). Gertrude was buried in the Belleville Cemetery close to me on Tuesday, August 21, 1917.

"It was not until September 8th, 1917, exactly one month after the loss of the *Marsh,* that the last body to be recovered was located, the other seven missing corpses presumed to be in the cabin of the ship where they supposedly sought refuge at the time of the sinking.

"The mate of the *Marsh,* Mr. William Watkins of Belleville, was found floating by an Amherst Island commercial fisherman named Thomas Smith (again, no relation to my family) just off that island. Undertaker R. J. Reid of Kingston was notified and the body was prepared for burial and sent to Belleville the next day. Poor Mr. Watkins was survived only by his grieving second wife in Belleville.

"The seven bodies of Captain John Smith, my siblings Eva, John, Clarence, and Lorraine, Mrs. Neil MacLennan, and her infant son, Douglas, did not surface or come ashore.

"Our deaths in the sinking of the *George A. Marsh* became the all-absorbing topic of conversation in Belleville and area, and left that city in deep grief. The city newspaper listed the final tally:

THE DEAD

Captain John W. Smith, aged 48 years.
Mrs. Smith (his wife), aged 22 years.
Greta Smith, aged 12 years.

Eva Smith, aged 8 years.
John Smith, aged 6 years.
Clarence Smith, aged 4 years.
Lorraine Smith, aged 1 year.
Mrs. Neil MacLennan, aged 25 years.
Douglas MacLennan, aged seven months.
George Greaves, Toronto, aged 4 years.
William J. Watkin, aged 66 years.
George Cousins, aged 59 years.

SAVED

Neil MacLellan.
William Smith.

One of our family friends in Belleville, Mrs. Hermans, took out her grief with her pen; her poem, which she named "The Wreck," appeared in the newspaper's "Poet's Corner" five days after our ship sank. This poem romanticized a different setting, but the theme of family loss was directly inspired by our tragedy:

All night the booming minute gun
  Had peeled along the deep,
And mournfully the rising sun
  Looked o'er the tide-worn steep.
A barque from India's coral strand,
  Before the raging blast
Had veil'd her topsails to the sand
  And bowed her noble mast.

The queenly ship! --- brave hearts had striven,
  And true ones died with her!
We saw her mighty cable riven,
  Like floating gossamer.
We saw her proud flag struck that morn---
  A star once o'er the seas,---
Her anchor gone, her deck untorn,
  And sadder things than these!
We saw the strong man still and low
  A crushed reed thrown aside;
Yet, by that rigid lip and brow,
  Not without strife he died.

And near him on the sea-weed lay---
Till then we had not wept---
But well our gushing hearts might say,
That there a mother slept!

For her pale arms a babe had pressed
With such a wreathing grasp,
Billows had dashed o'er that fond breast,
Yet not undone the clasp.
Her very dresses had been flung
To wrap the fair child's form,
Where still their wet long streamers hung
All tangled by the storm.

And beautiful, midst that wild scene,
Gleamed up the boy's dead face,
Like slumber's trustingly serene,
In melancholy grace.
Deep in her bosom lay his head,
With half-shut violet eye---
He had known little of her dread,
Nought of her agony!

O human love! whose yearning heart,
Through all things vainly true,
So stamps upon thy mortal part
Its passionate adieux---
Surely thou hast another lot:
There is some home for thee,
Where thou shalt rest, remembering not
The moaning of the sea!

"My earthly remains were taken to Belleville's St. Thomas Church where, previous to the service, they were sadly viewed by many sympathizing friends and relatives, the same people who adorned my white casket with numerous colourful floral tributes. The rector, Venerable Archdeacon Beamish, conducted the burial services of the Anglican Church and also officiated at the interment. I was buried on Saturday, August 11, 1917, in the Smith family plot at Belleville Cemetery.

"Unfortunately, no headstones were erected for either me or my stepmother. To this day, we lie in unmarked graves.

"On Sunday evening, August 12th, a solemn and impressive memorial service for us, the victims of the *George A. Marsh* sinking, was held in

Belleville's St. Thomas Church. Nearly all of the deceased had been members and communicants of that particular place of worship. The rector's address was quite fitting, urging the congregation to so pattern their lives that whether the summons into the Hereafter comes quickly or slowly, no apprehension need be felt of a glorious awakening in the Better Land.

"The music, too, was particularly appropriate, the hymns being well-known to my family: number 783: 'What a Friend We Have in Jesus,' number 735: 'Perfect Jewel,' number 592: 'On the Resurrection Morning,' and lastly, number 18: 'Abide With Me.' The hymn, 'Perfect Jewels,' was particularly appropriate because the drowning of the seven little children in the sinking of the *Marsh* was its saddest feature. The congregation sang with deep sympathy and tender feeling:

> *Little children, little children,*
> *Who love their Redeemer,*
> *Are the jewels, precious jewels,*
> *His loved and His own.*
> *Like the stars of the morning,*
> *His bright crown adorning,*
> *They shall shine in their beauty,*
> *Bright stars for His crown.*

"Twelve people were dead, and the ship was dead, too. Mr. Flint, my father's business partner who had stayed behind in Belleville, suffered a severe financial loss, since the *George A. Marsh* was not insured except against fire. Initially, he was told that the *Marsh* sank in only 25 feet of water, and that total salvage would be possible. When the depth was established at closer to 85 feet, the possibility of even partial salvage was greatly diminished. Mr. Flint concluded that the heavy coal cargo had given the *Marsh* only about 12 to 14 inches of freeboard when the gales developed. One pump on board was a powerful motor pump and, with an ordinary leak, would have sufficed to keep the schooner afloat until she reached dock or shore, but the heavy coal cargo conspired against the ship's survival.

"Coincidentally, over 80 years before the sinking of the *George A. Marsh,* the *Kingston Chronicle* of May 26, 1836, reported that "a schooner owned by Mr. Smith, of Belleville, laden with Wheat belonging to Bill Flint, Esq. and bound for Prescott, came in contact with the Steam Boat, *United States,* on Monday night, May 16, about one mile from Alexander's Bay, and sunk immediately...." Mr. Smith and Mr. Flint? This is indeed quite a coincidence!

"Life quickly returned to normal for most people in Kingston and Belleville. Ironically, five days after so many people drowned in the *Marsh* sinking, an 18-year-old Kingston woman named Isabel Nelson swam the span from Kingston to

Garden Island, establishing her reputation of being the greatest long distance female swimmer in the Kingston area by conquering those killing waters.

"My father's pride in the schooner, *George A. Marsh,* compels me to give her brief history. Built at Muskegon, Michigan, in 1882 by William Footlander for W. B. Ranson of Chicago, Illinois, the 118-foot schooner registered 174 gross tons. Named after lumber businessman, George Andrew Marsh (1834-1888), the vessel was sold by her namesake to West A. Walker in mid-August, 1883. During the winter of 1886-1887, the *Marsh* was rebuilt with 18 feet added to her length at a cost of $3000. Her last American owner was the Estebrooke Skeele Lumber Company of Chicago in 1913.

"Mr. Flint and my father purchased the *George A. Marsh* in 1913, changing her registration from the U. S. number (85727) to a Canadian one (133750) officially on April 17, 1914. She was one of the many Lake Michigan vessels brought down to Lake Ontario in the early part of the twentieth century for use as coal haulers or stone hookers, after a lifetime of usefulness in the western lumber trade. The *Marsh's* final dimensions were 139.1 feet in length, 26.4 feet in beam, and 8.1 feet in draught, with a gross tonnage of 215.

"The *Marsh* carried mainly coal cargoes during her final brief years sailing the Kingston area of eastern Lake Ontario when my father captained her. My narrative related our final moments on the ship's last day of operation.

"The government steamer, *Grenville,* which patrolled the waters around Kingston, launched an official investigation into the sinking of the *George A. Marsh.* Satisfied that the powerful forces of Nature had been responsible for the deaths of 12 people, the captain of the *Grenville* next had to determine if the wreck constituted a menace to navigation, and had to report to the Department of Marine with his findings.

"Shortly after our ship sank, the Kingston newspaper published two photographs of her masts protruding, intact and upright, from the lake. The masts on sailing ships were usually taller than the vessel was long, so it made sense that the *Marsh's* final resting place, in about 85 feet of water, would be marked by these telltale wooden posts. The location of the *Marsh,* west southwest of Nine Mile Point and north northwest of Pigeon Island, put her in a threatening position to the many other vessels navigating those waters. The *Grenville's* captain concluded that the wreck would have to be salvaged quickly by the remaining owner, or be blown up by the government. Money for a major salvage did not exist, so the future of the *Marsh* was determined.

"On October 2, 1917, a commercial hardhat diver named H. E. Poland, from Prescott, Ontario, attempted to reach the wreck of the *Marsh* for the purpose of removing those portions of her that posed a threat to safe navigation. Bad weather delayed him for several days. Finally, on a calmer day, he arrived at the site, with the masts and wire rigging complete and well out of the water. Underwater, he found the main sail and the fore sail still set, as they had been two months earlier during our frantic attempt to reach land. Mr. Poland lamented the work that would be required of him to do his job, for the rigging and the stays had also remained in place, attesting to the sound rebuilding of the Marsh. Mr. Poland was forced to wrap a tube of dynamite around the main mast just under the cross-trees where the rigging and stays were solidly attached. After this explosion, his second charge was placed lower on the mast, about 45 feet below the surface of the water. The mizzen mast had been carried away by foul weather by this time, and the third mast, the foremast, he removed from a point 27 feet below the water. Then he did several sweeps of the shipwreck site to ensure no obstacles were still in place above a safe depth for commercial navigation.

"Shortly after our ship sank, the Kingston newspaper published two photographs of her masts protruding, intact and upright, from the lake...." DAILY BRITISH WHIG (KINGSTON), Saturday, August 25, 1917.

"Mr. Poland then did an unspeakable thing. He placed a charge of dynamite down the main hatch of the hull, which, in his words, 'loosened up everything and brought a lot of wreckage to the surface.' I imagine he was hoping to locate and remove some of the remaining bodies which people believed were inside the ship's cabin area. Today their remains lie just off the shipwreck. Whether that is where they sank on their own, or whether the dynamite blast ejected them there, is not known. But our poor schooner! It saddened me to see the Captain's nautical pride and joy, already sunk by the forces of nature, further ravaged by a fellow human being with a load of dynamite!

"For fifty years after that, the *George A. Marsh* rested undisturbed, silently sitting in the slow current which gently deposited silt throughout the vessel's remains. Nature saw to it that the mortal remains of the seven storm victims unfortunate enough not to have received a Christian land burial, gradually disappeared, except for their bones, which still linger in small but distinguishable mounds just off the shipwreck's hull.

"The shipwreck, *George A. Marsh,* was relocated on October 7, 1967, by underwater explorers named Barbara Carson, Edward Donnelly, and Ted Symonds from Kingston using an invention called 'scuba' which allows humans to be guests in environments alien to them. In October, 1971, divers removed the large, graceful bow anchors from the *Marsh.* I understand this behaviour was the norm among their kind at that time, but it was another painful wound for my father, the Captain, a practical man who clearly understood the impracticalities of a schooner with no anchors, regardless of whether the *Marsh* was physically afloat, or sentenced to sail the silent seas of a spiritual world!

The Marsh's *wheel, the focal point of this beautiful, intact shipwreck, is viewed with fascination by visitor James Taylor, a commercial diver.* PHOTO BY CRIS KOHL

"The Captain did, however, feel quite honoured to have so many scuba divers visit his beloved schooner and appreciate her fine lines and antique hardware. Even though his half-interest in the vessel at the time of her sinking amounted to only $5,500, the ship was priceless to him. For years, the shipwreck was respectfully explored by appreciative people who were aware that the blocks and deadeyes, the pots and pans, the wheel and the windlass, the axes and the pumps, the dishes and the stove, the majestic bow chains and the noble bowsprit, belonged to us, not to them. The human remains of my beloved family and friends lay undisturbed off the wreck, veiled to curious visitors by poor water visibility.

Diver Dani Lee studies deadeyes on the Marsh's *starboard rail.* PHOTO BY CRIS KOHL.

"But then, one day, a curious thing happened in Lake Ontario. The milky, silty water cleared up, apparently due to another foreign invader called the zebra mussel. There was great excitement among scuba divers, for they could now see greater distances underwater than they had ever seen before. With this increased viewing ability, they developed confidence in themselves and explored the lake bottom immediately around the wreck of the *George A. Marsh.*

"It was only a matter of time before the human remains were detected and disturbed by visiting beings from the living world. This disrespect, this morbid attraction by a small minority to indignantly turn over human bones with casual, carnival-like curiosity, was the last straw for my father. The Captain lashed out and indiscriminately took personal revenge against these marauders. The 1990's were not good times for some scuba divers visiting the *George A. Marsh.* Five have died so far.

"I can understand my father's wrath and frustration. Both his wives rest safely with me in Christian ground, undisturbed at Belleville, while his remains, and those of other family members and friends, lie exposed to inconsiderate invaders in an open, watery grave. All this while two of the gravesites my father purchased in the Belleville Cemetery in 1914 remain unoccupied! Oh, it would be so good to have my father, the Captain, resting next to us. It would be so wonderful to be with my father and the others again!

"So wonderful...."

NOTE: The author purposely omitted footnotes in this particular story, concerned that little floating numbers between the printed words would distract the reader from the mood of the narrative. The sources of information for this story (the author's research notes on the *George A. Marsh* shipwreck grew to become the thickest of all his Kingston area shipwreck file folders; as a result, the story of the *George A. Marsh,* even by omitting time-consuming footnotes, took him over 20 hours to write) are:

Belleville Cemetery Company, computer printout information on the Smith family plots, provided on August 26, 1996.

George A. Marsh. Runge Collection, Ship Information and Data Records, Milwaukee Public Library.

George A. Marsh. Master Sheet, Institute for Great Lakes Research, Bowling Green State University, Ohio.

Golding, Peter. 'The Wreck of the *George A. Marsh."* *Diver Magazine.* Vol. 5, No. 8. Nov./Dec., 1979, pp. 38-40.

Greenwood, John O. *Namesakes 1910-1919.* Cleveland: Freshwater Press, Inc., 1986.

Jackson, Rick. "The *George A. Marsh." Save Ontario Shipwrecks Newsletter.* Fall, 1983, pp. 9-10.

Kohl, Cris. *Dive Ontario! The Guide to Shipwrecks and Scuba Diving.* Chatham, Ontario: self-published, 1990; revised edition, November, 1995.

McLeod, Ken. "The Schooner *George Marsh* Implicated in International Intrigue." *Save Ontario Shipwrecks Newsletter.* Spring/Summer, 1984, pp. 13-14.

Metcalfe, Willis. *Marine Memories.* Picton, Ontario: The Picton Gazette, 1975.

Hardhat diver H. E. Poland's report is from the Public Archives of Canada, R. G. 42, Volume 269, File 39326, and was reprinted in the Winter, 1985 issue of the *Save Ontario Shipwrecks Newsletter.* (Submitted to that publication by Rick Neilson.)

Newspapers:

Daily British Whig, Kingston, Ontario: August 8, 9, 10, 11, 13, 16, 20, 21, 24, 25, September 10, 1917.

Daily Intelligencer, Belleville, Ontario: August 9, 10, 11, 13, 1917.

Hallowell Traveller, Prince Edward County, Ontario: May 27, 1836.

Kingston Whig-Standard, Kingston, Ontario: Feb. 3, 1972.

Picton Gazette, Picton, Ontario: August 16, 1917.

The author seeks assistance from any individuals or organizations that could assist with the legal removal of all the human remains on or near the schooner, **George A. Marsh,** *for proper burial, possibly in the Smith family plot in the Belleville (Ontario) Cemetery. He can be contacted at (519) 351-1966, fax (519) 351-1753, or mail: Cris Kohl, 16 Stanley Ave., Chatham, Ontario N7M 3J2.*

HIAWATHA   (September 20, 1917)

A sole survivor remained after the 518-ton barge, *Hiawatha,* with seven people on board, sank on September 20, 1917, south of Main Duck Island. The victims were:

> Omer Hainault, who was the 24-year-old nephew of Capt. Joseph Leduc, of the barge, *Lapwing,* and resided in Valleyfield, Quebec,
>
> his wife, who was 24 years of age,
>
> their baby, who was five months old,
>
> Archille Hebert, 45, who left behind a wife and family in Montreal,
>
> Joseph Thivierge, an unmarried 19-year-old from Valleyfield, Quebec,
>
> Madame Monette, who was the wife of Capt. Zotique Monette, of the barge, Dorchester. Capt. Monette expected his wife to make this return journey by train, and when he discovered that she had been a passenger on board the *Hiawatha,* he was heartbroken. He and their 21-year-old son remained. Mrs. Monette carried quite a large sum of money with her on this trip.[330]

The sole survivor was the *Hiawatha's* master, Capt. Albene Lalonde.

The tug, *Magnolia,* towing the coal-laden barges, *Hilda* and *Hiawatha,* in that order, departed Oswego at ten o'clock on the night of Wednesday, September 19, 1917, heading for Montreal. All the vessels were owned by the Montreal Transportation Company. The tug and the barge, *Hilda,* weathered the gale, which came up with terrible suddenness, but the *Hiawatha* succumbed, sinking in 28 fathoms of water. The ship and her cargo were insured.[331]

Capt. Albene Lalonde of the *Hiawatha* loaded the two women, the baby, and Omer Hainault into a yawl boat just as his ship was sinking. The captain and the remaining two crewmembers were the last to leave the doomed vessel, clinging to a makeshift raft for survival. Two hours passed before the steamer, *McVittie,* commanded by Capt. Arthur Lalonde of Montreal (no relation to the other captain), picked up the only person left on the raft and returned him to Oswego. Mate Dauste of the *McVittie* talked to a reporter later:

> **...He said that about fifteen miles out of Oswego the wheelsman on the McVittie sighted a raft, made of three hatchway covers, upon which a man was clinging. Mate Dauste in a small boat rescued the man who was Captain Lalonde of the Hiawatha. Captain Lalonde said that A. Hebert, the mate of the Hiawatha and Joseph Thivierge, seaman, were with him on the raft but became exhausted a short time before and were washed into the lake and went down....**
>
> **Before the Hiawatha started to sink the bulkheads were knocked out by the crew to allow the water to run off her deck. The waves, however, crept into the hold....**

Captain Lalonde said that he blew the distress signal on his small engine six or seven times but could not make the crew of the barge Hilda or the tug hear it on account of the wind being against the sound. He cut the line when he saw that the boat was about to sink....

The steamer McVittie was but a short distance away when the last two survivors were seen to sink. The others, including the women and child, must have perished in the dark.

Captain Albert Lalonde, of the McVittie through his glasses saw the last two sink from sight. This was about 6 o'clock in the morning.

A curious feature of the tragedy was the meeting for the first time of the Captains Lalonde, the rescued and the rescuer. Though of the same name they are no relation to each other, the McVittie's captain coming from Montreal.[332]

The *Hiawatha's* captain spoke no English and told his story through an interpreter.[333] Two lifeboats were located near the scene of the sinking, a small one upside-down, and a large, flat-bottomed lifeboat with everything, including oars, intact. This led to the theory that those on board actually did not have enough time to get into the lifeboat to make a safe escape.[334] However, the *Hiawatha* sank so fast that it was a miracle that there was even a sole survivor.

The *Hiawatha,* built in 1890 by Thomas Brian at Garden Island near Kingston, measured 176' 5" by 30' by 11' 9" (53 by 9 by 3.5 metres).[335]

The unusual, multi-masted towbarge, Hiawatha *(left) and the small passenger steamer,* R. G. Stewart. GREAT LAKES MARINE COLLECTION OF THE MILWAUKEE PUBLIC LIBRARY.

BERTIE CALKINS   (October 7, 1917)

The Canadian schooner, *Bertie Calkins,* experienced a dramatic sinking after an unusual collision with the Bay Bridge at Belleville:

> On Sunday morning about 10 o'clock, a schooner while proceeding down the bay, light, had a mishap by colliding with a pier of the bay bridge. The schooner in question is owned by Capt. Bongard of Picton, and had discharged a cargo of coal at Trenton. The vessel was being guided through the swing of the bridge when she struck the pier with considerable force. It was apparent the schooner had sustained damages as she commenced to fill with water. Being in close proximity to the shore she was easily beached. Yesterday a diver from Kingston came to the city and made an inspection of the vessel. He ascertained that a large hole had been made through the hull, and this is being temporarily repaired, after which the water will be pumped out. When this is done the schooner will be taken to Picton and placed on the ways of the dry dock, where permanent repairs will be made. When the collision occurred a woman cook on the boat was thrown against a stove, sustaining a severe burn on the wrist.[336]

The *Bertie Calkins,* built in 1874 at Two Rivers, Wisconsin, by Hanson & Scove, measured 134' 4" by 27' 2" by 9' 3" (40.3 by 8.2 by 2.8 metres). She sailed under American registry from 1874 until 1908, Canadian registry from 1909 to 1911, American again in 1912 and 1913, and Canadian again from 1914 until 1931, when she was dropped from the records,[337] presumably abandoned.

The schooner, Bertie Calkins, *under full sail, sank after hitting part of the Belleville Bridge.* GREAT LAKES MARINE COLLECTION OF THE MILWAUKEE PUBLIC LIBRARY.

ALOHA   (October 28, 1917)

Tradition states that a captain must go down with his ship. This romantic fatalism, although not always the most practical or humanitarian notion, happened in the case of the schooner-barge, *Aloha,* but not by choice. The 76-year-old master of the vessel, Capt. Daniel McVicar, was the only fatality when his ship foundered in a severe storm off Nine Mile Point on October 28, 1917.

The 521-ton *Aloha,* built by William Dulac at Mt. Clemens, Michigan, in 1888, measured 173' (51.9 metres) in length, 32' 5" (9.7 metres) in beam, and 12' (3.6 metres) in draft. When she passed to Canadian ownership at Midland, Ontario, her official number changed from 106542 U. S. to Canadian 134264, with a Canadian measurement change to 517 tons.[338]

The barge, Aloha, *docked at Midland, Ontario, in 1916.* ARCHIVES OF ONTARIO. S13043.

In 1889, a year after her launch, the *Aloha* was owned by Hebard & Son of Pequaming, Michigan, and was classed A1 with a value of $26,000, which remained the same in 1890. In 1891, her value was listed as $24,000; in 1893, at $25,000; in 1894, as $20,000; in 1897, as $20,000. The ship was repaired in 1896 and 1899. In 1901, the ship was registered at Duluth, Minnesota. By 1906, the *Aloha* had changed owners to Luther P. Graves of Buffalo, New York, who owned her until 1913, and the ship was classed A1½ with a value of only $10,000. In 1906, repairs included the addition of steam power for pumping and working the ship, a steam pump well, and new deck and beams. Forward repairs had been made in 1904, and the ceiling had been recaulked in 1905. The Canada List of Shippping named the Midland Transportation Company Limited of Midland, Ontario, as the *Aloha's* owner from 1914 until 1916, and the Milnes

Brothers Coal Company of Toronto in 1917 when the vessel sank. From 1918 until 1924, the Donnelly Salvage and Wrecking Company Limited of Kingston was listed as the owner.[339] Launched as a schooner, the Aloha was converted to a bulk freight barge at the Empire Ship Building Company yards at Buffalo, New York, in 1902.[340]

The Toronto steamer, *C. W. Chamberlain,* towed the two-masted *Aloha,* loaded with 925 tons of coal heading for Kingston from Erie, Pennsylvania,[341] until the strong gales caused the barge to spring a leak about nine miles (15 kilometres) west of Kingston.

> ...The captain of the Aloha, Daniel McVicar, of Deseronto met death. He was seventy-six years of age and had been sailing on the lakes practically all his life, and was well-known at almost every port. His body drifted to shore at Simcoe Island and was...forwarded to his late home in Deseronto.
>
> The members of the crew who were saved are John Vale, mate, of Kingston; Frederick Hunt, wheelsman, of Wiarton, Ont.; Clarence Mills, of Portsmouth, deck-hand, and formerly a guard at the penitentiary; C. H. Ellis, cook, of Belleville.
>
> The four men had a close call for their life. Mills had the most thrilling experience, as for six hours he clung to one of the masts which he climbed when the barge went over on her side, and there he clung for all this time, until rescued by Capt. Esford and crew of the government steamer Grenville, which went from Kingston to his succor.

BARGE ALOHA FOUNDERED; CAPT. M'VICAR DROWNED

Crew Saved, Among Them Being John Vale of Kingston and Clarence Mills of Portsmouth— Barge Sank During Gale Off Nine Mile Point Sunday Morning.

VESSEL LOST.

Barge Aloha, coal-laden, on her way from Erie, Pa., to the Canadian Locomotive Works.

Loss of Life.

Capt. Daniel McVicar aged 76, residing at Deseronto.

master, lost no time in getting out to the scene of the wreck, and by some clever manoeuvering, was able to get Mills off the mast on to the steamer. He was suffering terribly from the cold, and it is doubtful if he would have been able to have held out much longer. Once on board the Grenville he was soon thawed out, and some time after the vessel reach-

Front page headlines on Monday, October 29, 1917, Daily British Whig *(Kingston).*

Vale and Ellis were rescued by Capt. William Stalker and crew of the steamer, Chamberlain, as they were struggling in the water, holding on to some of the wreckage. Hunt got on to the top of the cabin when the climax came, and drifted towards Simcoe Island, and was picked up by a gasoline launch near the shore....

The crew of the Chamberlain made a gallant attempt to save Capt. McVicar. The latter had on a life belt, but did not manage to get hold of any of the wreckage. He was thrown a line, but the wind was so strong that it did not get within his reach. Still another was thrown to him, but this too, he failed to get, and he was carried away and perished. When last seen by the men who had endeavored to save him, his body was doubled up, and it is believed that he sufferd cramps from his plunge in the icy waters, and that death was due to exposure. The men on the Chamberlain did everything possible to get him, but their efforts were fruitless.

As already stated, Mills took to the rigging....it was absolutely impossible for the Chamberlain to draw up very close to the wreck. Mills...waved to Capt. Stalker to go on to Kingston and send out another vessel to rescue him.... Capt. Stalker was loath to leave,...but there was nothing else left for him to do....

The tug, Mary P. Hall,...set out to rescue Mills, but after making a few miles, was forced to return to port.... The Grenville...lost no time in getting out to the scene of the wreck, and by some clever manoeuvering, was able to get Mills off the mast onto the steamer. He was suffering terribly from the cold, and it is doubtful if he would have been able to have held out much longer.... Mills is a strong, well-built fellow, and was able to stand the exposure....

The barge appeared to go to pieces all at once. One side was smashed, and the water rushed in and swamped everything. The little cabin blew up as if by an explosion.... With one side torn off, the barge lurched to the other side, and then foundered, throwing the crew into the cold waters to care for themselves. Just a short time before the crash, the tow line was cut in two, and the distress whistle blown....[342]

The Belleville newspaper added some details of the sinking and survivals:

...The Aloha sank at 6:30 Sunday morning.... The mate, Johnny Vale, of Kingston, saved his life by clinging to a pair of stairs washed from the deck.... When the barge sank the escaping air from the hold blew up in a regular explosion, blowing the hatches off and tearing the cabin from the deck, and it was on this cabin that Wheelsman Fred Hunt, of Wiarton, floated for three hours fighting the strength of the waves which several times washed him from his refuge, until he was rescued by George Eves and Robert Eves, of Simcoe island, who put out in a small gasolene [sic] launch and braving the terrors of the storm saved his life....

> Cook Ellis states that in his eighteen years of experience, off and on, as a sailor on the great lakes [sic] he never saw a worse storm, not even the big blow of 1913, which he was out in on the Midland Queen.... The crew of the Aloha lost everything....[343]

The Kingston newspaper summarized this and recent marine tragedies:

> Another wreck, with the loss of life, has been added to the already lengthy list to the credit of Lake Ontario, and this, like two others recently recorded, occurred within sight of Kingston and in the district which has become known to mariners as "The Graveyard of Lake Ontario."[344]

Local scuba divers and marine historians, Lloyd Shales and Barbara Carson, located the *Aloha* in August, 1964, in about 50 feet (15 metres) of water.[345] Most of the hull is intact, although presently being placed under great pressure from the weight of millions of zebra mussels. Most of this shipwreck's smaller artifacts were blissfully removed by visiting divers in the 1960's, blindly unaware that the *machismo* removal of these "tokens of accomplishment", which amounted to theft, was destroying a unique archaeological site, as well as dampening future scuba charterboat operations. However, anchor chain attached to a windlass still sits on the bow, and views of the original coal cargo can be seen in the ship's holds. In the sandy bottom at the stern lie a capstan, the steering quadrant, and the rudder post. More fish life in vast schools has existed at this site persistently over the years than on any other area shipwreck.[346]

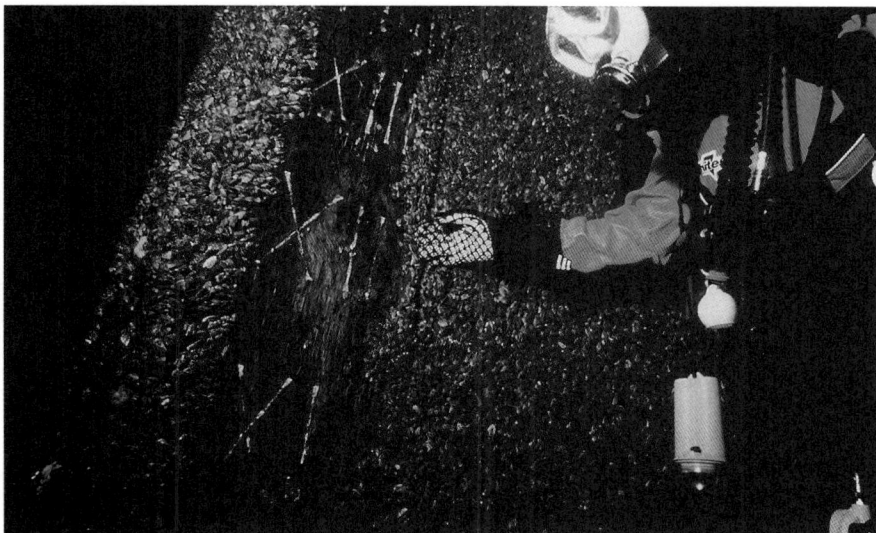

Scuba divers have not allowed the zebra mussel invasion of the Great Lakes to obscure the distinct Roman numeral draught markings on the bow stem of the barge, Aloha. *Diver Marcy McElmon takes a good look at the white paint still intact in these wooden grooves, while, sadly, zebra mussels cover the rich oak on the rest of the wreck.* PHOTO BY CRIS KOHL.

ABERDEEN   (March 11, 1918)

The 142-ton[347] Canadian steamer, *Aberdeen,* measuring 99' 6" (29.9 metres) in length, 22' (6.6 metres) in beam, and 8' 7" (2.6 metres) in draft,[348] burned to a complete loss on the south shore of the Bay of Quinte, below Picton, on March 11, 1918.[349] This small, bulk freight steamer operated in the Bay of Quinte area.

The Aberdeen *was built at Picton by John Tate in 1894.* AUTHOR'S COLLECTION.

NORTHWEST   (November 29, 1918)

Two sailors, Charles Jardine and George Tryon, both of Buffalo, died from exposure when the bow half of the huge, 385-foot (115.5-metre) steel freighter, *Northwest,* sank in 100' (30 metres) of water "a short distance off the Prince Edward county shore" near Trenton.[350] Their half-ship had been towed by the Toronto tug, *J. D. Burke,* across Lake Ontario after a passage through the old Welland Canal, for subsequent rejoining at Montreal with her stern half and service in World War One in Europe (which, ironically, had just ended!). The weather worsened, and Capt. McMinn cut his bow end loose from the tug off Rochester and dropped anchors to ride out the storm. But the *Northwest* bow broke away and drifted across the lake. When the gales worsened and the bulkheads broke in, the men took to a makeshift raft, which overturned once before they drifted to shore early Friday morning. They wandered for miles along the shore before finding shelter; Jardine and Tryon died on the beach.[351] The 4,244-ton *Northwest* was built at Cleveland in 1894.[352]

MANOLA   (December 3, 1918)

Four days after the bow half of the steel freighter, *Northwest,* sank with fatalities, the bow half of the steel freighter, *Manola,* sank with even more loss of life. Considering the rarity of immense, steel halves of ships cruising around the Great Lakes, this tragic double loss is indeed coincidental!

The 2,326-gross-ton *Manola,* built in 1890 at Cleveland by the Globe Iron Works Company for the Minnesota Steam Ship Co., measured 282' 4'" (84.7 metres) in length, 40' 2" (12.1 metres) in beam, and 21' 3" (6.4 metres) in draft. She was a duplicate of the *Maruba, Mariska, Masaba, Marina,* and *Matoa.*[353]

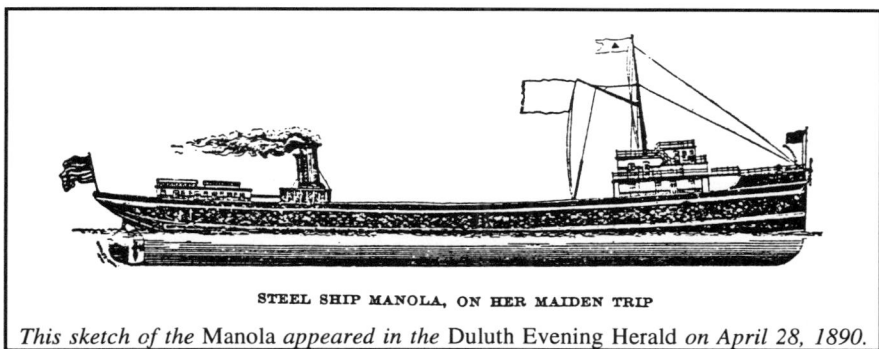

STEEL SHIP MANOLA, ON HER MAIDEN TRIP

This sketch of the Manola *appeared in the* Duluth Evening Herald *on April 28, 1890.*

The *Manola* was instrumental in rescuing the crew of the sinking freighter, *Joseph L. Hurd,* after that vessel collided with the *Cayuga* on Lake Michigan on May 10, 1895. The *Manola* successfully rode out the worst storm in recorded history on the Great Lakes, the Storm of November 9-10, 1913. Eight other steel ships were lost with all hands on Lake Huron during that storm, but the *Manola* reached refuge at Harbor Beach, Michigan. The captain ran his vessel full steam ahead while at anchor to maintain his position during the storm, and all eight of the thick lines running from the ship to the breakwall snapped.[354]

The *Manola* was sold on January 25, 1918, to the Emergency Fleet Corporation of the United States Government for war service.[355] At Buffalo, she was cut in two so she could be transported through the Welland Canal and on to Quebec, for reassembly and passage across the Atlantic Ocean. While being towed across Lake Ontario by the tug, *Michigan,* on December 3, 1918, the line parted just west of Main Duck Island in severe snowstorm conditions, and the bow half of the *Manola* sank suddenly, taking with it the eleven men who were on board.

> **Eleven men, comprising the crew of the bow section of the freighter Minola [sic], are believed to have been drowned when that section of the boat went down in Lake Ontario, near Duck Island, Monday night, in a terrific gale and blizzard.**

> News of the disaster was brought into Cape
> Vincent [New York] yesterday, by the Government
> tug Michigan, which was towing the Minola. The
> captain of the Michigan reports that within five
> minutes after the lines parted, the Minola
> foundered. The sea was heavy and no effort could
> be made to return to the scene of the disaster, or
> send a boat to search for the missing sailors. The
> Minola was one of the largest freight liners built
> for the United States Shipping Board in the upper
> lakes and towed in section to Montreal, where the
> boats are assembled and made ready for ocean
> traffic. The stern of the Minola safely weathered
> the storm.[356]

Nine days later, the body of Herbert McQueen, a sailor from the *Manola,*
washed ashore at Main Duck Island. It was the only body recovered from this
disaster.[357]

Manola's stern half was rebuilt and renamed the *Mapledawn,* which sank in
Georgian Bay on November 30, 1924.[358]

In 1976, Barbara Carson and Doug Pettingill found the *Manola's* bow half,
and many of the artifacts, such as the ship's brass bell and many chinaware items
bearing the Pittsburgh Steamship Company's name and logo (the company
which purchased the *Manola* in 1901) were recovered and are exhibited now at the
nearby Mariners' Park Museum in South Bay, Ontario.[359]

The bow half of the steel freighter, Manola, *lies upside-down on the rocky floor of*
Lake Ontario. GREAT LAKES MARINE COLLECTION OF THE MILWAUKEE PUBLIC LIBRARY.

The *Manola's* bow half is massive and impressive on the lake floor, offering visiting divers a fascinating shipwreck to explore and appreciate.

Picton diver Doug Pettingill hovers below one of the enormous hanging anchors on the Manola's *overturned bow at a depth of about 70' (21 metres).* PHOTO BY CRIS KOHL.

T. J. WAFFLE   (September 22, 1919)

The 202-ton steamer, *T. J Waffle,* built at Westport, Ontario, in 1914, and measuring 105 feet (31.5 metres) in length and 23 feet (6.9 metres) in beam, existed and worked for only five years before meeting a tragic demise.[360]

Her short history included close calls. On September 12, 1915, the year-old vessel, loaded with coal from Oswego, grounded at Salmon Point. Two vessels, the steamer, *Jeska,* and the tug, *Shanley,* pulled her off.[361]

"Is the steamer, *T. J. Waffle,* safe?" This was the question on hundreds of Kingston-area people's lips in 1917 just after the same storm which claimed the schooner, *George A. Marsh,* and the lives of 12 people on board her. Capt. Charles Beaupre, Mate O'Brien, his son, "an engineer, a woman cook, and probably others" were on board when the ship was overdue from Fair Haven with a cargo of coal.[362] The vessel finally arrived, safe and sound, three days later.[363]

Two years later, on September 22, 1919, the ship's luck ran out. Again under the command of Capt. Charles Beaupre of Portsmouth, Ontario, with a crew of eight this time, and again bound from Fair Haven for Kingston with a cargo of coal, the *T. J. Waffle* foundered with the loss of all hands. Wreckage from this unfortunate vessel washed ashore later near Oswego, New York.[364]

---

[281]Mills, op. cit., 33.

[282]John O. Greenwood. *Namesakes 1910-1919.* Cleveland: Freshwater Press, Inc., 1986: 97.

[283]Mills, op. cit.

[284]Greenwood, *Namesakes 1910-1919,* op. cit., 41.

[285]*Daily British Whig* (Kingston), July 8, 1913, quoting the *Montréal Herald.*

[286]*Daily British Whig* (Kingston), July 11, 1913.

[287]Metcalfe, *Canvas & Steam on Quinte Waters,* op. cit., 75.

[288]Greenwood, *Namesakes 1910-1919,* op. cit., 144.

[289]*British Whig* (Kingston), February 21, 1895.

[290]*King Ben.* Master Sheet, Institute for Great Lakes Research, Bowling Green State University, Ohio.

[291]Metcalfe, *Canvas & Steam on Quinte Waters,* op. cit., 99.

[292]John O. Greenwood. *Namesakes 1920-1929.* Cleveland: Freshwater Press, Inc., 1984: 326.

[293]*Daily British Whig* (Kingston), Friday, October 1, 1915.

[294]*Daily British Whig* (Kingston), Saturday, September 11, 1915.

[295]Ibid.

[296]*Daily British Whig* (Kingston), Saturday, September 25, 1915.

[297]*City of Sheboygan.* Master Sheet, Institute for Great Lakes Research, Bowling Green State University, Ohio.

[298]*City of Sheboygan.* Ship Information and Data Record, Runge Collection, Milwaukee Public Library.

[299]*Detroit Evening News,* June 9, 1887.

[300]Metcalfe, *Canvas & Steam on Quinte Waters,* op. cit., 48.

[301]*Daily British Whig,* Monday, September 13, 1915.

[302]Metcalfe, *Canvas & Steam on Quinte Waters,* op. cit.

[303]Quoted in Metcalfe, *Canvas & Steam on Quinte Waters,* op. cit.

[304]*Daily British Whig* (Kingston), Thursday, September 30, 1915.

[305]*Daily British Whig* (Kingston), Monday, September 27, 1915.

[306]*Standard* (Kingston), September 28, 1915.

[307]*Daily British Whig* (Kingston), Tuesday, September 28, 1915.

[308]*Detroit Free Press,* August 7, 1915.

[309]Metcalfe, *Canvas & Steam on Quinte Waters,* op. cit.

[310]*Daily British Whig* (Kingston), Thursday, October 7, 1915.

[311]*Daily British Whig* (Kingston), Tuesday, October 12, 1915.

[312]*Standard* (Kingston), September 28, 1915.

[313]Ibid.

[314]*Picton Gazette,* September 4, 1964, in an article about the *City of Sheboygan* titled "Spar From Old Schooner Recalls Story Of Wreck" by C. H. J. Snider.

[315]*Daily British Whig* (Kingston), Monday, August 13, 1917.

[316]*Kingston Whig-Standard,* Wednesday, July 24, 1963. Two photographs, one of the schooner, *Ford River,* "sister ship to the *City of Cheboygan* [sic]," under full sail, the other of Lloyd Shales and Barbara Carson, back on land with the ship's wheel. An abridged version of this article, containing a close-up photograph of Barbara Carson emerging from lake waters in full, 1963 scuba gear, appeared in the *Toronto Telegram* on Saturday, August 3, 1963.

[317]Kohl, *Dive Ontario! The Guide to Shipwrecks and Scuba,* op. cit., 62-65.

[318]Metcalfe, *Canvas & Steam on Quinte Waters,* op. cit., 49.

[319]*British Daily Whig* (Kingston), Thursday, November 18, 1915.

[320]Metcalfe, *Canvas & Steam on Quinte Waters,* op. cit., 66.

[321]*Daily British Whig* (Kingston), Thursday, November 11, 1915.

[322]*Picton Gazette,* Thursday, November 11, 1915.

[323]*Picton Gazette,* Thursday, November 25, 1915.

[324]*Daily Intelligencer* (Belleville), November 15, 1915.

[325]*Picton Gazette,* Thursday, November 25, 1915.

[326]*Picton Gazette,* Thursday, December 2, 1915.

[327]*Daily British Whig* (Kingston), Wednesday, November 10, 1915.

[328]*Frank C. Barnes.* Master Sheet, Institute for Great Lakes Research, Bowling Green State University, Ohio.

[329]Greenwood, *Namesakes 1910-1919,* op. cit., 375.

[330]*Daily British Whig* (Kingston), Friday, September 21, 1917.

[331]Ibid.

[332]*Daily British Whig* (Kingston), Saturday, September 22, 1917.

[333]Ibid.

[334]*Daily British Whig* (Kingston), Friday, September 21, 1917.

[335]Swainson, op. cit.

[336]*Daily Intelligencer* (Belleville), Tuesday, October 9, 1917.

[337]*Bertie Calkins.* Ship Information and Data Record, Runge Collection, Milwaukee Public Library.

[338]*Aloha.* Master Sheet, Institute for Great Lakes Research, Bowling Green State University, Ohio.

[339]*Aloha.* Ship Information and Data Record, Runge Collection, Milwaukee Public Library.

[340]Greenwood, *Namesakes, 1910-1919,* op. cit., 333.

[341]*Daily Intelligencer* (Belleville), Monday, October 29, 1917.

[342]*Daily British Whig* (Kingston), Monday, October 29, 1917.

[343]*Daily Intelligencer* (Belleville), Tuesday, October 30, 1917.

[344]*Daily British Whig* (Kingston), Monday, October 29, 1917.

[345]Interview with Mr. Lloyd Shales by the author at Kingston on August 15, 1995.

[346]Kohl, *Dive Ontario! The Guide to Shipwrecks and Scuba Diving,* op. cit., 54-55.

[347]Mills, op. cit., 3.

[348]*Aberdeen.* Master Sheet, Institute for Great Lakes Research, Bowling Green State University, Ohio.

[349]Greenwood, *Namesakes, 1910-1919,* op. cit., 58.

[350]*Daily British Whig* (Kingston), Monday, December 2, 1918.

[351]Ibid.

[352]Mansfield, op. cit., 867.

[353]*Mapledawn.* Ship Information and Data Record, Runge Collection, Milwaukee Public Library.

[354]Kohl, *Dive Ontario Two! More Ontario Shipwreck Stories,* op. cit., 52.

[355]Rev. Peter J. Van der Linden. *Great Lakes Ships We Remember II.* Cleveland: Freshwater Press, 1984: 203.

[356]*Daily British Whig* (Kingston), Wednesday, December 4, 1918.

[357]Metcalfe, *Canvas & Steam on Quinte Waters,* op. cit., 95.

[358]Greenwood, *Namesakes, 1910-1919,* op. cit., 42.

[359]Cris Kohl. "*Manola*--Half a Shipwreck." *Diver Magazine,* Vol 21, No. 9, February, 1996: 28.

[360]Mills, op. cit., 115.

[361]*Daily British Whig,* Monday, September 12, 1915.

[362]*Daily British Whig,* Friday, August 10, 1917.

[363]*Daily British Whig,* Monday, August 13, 1917.

[364]Metcalfe, *Canvas & Steam on Quinte Waters,* op. cit., 134-135.

Chapter Eight
The Roaring 1920's

JOHN RANDALL   (November 17, 1920)

Modern communication methods such as the telegraph and the telephone had long been invented and were in general usage for considerable time when the wooden steamer, *John Randall,* sank at Main Duck Island late in the year 1920. Yet, as incredible as it may seem to us today, the anxious outside world had to wait for over a week before the lighthousekeeper on the island could do something to communicate definite news of the crew's fate!

The *John Randall* was merely 15 years old when she met her end. Built in 1905 by the Shelby and Youlden Company of Kingston, Ontario,[365] and measuring 104' 4" (31.3 metres) in length, 22' 5" (6.7 metres) in beam, and 7' 7" (2.3 metres) in draft,[366] the *John Randall* was rebuilt only two years after her launch, with a resulting change in tonnage from 194 to 133.[367]

Well-known as a local carrier of bulk cargoes, the small steamer, *John Randall*, loaded 260 tons of coal[368] on Saturday, November 13, 1920, at the D. L. & W. trestle in Oswego, New York,[369] and waited for an opportunity to clear. The weather seemed to co-operate better by Tuesday, November 16, 1920, and the ship and crew left Oswego bound for Belleville, Ontario, at noon. At about that same time, the steambarge, *Jeska,* left Oswego heading for Kingston, arriving at her port of destination late that night after severe fall weather had set in. By noon the next day, the *John Randall* had not yet arrived at any harbour.[370]

Fears mounted. The Kingston newspaper communicated with the port of Belleville every three hours for word of the missing vessel and her four-man crew, all of whom resided in the Seeley's Bay area.[371] Captain Harry Randall, the son of the ship's namesake, Captain John Randall, was the only one on board who was married; John Brady[372] served as the ship's engineer, while the captain's cousins, Harry and Gilbert Smith, worked as crewmembers.[373] Captain Randall, for all his youth, "had a wide experience in navigation. He sailed with his father for years."[374]

Updates on the fate of the steamer, *John Randall,* were provided in the local newspaper:

> **Up till the time the Whig** (The *Daily British Whig* newspaper in Kingston) **went to press on Friday afternoon, no word had been received regarding the steambarge John Randall....**

> The Whig was in communication with
> South Bay Friday morning, but it was stated
> that nothing was known as to the
> whereabouts of the missing vessel. In local
> marine circles it was felt that the boat might
> have taken shelter in South Bay or Timber
> Island.
>
> There is also the belief that the members
> of crew [sic] may have been able to make their
> way to the Ducks and that they are safe. A
> heavy gale is still blowing, and it has not
> been possible for any search to be made.[375]

By the next morning, Saturday, November 20, 1920, the *Randall* had been missing since Tuesday evening, and no word had been received regarding her fate. One report from a man named Davis came in from Cape Vincent, New York, that the *Randall* had put in to shelter at Timber Island and laid alongside the steamer, *Keybell.*[376]

The small, wooden steamer, John Randall, *was built by Capt. John Randall at Kingston in 1905; she sank in a storm in that area in 1920.* AUTHOR'S COLLECTION.

Another despatch, this one from Oswego, New York, proclaimed that Captain Harry Randall's wife, "Mrs. Randall...telephoned from Belleville (Ontario), [and] stated that the boat had gone down off the Galloup [sic] Island."[377]

Six days after the *Randall* went missing, a despatch from Watertown, New York, stated that "the little steamer was last heard from Tuesday night, while sounding signals off Sackets Harbor."[378] Other residents of Sackets Harbor also claimed to have heard a vessel in distress, both on Tuesday night and on Wednesday morning. One woman, the wife of the engineer at the pumping station, claimed to have been awakened at 1:00 A. M. on Wednesday, November 17, 1920, by "cries from the lake. She said...that it seemed as if a man was crying 'Hello.' [She] awakened her husband,...but no further calls were heard."[379]

However, no wreckage of any kind washed up anywhere to verify any of these reports.

Captain John Randall, the father of Captain Harry Randall, was anxious to take a ship out and search at the Ducks, but the heavy gales held him back. He instead went to Kingston's Grand Opera House on Tuesday, November 23, 1920, to ask a visiting psychic and mind reader named Marjah about his missing son.

"That question was asked me last night," said Marjah, "and I again say that the *Randall* is at the Ducks."[380] Marjah also declared that the crew was safe.[381]

Captain John Randall became all the more determined to search the Ducks for his missing son, the ship, and her crew. Foul weather persisted, and the few steamers that were entering Kingston harbour had little to report. The steamer, *Aztec,* had passed the Main Ducks at night and could make out nothing in the way of a vessel or wreckage there.[382]

> **On Thursday morning** [November 25, 1920], **Claude Cole, Cape Vincent** [New York], **who owns the Main Ducks, left Cape Vincent with the intention of making the Ducks, providing the wind was not blowing too heavy. The Ducks consist of two islands known as the Main Ducks and the False Ducks. On the Main Ducks, there are eight hundred acres and on the False Ducks, about two hundred acres. Mr. Cole told Capt. Randall, father of the missing captain, that he would not return until he had made a thorough search of the whole shore...**[383]

Captain Mahoney of the steamer, *Rockferry,* declared his intentions of going directly to the Ducks to make a thorough examination of that area. His cousin was Engineer Brady of the missing *John Randall.* On board the steamer, *City of Hamilton,* Captain Alexander Patenaude reported that he had passed the Ducks on his way to Kingston on Tuesday, November 23, 1920, and "used his glass" to scan the horizon and the islands in an unsuccessful effort to locate any trace of the *Randall.*[384]

On the afternoon of Wednesday, November 24, 1920, Captain Randall Senior boarded the steamer, *Brockville,* in search of his missing son and crew. He planned to get off at Hick's Wharf and drive to Long Point, from where he hoped to be able to see the Ducks.[385]

Then, quite unexpectedly, a telephone call from Picton to Kington proclaimed the safe return of the *John Randall's* crew. Captain Harry Randall explained that he and his three crewmembers had remained on Main Duck Island for the past eight days after their ship sank in one of the inlets and they were forced to swim to shore. Main Duck Island's lighthouse keeper, Mr. Cecil Bongard, and his mother, Carrie, had sighted the *Randall's* spars and immediately hastened to the scene to offer assistance. With considerable difficulty, Mr. Bongard waded into the pounding surf and helped each man ashore. "The biggest job was to get the survivors to the lighthouse residence a mile away," confided Mr. Bongard later.[386]

The fact that Main Duck Island was inhabited by humans with shelter and adequate supplies of food ensured the crew's survival. Claude Cole had eleven deer and a small herd of cattle on the island that winter,[387] so food might not have been a problem, but it is doubtful that the men of the *John Randall* would have survived the cold had they been forced to stay in the freezing outdoors.

After that long period of safe isolation at the well-equipped lighthouse on the island only a few miles off the mainland, the lighthouse keeper took them in his small boat to South Bay, and then they drove to Picton.[388]

THANKFUL FOR ESCAPING

Capt. Randall Tells About Close Call of Himself and Crew.

Captain Harry Randall, master of the steambarge John Randall, with two members of his crew, Harry and Gilbert Smith, nephews of Ald. J. W. Smith, this city [Kingston], arrived home on Friday afternoon [November 26, 1920]. The fourth member of the crew, John Brady, remained at Picton. The captain and his companions were met by anxious relatives at the outer station and accompanied to the city.

When questioned about his experiences, Captain Randall stated that all were well and were very thankful for their escape from watery graves during the great storm that raged over the lake. They were on their way from Oswego to Belleville with coal when the storm compelled them to seek shelter at the Ducks. They made the Corby pier and tied up, and while the wind remained in the north east, they were safe, but on Tuesday night [November 16, 1920, the date they had left Oswego], it shifted to the east and made their position extremely dangerous as the water was shallow and the heavy seas let the steamer down on the bottom. The vessel was likely to be pounded to pieces, so early Wednesday morning, they cut hausers [sic] and drifted out to deeper water. but the storm drove her over a shoal and she grounded. Her back was broken and the water rushed over her. Only the wheelhouse was above the water and all hands were drenched by every sea. They put on life preservers and swam to the shore a distance of one mile. They made for the lighthouse,... and were taken care of by the lighthouse keeper, Mr. Bongard.

Captain Randall stated that the steamer is a total loss, but the machinery and fittings can be salvaged. The engine and boiler were good, he says. He spoke in strong condemnation of the life preservers, which almost strangled him while swimming, and his companions make the same complaint.[389]

In reality, the steamer, *John Randall,* sank much closer to shore than a mile, although when the crew were forced to swim to shore in heavy seas, the distance undoubtedly seemed a lot further than it really was.

When asked why it was that the members of the crew did not use the lifeboat, the captain stated that the sea was so heavy that it carried away the cabin and also the lifeboat which was near the cabin. The waves were so high that it was impossible for him to reach the cabin without being carried overboard....

Marine men, when speaking to the Whig, stated that the Randall case should certainly make the government realize that some life-saving protection should be given to mariners who sail these waters. Captain John Randall stated that the government should see to it that the lighthouse keeper on the Ducks be in telephone communication with

the mainland. Had the wind not dropped on
Thursday, nothing would have been heard of
the crew of the steamer Randall, perhaps, for
some days longer....

　　Captain John Randall is very grateful to
all the marine men who assisted him in the
search for his son and the members of the
crew of the Randall. Although the weather
was very stormy, the captains of several of
the boats, which were going up the bay, went
out of their way to try and get in sight of the
Ducks....[390]

The John Randall's *bow remained above water for a while.* AUTHOR'S COLLECTION.

KINGSTON, ONTARIO   FRIDAY,   NOVEMBER 26, 1920.

CAPT. RANDALL AND HIS CREW
EIGHT DAYS ON DUCK ISLAND

Steambarge John Randall Foundered Half a Mile From Island At 1:30 a.m. of 17th--Crew Swam to Shore--Stormy Weather Held Them on Island With Lighthouse Keeper--Reached Kingston on Friday.

Headline on the front page of the Daily British Whig *(Kingston), Nov. 26, 1920.*

Underwater videographer, Jim Stayer, captures the John Randall's *flattened remains on tape. The site is shallow enough not to require scuba equipment for exploration; the author was snorkeling when he took this picture.* PHOTO BY CRIS KOHL.

Much of the *John Randall's* heavy equipment and cargo was eventually salvaged, and the remains of the hull broke up shortly thereafter. Over the years, nature (ice, waves, wind) flattened these shipwreck remains onto the bay bottom at a depth of 12 to 20 feet (3.6 to 6 metres).[391]

A marine disaster had been averted, and family members were reunited. Since the story had a happy ending, cheerful observations could include the fact that the contemporary song, "Drifting Along on a Blue Lagoon" was on Columbia Records' "Song Hits" list, advertised in the Kingston newspaper at that time.[392] One wonders if Harry Randall and his crew ever listened to that song and connected it lightheartedly with their own recent experiences.

However, as "thankful for their escape from watery graves" as they were in late 1920, the year 1921 brought them great misfortune. Perhaps the captain had not had the time to rectify the problem with the lifejackets which he so strongly condemned when the *John Randall* sank. Perhaps it was a combination of numerous factors conspiring against him. The only thing known with certainty is that the luck of Captain Harry Randall and his family ran out when his next command, the steamer, *City of New York,* went missing near Kingston a year later.

That, however, is another story.

SCHOOLCRAFT   (December 3, 1920)

The 972-gross-ton[393] wooden steamer, *Schoolcraft,* built at the Linn & Craig Shipyard at Trenton, Michigan, in 1884, official number 115990 (later 134270), had a carrying capacity of 1,000 tons, or 700,000 feet of lumber.[394]

Measuring 185' 6" (55.5 metres) in length, and 34 feet (10.2 metres) in beam, the *Schoolcraft* was constructed to pull rafts and lumber barges on the strength of her 500 horsepower steam engine, usually towing the barges *George Nester, Keweenaw,* and *Mary N. Bourke* during the many years that she was owned by the Nester family of Baraga (1889 to 1911). In 1912, the vessel was owned by the Fairport Transportation Company of Cleveland, Ohio; in 1913, by Henry Brock of Cleveland; in 1914-15, by N. D. Childs of Cheboygan, Michigan. In 1915, when Manley Chew of Midland, Ontario, purchased the *Schoolcraft,* the aging vessel passed into Canadian registry.[395]

The oak-timbered *Schoolcraft,* upbound light from Montreal to Kingston for lay-up at the very end of the navigation season after delivering her final load of coal to Montreal, caught fire off Wolfe Island, about 14 miles (22 kilometres) east of Kingston. The vessel was purposely beached, and all 14 people on board escaped unharmed. After burning to the waterline, the ship was abandoned in place.[396]

The *Schoolcraft* was named after Henry Rowe Schoolcraft (1793-1864), explorer and founder of the Michigan Historical Society.[397]

The steamer, Schoolcraft, *often carried full loads of lumber, as this 1912 photograph indicates.* GREAT LAKES MARINE COLLECTION OF THE MILWAUKEE PUBLIC LIBRARY.

VARUNA (1920)

In late 1879, the *Kingston Whig* newspaper described the construction of the new steamer, *Varuna,* at Picton:

> The *Veruna* [sic] now building, has a length of 100 feet, beam 16 ft. 6 in., depth of hold 6 ft. 6 in. Her speed, it is anticipated, will be from 14 to 15 miles per hour; her hull is planked with $2^1/_2$ inch white oak and elm and is now ready for laying the deck. She is to be finished in first class style as a passenger boat, to ply between Trenton and Picton, on which route she is to replace the *Utica,* which was also built by Mr. Davis in 1873, but is not fast enough and is to be replaced by the *Veruna.* The engine of the *Veruna* is now being made at the Kingston Foundry. The cylinder will be 14 x 14, and the boiler will have 600 feet of heating surface which, it is calculated, will give any amount of steam requisite. The *Veruna* is for Jonathan Porte, of Trenton, the present owner of the *Utica,* the third steamer built for the same party by Mr. Davis in the past ten years.[398]

The passenger steamer, Varuna, *plied the waters between Picton, Belleville, and Deseronto for about 40 years before being scuttled.* AUTHOR'S COLLECTION.

This 134-ton[399] steamer, *Varuna,* was valued at $6,200[400] when she was launched in 1880. By 1920, this faithful, but tired, old ship was partially dismantled at Collins Bay and the hull was sunk in about 70 feet (21 metres) of water in the ships' graveyard off Amherst Island.[401] The *Varuna's* hull sits upright, with several hatches opening to a silt-filled interior.[402]

Str. "VARUNA"

A. HICKS, Captain.

WILL leave Trenton every morning (Sunday excepted) at 7:00 o'clock calling at Rednerville and all points between the head of the bay and Picton leaving Belleville at 8:30 a. m., Deseronto at 10:20 a. m.

Will connect at Picton with stage for Sand Banks,

Parties wishing to arrange for excursion rates will see Capt. Hicks on board.

Will leave Picton at 1 p. m. on return for the head of the bay ; Deseronto, 2:30 p. m. Belleville, at 4:30 p.m., and Trenton, at 6.

Meeting all trains going west and north.

This advertisement for the Varuna *appeared in the Belleville newspaper on July 22, 1899.*

NICARAGUA (1921)

In 1921, the 27-year-old wooden steamer, *Nicaragua,* owned by the Montreal Transportation Company, lay abandoned at Kingston. Her engine was removed and placed in the steamer, *Thunder Bay,* and her hull was towed to Montreal. Built at the James Davidson Shipyard at West Bay City, Michigan, in 1894, the *Nicaragua* measured 249' 9" by 37' by 22' 8" (75 by 11 by 6.7 metres).[403]

The Nicaragua's *oak timbers were abandoned in 1921.* AUTHOR'S COLLECTION.

ATLASCO and CONDOR   (August 7, 1921)

The barge, *Atlasco,* slid down the launchramp originally as the steamer, *Russell Sage,* in Buffalo, New York, on May 21, 1881. Built by the Union Dry Dock Company, this 1,224.25-gross-ton wooden propeller measured 218' (65.4 metres) in length, 32' 8" (9.8 metres) in beam, and 13' 4" (four metres) in draft.[404] Few expenses were spared in her fine construction, and when she first hit the water, she was valued at $88,500,[405] a large sum for a vessel at that time.

Her powerful steeple compound engine, built by the King Iron Works in Buffalo in 1881, fired up 650 horsepower, while her two boilers, also built that year in Buffalo, were of the fire box type measuring seven feet (2.1 metres) by 14 feet (4.2 metres); these were later replaced by a single Scotch boiler built by the Globe Iron Works Company in Cleveland in 1899.[406]

The *Russell Sage* was one of the old-style package freight steamers without arches, a duplicate of the steamer, *John C. Gault,* plying mostly package freight for the Wabash Railroad on Lake Erie between Toledo and Buffalo. In 1906-07, Frank Upton of Charlotte, New York, purchased the *Russell Sage,* removed her upper deck, and converted her into a coarse freight carrier.[407]

A pre-1899 photo of the steamer, Russell Sage, *carrying a smokestack for each boiler.* GREAT LAKES MARINE COLLECTION OF THE MILWAUKEE PUBLIC LIBRARY.

The *Sage* caught on fire at her dock at Oswego, New York, on November 2, 1912, and she burned to the waterline, her upper works totally destroyed. So badly damaged was she that her final U. S. enrollment (#110472) was surrendered at Ogdensburg on March 17, 1914, and endorsed "burned."[408] The hulk remained at Oswego until 1917, when the Barge Ireland Company of Montreal purchased the remains of the *Russell Sage* for rebuilding as a barge. Her new Canadian number was 138234,[409] and, when she was purchased by the Atlas Transportation Company of Montreal, she was renamed *Atlasco*,[410] a name under which she sailed for four years before that fateful day in August, 1921, while being towed, along with the schooner-barge, *Condor,* by the steamer, *Macassen.*

A violent, summer storm surprised the crews and passengers of the three vessels on the night of August 6-7, 1921, and the barges, *Atlasco* and *Condor,* began to sink. The steamer towing them, the *Macassen,* hastily rescued the people on board, cut loose her tows, and headed for safe harbour. The next day, the Kingston press related the harrowing tale of rescue:

WOMEN AND CHILDREN
TAKEN FROM WRECKS

Thrilling Rescue in Dead of
Night, About Thirty Miles
From Kingston

With the waves beating ten feet high against the steamer Macassen on Sunday morning at two o'clock a thrilling rescue was effected of nineteen men, women and children on board the barges Condor and Allasco [sic] in tow of the Macassen. The steamer was plunging through the heavy waves about six miles above South Bay Point or thirty miles up the lake from Kingston when distress calls were sent out from each of the barges. The lake was so rough that it was difficult to establish communication with the men on the barges but finally word was received that each of them had sprung a leak in the heavy storm and that there was six feet of water in the Condor and four feet of water in the Allasco. In addition the former's steering gear was smashed.

Realizing that it would be of no use to save the barges, Capt. Clark of the Macassen immediately endeavored to rescue the crews which included a number of women and children who had been sleeping on the barges. Life boats could not be lowered and it was an exceedingly difficult task in face of the wind and waves to bring the Macassen alongside of the barges.

However, the crew of the steamer were able to get a line on the Condor and the women and children were brought over first. Some of the latter were very frightened and it was over two hours before a complete rescue was made.

Capt. Clark then cut off from the barges and made for Kingston to report the accident.... The Condor was loaded with grain and the Allasco with wire. Local mariners were to-day anxiously awaiting further details of the wreck and Capt. Clark was being complimented upon his masterly handling of the situation....[411]

This 1912 view shows the steamer, Russell Sage, *later the barge,* Atlasco, *prior to her Oswego burning that year. No photos of her as the* Atlasco *are known to exist at this point in time.* GREAT LAKES MARINE COLLECTION OF THE MILWAUKEE PUBLIC LIBRARY.

Captain Clark left Kingston at daybreak on Monday, August 8, 1921, to search for his two barges which he had to cut loose during the severe storm the day before. The gale, however, was still strong, and Clark had to put in to shelter until the next day.[412] On Tuesday and Wednesday, he searched the area for his missing tows. Rumours about the fate of the unmanned barges included the story of the *Atlasco's* decks coming ashore near South Bay Point.[413]

By Friday, August 12, 1921, it was well-known that the *Condor* was "breaking up at Poplar Point near South Bay Point, and that the grain cargo is being washed away," that the *Atlasco's* decks had indeed washed ashore, and that the *Atlasco* was "sunk in about thirty-five feet of water."[414]

Very quickly, the Donnelly Salvage and Wrecking Company was awarded the contract to salvage the barge, *Atlasco.* "Efforts will be made to complete the salvage this week."[415] Weather proved favourable, and good progress was made in salvaging the coiled wire cargo on the *Atlasco*.[416] Two weeks later, another of the Donnelly Wrecking Company's steamers, the *City of New York,* returned to Kingston harbour after helping load some of the wire cargo.[417] That same steamer carried 400 tons of salvaged wire cargo to Montreal,[418] while the steamer, *Cornwall,* worked on salvaging more cargo from the *Atlasco* until the *City of New York* returned.[419]

A year later, in the summer of 1922, the barges, *Mary P. Hall* and the *Mary Daryaw,* owned by the Donnelly Wrecking Company, worked on salvaging the last of the wire cargo from the wreck of the *Atlasco*.[420] By mid-October, 1922, the company had disposed of a total of 600 tons of *Atlasco* wire to the Steel Company of Canada in Montreal.[421] The remaining half of the cargo remains on the shipwreck to this day.

The *Condor,* the other barge destroyed in the same storm as the *Atlasco,* was built in 1888 in Montreal by Cantin for the K. M. & F. Company, and given the official number 92553. Her dimensions were 180' 7" (54.2 metres) in length, 34' 5" (10.4 metres) in beam, and 11' 6" (3.5 metres) in draft, with a tonnage of 567[422] and a value of $20,000 at the time of launch.[423] For 33 years, the *Condor* served her owners faithfully, requiring only one rebuild, in 1915. Loaded with wheat at the time of her stranding in 1921, the *Condor* soon broke up from the violent action of wind and waves.

The barge, Condor, *with her name in white letters just to the right of centre, is hidden by other vessels in this busy 1912 scene of Montreal harbour crowded with local, as well as ocean-going, ships.* AUTHOR'S COLLECTION.

Above, *diver Doug Pettingill, from Picton, peers between the spokes of the* Atlasco's *wheel. Much of the red paint that was used on the hub is still in place. On a tip from commercial fisherman, Doug Harrison, that gave away this shipwreck's location in the summer of 1990, Doug Pettingill became the first scuba diver to visit this site.* Below, *commercial diver James Taylor, also from Picton, glides through the valley of wire, one of the most impressive cargo sights I have ever seen. About 600 tons, or half of the* Atlasco's *coiled wire cargo remains at the site. This shipwreck sit in about 43' (13 metres) of water. There are four anchors on this site, plus the ship's rudder, winch, bollards, and many other items.* PHOTOS BY CRIS KOHL.

The author explores, photographs, and comments on various aspects of the wrecked barge, Condor, *ashore on the south side of Point Traverse facing Lake Ontario's Gravelly Bay between Gravelly Point and Ostrander Point. The immense size of this vessel is reflected in the seemingly endless keelson and rows of ribs which are usually left totally dry by the end of the summer season (this photograph was taken in July). The* Condor's *keelson acts as a low breakwall keeping stones piled up on shore and maintaining luxuriant plant growth, particularly flowers, in the summer. Dozens of ribs point into the lake, the many white stones in between giving the semblance of railroad ties. Scores of long bolts, most bent inwards towards shore by the 75+ years of nature's wear and tear on this hull, beckon visitors.* PHOTO BY KATHY EVERSON.

H. N. JEX   (August 16, 1921)

The freight steamer, *H. N. Jex,* was in her 54th year of service on the Great Lakes when her aging hull sprang a leak and she sank in deep water ten to fifteen miles (16 to 24 kilometres) southeast of Point Petre, Ontario, on August 16, 1921. She had departed Sodus, New York, bound for Kingston with a load of coal at 11:45 that morning, but she foundered around the set of sun.[424]

Captain Malcolm Shaw, of Kingston, and his crew of seven "put up a gallant fight with the pumps to keep the *Jex* afloat, but the vessel was doomed."[425] The *Jex* sank at about 8:00 P. M. All eight people on board took to their yawlboat and were picked up within half an hour by the passing steamer, *Lehigh,* of Ogdensburg, New York, arriving at Kingston at about one o'clock on Wednesday morning (August 17, 1921). It was the first time in the long career of 64-year-old Capt. Shaw that he "was forced to take to the boats" after the *Jex* "took the final dive into Davy Jones' locker."[426]

Built by Ira Lafrinier and launched in 1868 at Cleveland, Ohio, as the wooden passenger steamer, *Lawrence,* the *H. N. Jex* measured 170' 2" (51 metres) in length, 26' 5" (8 metres) in beam, and 10' 3" (3.1 metres) in draft. The *Lawrence* became the *Frontenac* in 1902, and finally, in 1910, the *H. N. Jex,* named after her new owner, a Port Huron, Michigan, captain (1854-1928). In spite of the vessel's history of numerous groundings and burnings,[427] John F. Sowards, a well-known coal merchant from Kingston, became the *Jex's* 13th and final owner in 1915.[428] Apparently he was not superstitious.

The wooden freighter, H. N. Jex, *seen plying the waters of the St. Clair River with a load of coal late in her career, sank near Kingston in 1921.* AUTHOR'S COLLECTION.

OLIVER MOWAT   (September 1, 1921)

The year 1921 saw renewed optimism in the world, with counter-balancing doses of gloom: World War I had been over for three years, and the initial joblessness of returning soldiers was being resolved, but British Labour leader, Peter Wright, predicted another World War by 1931, with Germany, Russia, and Japan attacking the United States[429] (he was only about ten years off in his alarmingly correct prophecy); silent film star, Charlie Chaplin, took London, England, by storm on a visit and had to be guarded from admirers by 50 British "Bobbies",[430] but another Hollywood comedian, Roscoe "Fatty" Arbuckle, was found guilty of manslaughter in the California party death of a young actress.[431] The "Roaring '20's" was a decade of contrasts; some people lived their lives with well-publicized self-indulgence for their 15 minutes of fame, but more people worked hard just to earn a living. The automobile became the most popular purchase in those years; a Chevrolet Four-Ninety Special, f.o.b. Oshawa, cost a relatively affordable $895.00.[432] North American society was changing rapidly.

The modern era was changing the look of the Great Lakes as well. By the 1920's, the age of sailing vessels dominating the inland seas was long over; commercial sailing ships active anywhere on the Great Lakes were a rarity, and those few remaining schooners were aging fast and fading quickly.

From the few left among them, the schooner, *Oliver Mowat,* met a tragic end. Named after the prominent Sir Oliver Mowat (1820-1903), Kingston-born politician who served first Upper Canada and, later, the province of Ontario, this schooner serviced the Kingston area for almost 50 years.

The Oliver Mowat *was one of the few sailing vessels left operating under sail in the 1920's.* INSTITUTE FOR GREAT LAKES RESEARCH, BOWLING GREEN STATE UNIVERSITY, OHIO.

The *Oliver Mowat,* loaded with a coal cargo, was plowed into by the steamer, *Keywest,* on the waters just east of Point Traverse, near the Pennicon Shoal, between False Duck Island and Main Duck Island in eastern Lake Ontario, at about 11:00 P.M. on Thursday, September 1, 1921.[433]

The steamer, Keywest, *sliced halfway through the* Mowat. AUTHOR'S COLLECTION.

Three people from the *Oliver Mowat* drowned: 65-year-old Captain Thomas Lake Vandusen of Picton, the vessel's owner; the 23-year-old mate from Deseronto, Ontario; and the initially unidentified woman cook from Niagara Falls. The Belleville newspaper carried the most detailed report of the losses:

> A cloudless night, only a light wind blowing, and visibility at its best on Lake Ontario, and yet a large steam freighter cut a sailing schooner in two and three human beings went to watery graves. Such is the basis of the mystery of the sinking of the sailing schooner Oliver Mowat, a frequent visitor to Belleville port, having sailed from this harbor less than two weeks ago, after discharging a cargo of coal for the Schuster Co. Another strange feature of this tragic story of the lake is the fact that the large steam freighter, the Key West [sic], after sinking the Oliver Mowat near the Main Ducks in Lake Ontario Thursday night, did not immediately, after doing everything possible to rescue survivors, proceed to the nearest port and make report of the accident as is customary under Marine Law and usage. Instead Capt. Wattley, after cruising about the scene until all hope was gone of rescue of the three missing ones...resumed the course after picking up George Keegan, of Belleville, and another sailor named

John Wannacott, of Picton, and the tragedy was not reported until the Key West made Port Dalhousie, whence the survivors returned home by rail. The collision occurred Thursday night and the first news of it was brought to this section by Keegan when he returned home on Saturday.

Keegan's Story

George Ernest Keegan, the sailor who so narrowly escaped death, lives with his wife and baby on Brock street....Keegan's story of the tragedy is that the schooner Oliver Mowat left Picton at noon on Thursday light for Oswego to bring back a cargo of coal for either Belleville or Picton. The schooner was making fair headway under a light wind, there was hardly a cloud in the sky and the lookout could see a long distance. Off the Main Ducks a large steam freighter was observed approaching. Keegan says that Capt. Vandusen of the Mowat flashed the signal light repeatedly but the steamer seemed to pay no attention and came steadily on crashing into the schooner amidships at 10:57 P.M. and cutting half way through. Water poured in and the Oliver Mowat sank in a few minutes.

Piercing Screams

Keegan heard piercing screams coming from the cabin where the cook, a Niagara Falls woman was imprisoned. He judged that the collision had caused the doors to jam and imprison the woman. Capt. Vandusen and Mate Jacob Corby, of Deseronto, went to the assistance of the woman, and no doubt gave their lives to their courageous attempt at rescue. Keegan says that he saw Capt. Vandusen later swimming but just for a moment and the waters closed over the gallant captain and mate who had braved many storms and always before conquered the elements.

Sole Survivors

Keegan and Wannacott jumped into the water so as not to be drawn down by the sinking schooner and were picked up by a boat launched from the Key West. Wannacott had a life preserver and found a plank for Keegan....

A son of Capt. Vandusen who had been sailing on the Oliver Mowat this summer passed up the last trip to go to Toronto Exhibition and in so doing may have saved his own life. He was in Belleville Monday conferring with George Keegan, who accompanied him back to Picton where plans were to be made in regard to a search for the bodies.

Keegan sailed last summer on the Grace M. Filer, Capt. Fegan, but this year transferred his allegiance to Capt. Vandusen.

Key West Story

Capt. Wattley, of the Key West, interviewed at Port Dalhousie, said that the Oliver Mowat apparently had not been carrying lights and was not seen by the Key West until she was right on her. This is directly at variance with the story of George Keegan that the Oliver Mowat was showing the regular lights and that Capt. Vandusen repeatedly flashed a light signal to warn the Key West....[434]

Records at the Oswego custom house, where the *Mowat* last cleared, shows that the female cook was Carrie McGuiggan.[435] This Niagara Falls, New York, woman had been sailing on the *Oliver Mowat* for seven years.[436]

The steamer, Keywest, *sliced through the schooner,* Oliver Mowat, *at the schooner's midship point on a clear night off False Duck Island.* ARTWORK BY MARCEL BLANCHETTE (For information on obtaining prints of this and other nautical subjects, contact Mr. Blanchette at Black River, Ontario K0K 2P0, telephone 613-476-6585.)

The Dominion of Canada publication, "Notice to Mariners," No. 60 of 1921, noted that "The wreck of the schooner 'Oliver Mowat' lies sunk between False Duck islands and Main Ducks islands and will, without further notice, be marked by a gas buoy...." The publication proceeded to give the wreck location as "West of Psyche shoal and about 3 miles 113 degrees 15 minutes (South 56 degrees, 15 minutes East magnetic) from False Ducks islands lighthouse on

Swetman island [the old name for False Duck Island], latitude North 43 degrees, 55 minutes, 40 seconds, Longitude West 76 degrees, 44 minutes, 5 seconds..."

Front page headline in The Daily Intelligencer *(Belleville), Tuesday, September 6, 1921.*

About three weeks later, Wreck Commisioner Demers in Ottawa gave judgment fixing responsibility for the collision on the steamer, *Keywest*. The speed of the steamer on the night of the collision "was justified in view of the weather," but Captain D. W. Whiteley,

> though it was his watch, was resting on a sofa within the wheelhouse, and could not by any means view the exterior surroundings. He was not asleep, but was in such a position that he could not be considered as keeping his watch....The master's action in remaining in the gap [the *Keywest's* bow held in place in the schooner's side] to clear from the sinking schooner was...timely seamanship. The distance he withdrew was, according to the evidence, vague, and the court considered it nearer a quarter than a half mile, but why, when clear of the schooner's rigging he did not bring his ship to a stop, and promptly lower a [life] boat, is surprising. If this had been done, another life might have been saved. The time taken, when the boat was eventually lowered, was considered by the court to be too long....[437]

The captain of the *Keywest* had his certificate suspended for a year and, while the second officer, C. F. Gildnan, "a man of limited navigation experience,"[438] was also blamed, he was given only a severe reprimand, as he held no certificate which could be suspended. It was also determined that the schooner, which had been travelling at a speed of four miles per hour and was being navigated properly, contributed indirectly to the accident by "the non-effectiveness of the torch light"[439] and indifference on the part of her lookout.[440]

Two of the *Mowat's* three masts protruded from the lake waters,[441] telltale signs of the shipwreck's location. One newspaper account incorrectly stated that the *Mowat's* masts showed that the water was 140 feet deep.[442] These masts were later dynamited by a hardhat diver to remove them as a menace to navigation.

The three-masted, 295-net-ton schooner, *Oliver Mowat,* built by E. Beaupre at Mill Haven, near Kingston, Ontario, in 1873, measured 131' 2" (39.3 metres) in length, 25' 9' (7.6 metres) in beam, and 10' 8" (3.2 metres) in draft. Those were her original dimensions. Some time prior to 1905, the vessel was rebuilt and shortened to her final dimensions, listed from 1905 to 1920 as being 116' (34.8 metres) by 23' 8" (7 metres) by 9' 8" (2.9 metres).[443]

The British-built (1909) canal-size steamer, *Keywest,* which collided with the *Oliver Mowat,* served the Great Lakes for another 25 years, retiring from service in 1946 and being scrapped at Kingston in 1947. The name, *"Keywest,"* incidentally, was not influenced by that historic and colourful party town at the tail end of the Florida Keys, but rather by a part of the name of the ship's owner (Keystone Transports, Limited) and the direction "west," which was where half of the vessel's tonnage headed in the course of her work.[444]

The *Oliver Mowat* left a lively legacy. After she sank, old-timers recalled

> ...that in 1873, on the 11th day of July, the sailing vessel Oliver Mowat was launched at Millhaven, near Bath. The event was a big one in the minds of the people of Kingston, Millhaven, Bath, and surrounding district, and there was a very large crowd who witnessed the launching of the Mowat. Sir Oliver Mowat, Lady Mowat, and Miss Mowat came from Toronto for the launching, Miss Mowat breaking the bottle of wine over the bow of the boat, thereby christening it.
>
> The boat had been built for the firm of Fraser & George, a hardware firm of Kingston. It was let out for use in the grain trade from Chicago to Kingston and was considered one of the fastest boats on the lakes. For years it was owned by the Folger Steamboat Company and during that time was in command of Captain Edward Beaupre Jr. and Captain Saunders, a son-in-law. The timber in the Mowat had been brought from Amherst Island and the vicinity of Bath, and it was a very sturdy craft.
>
> The Folger Company sold the Mowat to a Toronto firm, and then it passed from the command of the Beaupre family. Captain R. Henderson of Portsmouth, marine artist, made several trips on the Mowat, and on one of these trips he made an oil painting of the Mowat weathering a gale. Mr. Beaupre still has that painting.
>
> The Mowat was considered a very lucky boat by mariners, and in only one instance can it be recalled

that she ever came into trouble. About ten years ago she went ashore near Cobourg, but she was so strong that all that was required after she had been released was a little caulking and she was as good as ever.

A very strange coincidence recorded by Mr. Beaupre was that, when his father died in Portsmouth in 1908, the Mowat was anchored in the harbor in full sail. The boat he had sailed and loved so well was near when he passed away.

Today the Mowat lies cut in two in her watery grave near the Main Ducks and with its passing many pleasant memories are brought to the minds of old sailors who had watched her career from the time when she was first built to the present day.

The Oliver Mowat was owned by Captain Vandusen of Picton. She had been repaired in Kingston early in the season very extensively.[445]

The press frequently described the *Oliver Mowat* as a fast vessel, particularly on one occasion early in her career in 1882:

The run made by the schr. Oliver Mowat from Charlotte to Kingston was accomplished in 6 hrs. 35 min., the fastest time on record. Captain Saunders is very proud of the fact. The distance is 90 miles, so that the vessel made about 14 miles an hour. Captains in the city were loathe to believe the statement and one, after reading the item in last night's Whig [Kingston newspaper], asked Captain Saunders:

"What time did you leave Charlotte?"

"At 6:30 o'clock."

"I don't believe you."

"Here gentlemen," said one of the owners, "is the proof,' and he held to view a telegram, just received, and which read: "Schr. Oliver Mowat left between 6 and 7 o'clock this morning." It was from Charlotte and had been sent in reply to a message from the owners, who had felt anxious about the craft and telegraphed asking about her whereabouts. The telegram settled the discussion.[446]

The *Mowat* had her share of problems, too, one of which was reported in 1889:

The schooner O. Mowat has been seized at Kingston, Ont., for having repairs done in the United States and not reporting. She was fined $50.[447]

The remains of the *Oliver Mowat,* heavily damaged by the dynamiting shortly after her loss, has a relief of only about five feet (1.5 metres) off the bottom of the lake. Sitting in about 100' (30 metres) of water, this shipwreck was located by scuba divers in the early 1960's,[448] and they immediately removed many of the artifacts, such as the ship's port and starboard lanterns, as souvenirs, or "tokens of accomplishment." Contrary to some of today's divers who make up special T-shirts bragging about their shipwreck discoveries, those people who first explored the *Oliver Mowat* in the early 1960's did so quietly and without fanfare. The shipwreck has been infrequently visited since its initial discovery.

CITY OF NEW YORK   (November 25, 1921)

November, 1921. The Great War (World War I, 1914-1918), had been over for three years, and the era which later became known as the "roaring '20's" was accelerating into peace-time pleasure. Ten-inch double-sided R.C.A. ("His Master's Voice") records, which had formerly sold for $1.00 each, were now reduced to 85¢, "less than pre-war price."[449] Charlie Chaplin's silent film, "The Kid," billed as "the biggest comedy the world has known" and which "took one year to complete,"[450] played to packed houses in local movie theatres. Philip Morris navy cut cigarettes cost 15¢ for ten, or 25 for 35¢[451] (keep in mind that average wages in 1921 were considerably lower than today's, but life was still good.) A Bell Telephone Company advertisement depicted a giant hand reaching towards a local merchant, with the heading, "Reach out For More Business"[452] (this slogan much later evolved into the less materialistic and more humanly sensitive "Reach out and touch someone.") But in 1921, as a sign of the times, the main focus in society was on dollars and cents and fun. The war was over.

In late 1921, Captain Harry Randall reached out for more business, and ended up wishing that a hand of divine origin would reach out and help him and his crew. They were definitely not having fun. His ship, the old wooden bulk freight steamer, *City of New York,* was savagely at war with the elements, being tossed about in a severe storm on Lake Ontario.

A year earlier, in late 1920, Harry Randall and another crew were fortunate in surviving the storm-caused sinking of the steamer, *John Randall,* at Main Duck Island (read that story earlier in this chapter). To replace that lost vessel,[453] he purchased one of the oldest steamers on the Great Lakes, the *City of New York,* in late 1920 for $15,000 from the Lake Shore Sand and Gravel Company of Toronto.[454] He sank several thousand dollars more into making his aging ship seaworthy at Toronto in the spring of 1921.[455] Then his troubles really began!

On the first trip of this newly-acquired vessel, in May of 1921, while carrying coal from Oswego to Toronto, the Toronto Lifesaving Station had to rescue the *City of New York* after her manhole had been blown out of her boiler. The steamer had drifted helplessly for hours with four men, one woman, three children, and a deckload of horses on board.[456] This was, indeed, a bad omen.

On the American Thanksgiving Day holiday,[457] Thursday, November 25, 1921, Captain Harry Randall, light of wallet and heavy with financial worry, guided the *City of New York* out of Oswego harbour, New York, loaded with 350 tons of phosphate (a heavy load, but not overloaded, since the vessel's claimed carrying capacity was 500 tons),[458] heading north towards Trenton, Ontario, about an hour behind the steamers, *Hinckley* and *Louis Pahlow*,[459] which, Coast Guard records at the Oswego station indicate, left the harbour at 3:15 A. M.[460] Somehow, the *City of New York* almost caught up with the earlier vessels just as a brewing storm broke. The *Hinckley* reported last seeing the *City of New York* turn and head east towards Galloo Island at 6:30 A. M.,[461] when the storm worsened. The *Hinckley* and *Louis Pahlow* fled for the protection offered by Main Duck Island; the *City of New York,* however, disappeared.

For her first 18 years (1863-1881), the triple-decked freight and passenger steamer, City of New York, *operated as the flagship of Cleveland's Northern Transportation Company between Ogdensburg, New York, and Chicago, Illinois.* INSTITUTE FOR GREAT LAKES RESEARCH, BOWLING GREEN STATE UNIVERSITY, OHIO.

The *Hinckley* and the *Louis Pahlow* reached Trenton on Friday morning after their layover to ride out the worst part of the storm at Main Duck Island. To their grave concern, the *City of New York* had not yet arrived. Captain Augustus Randolph Hinckley, the Wolfe-Island-born Oswego transportation entrepreneur, salvager, and captain of his namesake vessel, the *Hinckley,*[462] telephoned his Oswego office from Trenton. There was no news of the *City of New York.* Various harbours were contacted on the south side of the lake, but no word of the missing steamer was heard.

Then, the steamer, *Isabella H.,*[463] arrived at Oswego at about 11:00 A. M. on Saturday, November 26, 1921, with a grisly cargo. Both lifeboats from the *City of New York* had been located in the lake and retrieved, one of them containing the lifeless bodies of four men and a woman, the other one, upside-down and empty. The bodies had been picked up at about eight o'clock that morning about ten miles (16 kilometres) southwest of Stony Point Light.

The City of New York *was converted to a bulk freighter in 1881 and worked on the Great Lakes in that capacity for the remaining 40 years of her life until she tragically sank in 1921. This photograph shows the steamer in Racine, Wisconsin, harbour in 1890.* INSTITUTE FOR GREAT LAKES RESEARCH, BOWLING GREEN STATE UNIVERSITY, OHIO.

Four of the five bodies were identified almost immediately as those of Mrs. Harry Randall, 31, clad in her nightgown with a wrap about her;[464] First Mate Wesley Warren, 30, also of Seeley's Bay (described as a "lover of clean sport" who played on the hockey team at Seeley's Bay; the watch found on his body had stopped at 7:48); and the Dorey brothers of Kingston, Robert Henry Dorey, 31, who had served three years with the Canadian army in France and who had, ironically, come home without a scratch, and his younger brother, Gilbert James Dorey, 17, on his first trip ever on the lake. The fifth body, that of a fair-haired young man, awaited identification.[465]

The bodies of the men were found huddled under the seats of the lifeboat, while Mrs. Randall's body was "hanging over the side of the boat, with her hands in the water."[466] It was suggested that she had died in a posture of beckoning towards, or attempting to rescue, one of the missing victims of the sinking, possibly her baby daughter or her husband.

The lifeboat itself was holed at the bow and contained about eight inches of water, with only the airtight compartments at the bow and stern keeping it afloat. A sea anchor trailed from it. The davits had been ripped from the steamer and were still attached to the lifeboats, indicating that there had not been time to lower the lifeboats properly, but rather that they were yanked from their mounts when the *City of New York* sank. All five of the victims had frozen to death.[467]

Missing and never located were the bodies of Captain Harry Randall, 31, his ten-month-old daughter, and Stanley Pappa, 14, of Seeley's Bay, who was working as a cabin boy and assistant to Mrs. Randall in the ship's galley.[468]

Mystery surrounds the presence of young Stanley Pappa on board the lost ship. Some newspaper reports assumed that he was the adopted son of the Randalls, yet the Kingston newspaper told a considerably different story:

> **John Pappa, 59 Queen street [Kingston], is the father of Stanley Pappa, the fourteen-year-old boy who was lost with the other members of the crew of the steambarge City of New York. He says that he lived in Gananoque nineteen years and in Kingston for the past nine years. He had allowed his boy Stanley to live with the Culvert family of Seeley's Bay whom he knew well. Mrs. H. Randall, wife of Capt. H. Randall, was a Culvert. Mr. Pappa told the Whig [the Kingston newspaper] on Wednesday morning that he did not know his boy was aboard the City of New York on its last trip. He had heard that the boy was taken on former trips by the steamer and he says he asked Capt. Randall last September not to take the lad again. Hence he was greatly surprised when he heard of the catastrophe to learn that his son was among the missing. Mr. Pappa says that Capt. Randall did not want to take his wife on the steamer so late in the fall, but Mrs. Randall insisted upon accompanying him.[469]**

Captain Harry Randall's father, Captain John Randall, who had a financial share in the steamer, *City of New York,* was informed of the vessel's loss at about noon on Saturday, November 26, 1921, only an hour after the lifeboat bodies had been brought ashore at Oswego. He repected his son's navigational abilities, and he had been a trusting business partner with him in several recent ventures. Most importantly, he loved his son. The older captain's struggles to reach Oswego as quickly as possible show his parental concerns: from his home at Seeley Bay, Ontario, he immediately went to Kingston, and, finding that the ferry to Cape Vincent had departed, boarded the Wolfe Island ferry. Then he was driven 12 miles (18 kilometres) across Wolfe Island in a buckboard to a fishing hamlet opposite Cape Vincent, New York. Unable to obtain passage on a motorboat, Captain Randall senior persuaded two fishermen to help him row a boat to the U. S. shore, an undertaking which took two hours of strenuous work to accomplish, the wild spray dashing over them constantly as one of the men kept bailing the small boat. By the time they reached shore, they were soaked to the skin and their outer garments were a mass of ice.[470] From there, the determined but tired Captain Randall found accommodations for the night and arrived at Oswego the next day, Sunday, November 27th, at about 2:00 P. M.

When he claimed the four identified bodies at Dain's undertaking parlor in Oswego, Captain John Randall stated:

> **From the information I secured before leaving Canada, I am confident that the [City of New York] foundered in the vicinity of the Galloup [sic] islands. Harry, I believe, was at the wheel and when the storm set in, he no doubt made up his mind to get into shelter in the lee of the nearest island. But the storm was too much,...and she probably broke in two and sunk [sic] within a few minutes.**
>
> **Harry knew every inch of the lake and I am sure he tried hard to prevent a reoccurrence of the fate which befell our barge, the John Randall, which foundered off Duck islands last November. Although having seen many years of service, the City of New York was in good shape.**[471]

For as long as possible, Captain John Randall kept the news of the disaster a secret from his ailing wife, who suffered from heart disease.[472]

Front page headline in The Daily Intelligencer *(Belleville), Saturday, November 26, 1921.*

The four identified bodies were taken to Kingston on board the steamer, *Waubic.* The fifth body was later positively identified by his mother and his sister as being that of 19-year-old Frank Gallagher.[473] Mrs. Randall and Wesley Warren were buried at Seeley's Bay (each funeral having over 700 people in attendance, attesting to the high esteem in which the victims were held)[474]; Robert and Gilbert Dorey, and also Frank Gallagher, were buried at Kingston.[475]

Wreckage from the missing vessel was reportedly seen in more than one location: the *Hinckley* "passed through wreckage believed that of the *City of New York*" when the ship "stopped at McDonald's Cove on the Bay of Quinte, just inside of Indian light...."[476] The steamer, *M. Sicken,* reportedly passed some wreckage between Stony Point and the Galloup [sic] Islands consisting of "a couple of doors, some small pieces, and a tin can. The crew tried to pick up the can believing it might contain a message but the sea was high and they finally concluded that it was only an ordinary oil can."[477]

Captain Hinckley, the last man to see the *City of New York* afloat, conjectured that the ship "perished between the Main Ducks and the Galloups [sic]. There is a passageway of about nine miles between the two islands." In Hinckley's estimate, Captain Randall had, for some strange reason, attempted to reach the shelter of Galloo Island rather than Main Duck, "with fatal results."[478]

C. W. Cole, resident of Cape Vincent, New York, but owner of Main Duck Island, Ontario, revealed that he had the equipment necessary for the establishment of a wireless station at his island, but that it would not be put into service until the next year. The press commented that the crew and families of the *John Randall,* which sank there a year earlier, would have benefitted from its existence.[479] The current loss made the area even more rescue-conscious.

The *City of New York* was originally a passenger and freight steamer for the Northern Transportation Company of Cleveland, Ohio, but was converted to a coal and lumber carrier in 1881 at Dunford & Alverson Dry Dock in Port Huron, Michigan.[480] Built in 1863 at Cleveland by Stevens & Presley with official number 4377, the 292-gross-ton *City of New York* measured 136' (40.8 metres) in length, 27' 6" (8.2 metres) in beam, and 11' 6" (3.5 metres) in draft. The ship's value in 1882, when she was already 19 years old, was $15,000, and her underwriter's rating was B1, far from the best for insurance rates. Two years later, this value had diminished to $13,000, with a slightly worse rating of B1½, with the provision that she could haul coarse freight only. By 1889, when the *City of New York* hauled lumber for her owner, the Chicago Lumber Company, her value was only $12,000. In 1893, after Mr. M. S. Green of Chicago, her new owner, added steel arches and a relatively new fire box type boiler, built by the American Boiler Works in Chicago in 1889, she was valued at an increased $17,000 with an improved A2 rating. Her rating remained the same by 1897, but her value had slipped to $12,000 again when Thomas Curry of Port Huron, Michigan, became her owner. Drifting through a total of seven owners by 1897, the *City of New York* was sold to a Canadian named George Wilkinson of Sarnia in 1903 and became Canadian vessel #116393.[481]

By 1921, the high-pressure, non-condensing steam engine capable of producing 425 horsepower and built by the Cuyahoga Iron Works in Cleveland in 1863[482] was getting a bit tired. Perhaps that situation helped sink the vessel. Also, Harry Randall's desperation to recoup the cost of his ship had coerced him onto Lake Ontario late in the season to transport phosphate to Trenton.

Harry Randall had cheated the lake in 1920, but he lost heavily in 1921. Besides the immense loss of lives, the *City of New York* carried no insurance.[483] The contemporary press dramatically, but incorrectly, reported that the *City of New York* was a sister ship to the ill-fated steamer, *H. N. Jex,*[484] which sank near Kingston just a few months earlier (see that story earlier in this chapter).

HORACE TABER   (November 26, 1922)

Grounded in the same storm which drove ashore the schooners *Mary A Daryaw* and *Lyman M. Davis*, and which eventually sank the schooner, *Katie Eccles*, the three-masted schooner, *Horace Taber*, was pounded to pieces before she could be removed from the north side of Simcoe Island just to the west of Four Mile Point. Her crew escaped without mishap;[485] her cargo was salvaged.

The *Horace Taber*, under the command of Captain Henry Daryaw with three male crewmembers and a female cook, had left Oswego loaded with coal for Kingston on the afternoon of Sunday, November 26, 1922. The *Mary Daryaw*, under the command of Captain Frank Daryaw with three male crewmembers and a female cook (who happened to be Mary Daryaw, the vessel's namesake!) accompanied the *Taber* with a similar cargo for the same destination.[486] By nightfall, a severe snowstorm grounded both Kingston schooners at Four Mile Point. The *Daryaw* remained undamaged and was towed off within two days and returned to service, but the *Taber* commenced to break up immediately.

SCHOONER HORACE TABER
MAY BE A TOTAL LOSS

There appears to be no doubt that the schooner Horace Taber...is a total loss. The weather has been too rough for the tugs to get very close to the stranded schooner. Marine men are convinced that she is a total loss, and the coal will probably be taken off and the wreckage will have to stay on the shore until spring. It is feared that the boat is broken in two pieces and the use of pumps will not take the water out of the hull. It will certainly be a great loss to the owner, as it was impossible to carry insurance on the schooner at this time of the year.

Anthony Rankin, M. P. P., Collin's Bay, who owns the cargo, has arranged for the Pyke tugs to go out to the stranded vessel and try and take the coal off. Unless the coal is taken off at once there is a chance that the heavy winds will break the boat to pieces and then all the coal will be lost.[487]

Originally named the *Amoskeag* when she was built by Simon Langell and launched at St. Clair, Michigan, in 1867, on April 20, 1883, she was purchased by the firm of Horace Taber & Sons and renamed the *Horace Taber*, after the founder of that Michigan lumber company who lived from 1827 until 1914.[488] Measuring 135' 8" (40.7 metres) in length, 26' 6" (7.9 metres) in beam, and 9' 6" (2.9 metres) in draft (1911 Canadian measures), the 236-ton *Taber* was "sold alien" (in this case, to a Canadian) in early 1911; her final U. S. enrollment was surrendered at Chicago on April 24, 1911, when her official number changed from U. S. 1123 to Canadian 130324.[489] Her Canadian purchaser was Frank R. Barnhardt of Deseronto, Ontario, who registered the ship at Kingston.[490]

Many pieces of the *Horace Taber* rest in shallow water, between five and fifteen feet (1.5 to 4.5 metres) off Simcoe Island. A rudder, claimed to be that of the *Taber,* was located about 400 yards (360 metres) off the main wreckage and "salvaged" in the spring of 1984 by local divers, who planned to donate it "to a Lake Ontario museum."[491] More recently, one marine expert has indicated that, besides the *Taber* having a unique double centreboard system, her interesting rudder lies approximately 250 feet (75 metres) away from the main wreckage.[492] This is truly a case of the disappearing/reappearing rudder!

The beautiful lines of the three-masted schooner, Horace L. Taber, *can be appreciated in this scene.* GREAT LAKES MARINE COLLECTION OF THE MILWAUKEE PUBLIC LIBRARY.

KATIE ECCLES (November 28, 1922)

The loss of a small vessel in late 1922 helped spawn a series of local newspaper editorials, particularly one on the role of a woman on board a ship.

The old, but still beautiful schooner, *Katie Eccles,* carrying 300 tons of coal bound for the Schuster Coal Company of Belleville, Ontario,[493] sailed out of Oswego harbour, following the Napanee-bound schooner, *Lyman M. Davis,* at four o'clock on Sunday afternoon, November 26, 1922.[494] About five miles (eight kilometres) out into the open lake, two disturbing things happened: a blizzard began, and the *Katie Eccles'* rudder fell off. The first event was considered normal for this time of year, while the second was extremely unusual, awkward, and debilitating. Undaunted, however, casual Captain Harry Michell, summoning up all of his experience and navigational skills, and with assistance from Mrs. Mary Lloyd, the female cook from Kingston,[495] and the cabin boy named Hugh Hanna (this was a small operation), sailed the rudderless *Eccles* through winter conditions across Lake Ontario to the shelter of uninhabited Timber Island. There, they dropped anchor and waited.[496]

This same storm had cast other schooners in the area ashore: the *Mary Daryaw* (eventually returned to service), the *Horace Taber* (a total loss) and the *Lyman M. Davis.* (also returned to service, only to become the Christian-thrown-to-the-lions in a public burning spectacle at Sunnyside Park in Toronto in 1934.)[497] However, no one knew what had happened to the *Katie Eccles.* The captain of the *Davis,* stranded on Waupoos Island, claimed to have seen the *Eccles* with a broken boom and at the mercy of the sea on Sunday evening.[498]

The crew of the passing tugboat, the *Mary P. Hall,* saw the *Katie Eccles* ashore on the east side of Timber Island. Initial reports placed the little schooner "up so far on the shore that it will be impossible for a tug to get close enough to pull her off."[499] Smoke emerging from the schooner's smokestack indicated that the crew was on board and safe. However, during another storm on Wednesday night, November 29, 1922, "the schooner was refloated and went adrift. The crew were on the island and are safe."[500] The small crew was soon rescued from Timber Island, but the *Eccles* was adrift.

> The direction of the wind was such that she drifted North-East....The extent of the damage to her hull is...not known, but evidently she will be leaking badly after her grounding. Attempts were made to locate her and save her cargo because if allowed to drift indefinitely she might sink or go to pieces when she drifted ashore.[501]

And sink she did, before the cargo of coal could be removed. Another report gave this information about the loss of the *Katie Eccles:*

> ...after unshipping her rudder...the skipper...worked the
> schooner by sail into the shelter of Timber Island...,
> dropped her sails and anchored. However a change in the
> wind began to move the ship and with the anchors dragging,
> the captain and his crew of two rowed ashore to Timber
> Island where they spent the night. During the night the ship
> was carried away by the wind coming from the southwest and
> was never seen again....[502]

The modest-sized, twin-masted schooner, *Katie Eccles,* was built by
William Jamieson (who also built his namesake schooner described later in this
chapter) at Mill Point (Deseronto), Ontario, in 1877. She measured 95' (28.5
metres) in length, 24' 6" (7.4 metres) in beam, and 9' 6" (2.9 metres) in draft,
with a gross tonnage of 122. The *Eccles,* official number 75911, had been
rebuilt but once, in 1889.[503]

The graceful, gaff-rigged schooner, Katie Eccles, *sailed the waters of the Great Lakes
for 45 years.* GREAT LAKES MARINE COLLECTION OF THE MILWAUKEE PUBLIC LIBRARY.

Because the Toronto newspapers had been publishing editorials about the fact that lake boats were as heavily loaded in the late fall as they were during the milder summer months, thereby putting them at risk to the heavy gales, the Belleville *Daily Intelligencer* jumped onto the bandwagon in early December, 1922. Topics varied, such as "Disasters on Lake Ontario," "The Main Duck Islands," and "Salvaged Coal,"[504] but the most interesting editorial was titled "The Safety of Lake Sailors":

> ...Are these boats undermanned? Take, for instance, the case of the Katie Eccles. She is a two masted schooner capable of carrying a load of two hundred and fifty tons. She carried a crew of three, one man, a boy, and a woman cook. This woman cook is the mother of three children, according to her own story, [sic] took her spell at the wheel, handled ropes and sails and took soundings, on the last trip of the ill-fated vessel. This does not seem in keeping with our ideas of a woman's sphere. Now a vessel trading across Lake Ontario has often to make runs exceeding twenty-four hours, and how can a crew of three handle such a craft, especially if only one of the three is a man? It does seem a case of a boat being pitifully undermanned.
>
> Of course the woman was a heroine and was able to assist in a way that was effective. Supposing she had been an ordinary woman, and could not have rendered such skilled assistance, the vessel might not have been able to reach shelter, and today there would have been mourning in three households, and in one of them there would be three little motherless kiddies. Mrs. Lloyd is indeed a heroine and her name should go down in marine annals as one of our illustrious Canadian daughters. Mrs. Lloyd in her modest way claims the vessel was fully manned. This might be true in this case, but it is hard to be convinced of the fact. It does appear that we need more legislation to prevent vessels from sailing with too heavy loads and with too small crews. We cannot afford to lose our sailors at the rate we have been doing the last few years.[505]

The newspaper need not have worried. The days of private, commercial, wooden schooners, such as the recently lost *Katie Eccles,* sailing the inland seas were sadly numbered, symbolic of a slower, more relaxed way of life that was disappearing forever, and the larger, faster, stronger, overbearing, corporate fleet of steel steamers on Great Lakes waters all had their full complements of men to man them.

The *Katie Eccles* sits in about 100' (30 metres) of water off Timber Island and has been explored secretively by a clandestine group of scuba divers who located her several years ago. One identifiable feature of the *Katie Eccles* is "a steel hatchcombing on number three, the after hatch."[506]

WINNIE WING (1923)

Built by Arnold Johnson at Fort Howard, Wisconsin, the oak-hulled schooner, *Winnie Wing,* measured 120' (36 metres) in length, 28' (8.4 metres) in beam, and 10' (3 metres) in draft, and slid down the launchramp on July 18, 1867. Captain John Saveland commissioned the *Winnie Wing* to be built, and he named this ship after his late grandmother (1788-1860).[507]

Working for many years in the lumber trade on Lake Michigan, the *Winnie Wing* eventually made her way to the Kingston area, where she laboured until she grew too old, finally being abandoned at Kingston in 1923.[508]

In the course of the Kingston area part of her long career, the coal-laden *Winnie Wing* sank in the Napanee River after colliding with a scow, but the schooner was raised, repaired, and returned for a few more years of service.[509]

The old schooner, Winnie Wing, *was abandoned in the Kingston area in about 1923 after almost 60 years of working on the Great Lakes.* AUTHOR'S COLLECTION.

ST. LOUIS (1923)

In 1909, at Buffalo, New York, a 45-year-old passenger and freight freighter named the *St. Louis* was converted to a simple towbarge. Originally built by the Peck & Martin Shipyard and launched in 1864 at Cleveland, Ohio, the steamer, *St. Louis,* measured 202' (60.6 metres) in length, 31' 9" (9.5 metres) in beam, and 11' 7" (3.5 metres) in draft. As a towbarge, the ship worked for only another five years, then lay idle at Cape Vincent, New York, until being towed to an area off Amherst Island in 1923 and scuttled.[510]

WILLIAM JAMIESON   (May 15, 1923)

The 45-year-old schooner, *William Jamieson,* rode low in the water with a heavy load of coal when she showed her old age and opened her seams during a spring storm on Tuesday, May 15, 1923.

Every person on board the *Jamieson* was from Picton, Ontario; that town's newspaper described this first loss of the 1923 shipping season thusly:

> The schooner W. J. Jamieson of Picton sank on Tuesday while returning from Oswego with a load of coal for Hyatt and Hart. The crew are all safe in Picton but the vessel with her cargo is a total loss.

The schooner, William Jamieson, *sank with a load of coal.* AUTHOR'S COLLECTION.

> The Jamieson left Oswego on Tuesday morning [May 15, 1923] at five o'clock with 250 tons of stove and nut coal for Picton. The weather was fine in the forenoon and she made a quick run across the lake. Just about noon when the schooner was between False Ducks and Indian Point she was hit by the gale, and driven through the upper gap. She lost her main mast and most of her canvas but fortunately she was not far from land and the crew managed to beach her on the north shore of Amherst Island. The anchor was thrown out but it would not hold as the vessel was in an exposed position, and she drifted out into the channel between Amherst and the mainland, where she broke up in the seas and sank. The vessel was leaking badly when she was beached, the crew being unable to keep the water down with the pumps.

Realizing that it was hopeless to attempt to save the schooner the crew landed in their yawl boat coming up to Picton Wednesday morning.

The Jamieson was owned by Captain W. Savage and Mate P. McManus of Picton. She was an old vessel and one of the few surviving schooners on the lake.

The crew was composed of Captain Savage, Mate McManus, Philip Haskell, Richard Woodward, and Mrs. Tierney, cook, all of Picton.[511]

Although situated in a silt-rich area and showing extensive zebra mussel coverage, the wreck of the schooner, William Jamieson, *offers an intact hull in 80' (24 metres) of water for visiting divers, such as Marcy McElmon, to explore.* PHOTO BY CRIS KOHL.

Initial reports indicated that the *Jamieson* sank in about 40' (12 metres) of water,[512] and that this "speaks well for [Captain Savage's] bravery and presence of mind"[513] because the coal cargo could be salvaged. However, the vessel sank in water twice that deep, so the cargo stayed where it was.

Launched on July 3, 1878 at Mill Point (Deseronto), Ontario, the 143-ton schooner, *William Jamieson,* was built by her talented namesake, William Jamieson (1823-1901), a Deseronto man all his life, working first as a sailor, then as a shipbuilder, and finally, as the owner/manager of the Empress Hotel in Deseronto, where he died.[514] This ship, official #75912, measured 100' (30 metres) in length, 25' 4" (7.6 metres) in beam, and 8' 6" (2.5 metres) in draft.[515]

On July 31, 1963, Kingston scuba divers Lloyd Shales, Barbara Carson, Ron Hughes, and John Birtwhistle, members of the Aqua Fins Scuba Club, located the wreck of the *William Jamieson* about a quarter of a mile off the north shore of Amherst Island using a depth sounder and a boat. That same team had found the wreck of the *City of Sheboygan,* four miles away, earlier that summer (see chapter 7). In those pre-conservation days, the divers brought up artifact after artifact, including the ship's bell, a brass whistle that was on a small boiler used for hoisting sails, crockery and glasses, and the schooner's brass compass, the glass face of which promptly exploded on the dive boat due to the sudden change in pressure and temperature, sending glass slivers flying![516] Fortunately, no one was injured. Several descendents of the *Jamieson's* crew requested small items from the shipwreck as keepsakes.[517]

The *William Jamieson* sits upright and intact (except for the bow, which apparently hit the bottom first and hardest when she sank) in about 80' (24 metres) of water. Rigging and bow pumps remain at this often-silty site.[518]

W. J. CARTER   (July 28, 1923)

Born on the western edge of the Great Lakes, the steamer, *W. J. Carter,* died on the eastern side. Constructed at the Wolfe & Davidson Shipyard at Milwaukee in 1886, the *Carter* passed into Canadian ownership in 1920[519] at the age of 34, and, three years later, her career ended. While enroute from Oswego to Cobourg, Ontario, the 317-ton *W. J. Carter* sprang a leak about 20 miles (30 kilometres) south of Point Petre, west of Kingston.

The steamer, W. J. Carter, *sank in deep water in Lake Ontario.* AUTHOR'S COLLECTION.

Captain Quinn of Toronto, co-owner of the ship, ordered the two lifeboats lowered, but befouled lines in the davits prevented the launching of one. The crew of nine (eight men and the cook, Mrs. Catharine Readman) crowded into the other, just as the *Carter* sank "practically without warning in 150 fathoms [900 feet] of water."[520] The sinking occurred at 10:30 P.M. on Saturday, July 28, 1923, and the crew drifted in the one lifeboat all night until their little craft was sighted by Captain McKee of the steamer, *Keyport,* who conveyed the wrecked crew to Cape Vincent. They were taken to Kingston on Sunday afternoon, July 29, 1923. "Owing to the great depth of the water at the place where [the *W. J. Carter]* sank,...she must...be regarded as a total loss."[521] Some understatement!

Named after Lake Michigan lumber-hauling entrepreneur, William J. Carter (1842-1936), this steamer measured 130' by 28' by 10' (39 x 8.4 x 3 metres).[522]

SENATOR DERBYSHIRE   (October 11, 1924)

The real-life Senator Derbyshire was a Canadian politician born at a place called Plum Hollow, Canada West. This one-time mayor of Brockville, Ontario, lived from 1846 until 1916.[523] His namesake vessel outlived him by eight years.

Travelling light upbound, the steamer, *Senator Derbyshire,* owned by the George Hall Coal Corporation of Ogdensburg, New York, caught on fire about 25 miles (40 kilometres) west of Kingston, on Saturday, October 11, 1924.[524] Under Canadian registry, the wooden steamer was "in first class condition" and was valued at $25,000.[525]

The steamer, Senator Derbyshire (ex-Bermuda), *caught on fire and sank off Prince Edward County.* GREAT LAKES MARINE COLLECTION OF THE MILWAUKEE PUBLIC LIBRARY.

...The steamer took fire at an early hour on Saturday morning as the farmers who live along the main shore could see a bright fire in the distance when they arose. The blaze

continued until about two o'clock in the afternoon and then suddently went out. The steamer was in command of Capt. J. W. Scarrow.

The Hall Company, Ogdensburg, was called on the long distance telephone and learned that the members of the crew had been picked up by the steamer Maple Bay, owned by the Tree Line, and were taken to Montreal. The men had a very narrow escape. The crew stayed with the steamer as long as they could and then the blaze got so bad that they were forced to the life boats and were travelling at the mercy of the seas when picked up by the Maple Bay on Saturday morning. The members of the crew lost all of their personal belongings.[526]

The wooden steamer, *Senator Derbyshire,* built by James Davidson at West Bay City, Michigan, as hull number 83 and launched as the *Bermuda* on September 18, 1897, official #3729, measured 220' by 41' by 16' 6" (66 by 12.3 by 4.9 metres). Passing into Canadian ownership in 1910, her name was changed to *Senator Derbyshire*, official number C.112351. Her final U. S. enrollment was surrendered at Ogdensburg on March 15, 1910, and endorsed "sold alien." Her steeple compound engine, built at Chicago by the Vulcan Iron Works in 1896, could produce 395 horsepower. Her first boiler was built in 1890 by F. L. McGregor at Milwaukee, but this was replaced in 1914 by one from the Polson Iron Works in Toronto. Lastly, her gross tonnage was 1,246.[527]

"GLENDORA" (1925)

Scuba divers began calling one of the unidentified steamers in one of the Kingston area ships' graveyards the *"Glendora"* or *"Glenora."* In my research, I have not located any vessel of such a name being abandoned and/or scuttled anywhere in the Kingston region. This wooden steamer retains a relatively intact hull, a rudder, and a four-bladed propeller; all other machinery and fittings were removed,[528] strong evidence that this ship was scuttled. More than likely, the *"Glendora"* is really one of the other old steamers scuttled in the two major clean-ups of 1925 and 1937.

MAPLEGLEN (June 19, 1925)

Several abandoned steamers were scuttled in 1925 (the *Mapleglen,* the *Maplegreen,* and the *Maplegorge;* several more met that end in 1937 and at times in between those dates) in deep water to the west of Kingston in order to eliminate the "eyesores" that ships in this category had become in municipal harbour areas. People viewed sunken, abandoned ships as health nuisances and scenic blights, and thus municipalities were urged to raise the wrecks, tow them out into deep water, and sink them. At least they would be out of sight, if not out of mind. Similar scuttlings took place in the 1920's and the 1930's off

Toronto, off Sarnia in lower Lake Huron, off present-day Thunder Bay, Ontario, in Lake Superior, and several other locations around the Great Lakes. It was the most convenient way of solving the problem in thosepre-conservation, environmentally worry-free days.

The problem of what to do with old vessels that had outlived their usefulness had existed in the Kingston area since the close of the War of 1812. Several of those warships lay idle for so long that they rotted and sank! (See chapter two.) Beginning in the mid-1800's, Kingston City Council was expected to take action regarding abandoned vessels in the harbour. Some barges were ordered to be removed as early as 1851.[529] With the onset of winter in late 1863, the poor people of Kingston were encouraged to remove old, rotten barges and durham boats from the harbour for use as firewood.[530] Two years later, in an apparent disagreement with City Council because the latter wished to someday use these derelict hulls as town docks, the local press argued:

> The fleet of old rotten hulks lying in the mud...should be burnt up, as in the event of contagion visiting the city they would afford a great comfort and sustenance. It is a matter of surprise that the military authorities have allowed them to rot and fester in the sun under the nostrils of the Garrison so long....We did invite the poor people of the city last year in want of fuel to smash up these old hulks and burn them....We renew the invitation this year....[531]

By the beginning of the twentieth century, increasing numbers of abandoned vessels prompted Kingston Harbourmaster, William McCammon, to declare:

> I would like to see the city council choose some spot in the harbor as a graveyard for derelicts. Such a place is badly needed. For years now, worn-out vessels have been towed to various parts of the harbor and there left. In all such cases they are a menace to navigation.... Mr. Calvin, at Garden Island, has a graveyard for such old vessels, and the city should have one, too. Or if the derelicts were taken out into deep water and sank [sic], it would not be so bad.... In my opinion it would be a wise move on the part of the city to choose a place as a graveyard for old vessels, and then made it compulsory for every derelict to be buried there.[532]

By the 1920's, Kingston's inner harbour had become such an eyesore due to abandoned ships that several of them were removed and scuttled in deep water.

Generally, there are three ships' graveyards in the Kingston area where inoperative vessels were purposely and legally sunk to get them out of the way. The Amherst Island graveyard lies due west from the extreme western point of Simcoe Island (and, as the name implies, is actually closer to Amherst Island), while the Nine Mile Point graveyard is due south of the extreme western point of Simcoe Island. The latter seems to have been used in the 1937 clean-up, while the former seems to contain all the vessels, plus more, from the 1925 clean-up. The third graveyard is the private one established by the Calvin family at Garden Island, and used for the derelict vessels that had been associated with their business.

The first of the derelicts that Canada Steamship Lines eliminated from Kingston's harbour area in 1925 was the wooden steamer named the *Mapleglen*.

Sank Old Hulk

> The steamer Mapleglen, the first of the old boats in the grave yard below the causeway to be removed, was towed by the Donnelly Wrecking Company on Friday morning up the lake near Amherst island where it was sunk. The same will be done with the rest of the boats.[533]

The scuttled Mapleglen *began her life in 1887 as the 250-foot package freighter,* Wyoming. GREAT LAKES MARINE COLLECTION OF THE MILWAUKEE PUBLIC LIBRARY.

Robert Mills & Company built the *Mapleglen* (launched as the *Wyoming)* at Buffalo in 1887, official number 141589. This wooden-hulled package freighter measured 250' 4" (75.1 metres) in length, with a beam of 40' 1' (12 metres), and a draft of 14' 6" (4.4 metres). Originally, the *Wyoming* had three masts and two smokestacks. She was converted to a bulk freighter in 1906 by the Abram Smith & Sons Company of Algonac, Michigan. The *Wyoming* was sold Canadian in January, 1920, when her name was changed to *Mapleglen* and she received the new official number C.141589. She lasted one season, after which she sat idle with several other abandoned vessels at Kingston. She was last shown on the Canadian register of 1924.[534]

Today, the *Mapleglen* is quite an interesting shipwreck to explore underwater. She sits upright in about 80' (24 metres) of water. The hull has collapsed and is in disarray, with frames, planking, hanging knees, and other wood aiming in all directions. The two boilers and the four-bladed propeller are definitely highlights of this underwater exploration. The intact bow area is also of interest. Marine life, such as bass, perch, ling cod, and American eels, can be seen at this site, particularly around the massive boilers.[535]

The Mapleglen's *boilers are a highlight of any visit to this site.* PHOTO BY CRIS KOHL.

MAPLEGREEN   (June 23, 1925)

"The hulk of the steamer *Maplegreen* will be towed up the lake Tuesday [June 23, 1925] and sunk by the Donnelly Wrecking company."[536]

These words formed the obituary of a 37-year-old wooden steamer which had been abandoned at Kingston. The *Maplegreen,* built by the Milwaukee Ship Yard Company for J. B. Merrill, et. al., Milwaukee, in 1887, official #155146, was launched as the *Omaha.* Her 485 horsepower fore & aft compound steam engine could easily propel her 222' 8" (66.8 metre) hull across the waters of the inland seas. Her beam measured 34' 8" (10.4 metres) and her draft was 18' 7" (5.5 metres). In June, 1914, she was sold to Canadian interests and was registered at Montreal with official Canadian number 134350. In 1917, the *Omaha* was purchased by the Canada Steamship Lines, which finally renamed her the *Maplegreen* in April, 1920.[537]

As with so many other old vessels, the *Maplegreen's* aging wooden hull and diminutive size as a modern cargo carrier rendered her obsolete, so she was towed out of Kingston harbour to join her scuttled sister, the *Mapleglen,* in the Amherst Island ships' graveyard on June 23, 1925.

The Maplegreen *was valued at $75,000 at her launch in 1887. She was worthless by 1925.* GREAT LAKES MARINE COLLECTION OF THE MILWAUKEE PUBLIC LIBRARY.

MAPLEGORGE (July 8, 1925)

The 1,367-ton wooden steamer, *Maplegorge,* launched as the *Ionia* at Grand Haven, Michigan, in 1890,[538] official number 100473, measured 209' (62.7 metres) in length, 38' (11.4 metres) in beam, and 21' (6.3 metres) in draft. Later in the year of her launch, she suffered severe damage in a fog-induced collision with the steamer, *Monteagle,* near Waugashance, Lake Michigan, and had her bow twisted. Repairs cost $18,000. In 1912, the *Ionia* was sold to Canadian interests, and her name became the *Fairfax,* with official number C.111966 registered at Picton. The *Fairfax* was sold to Canada Steamship Lines in April, 1916. In 1920, near the end of her career, she was renamed the *Maplegorge*.[539]

The newly-named *Maplegorge* was on her last legs, so to speak. She did not operate too often under her final name due to structural instability. She was stripped (or "dismantled") of any usable equipment, towed out into Lake Ontario near Amherst Island, and scuttled in early July, 1925.[540]

The wooden steamer, Ionia, *later renamed the* Maplegorge, *was launched in 1890 and scuttled in 1925.* GREAT LAKES MARINE COLLECTION OF THE MILWAUKEE PUBLIC LIBRARY.

YEWBAY   (1926)

Her value was an incredible $110,000 during her first inspection on June 15, 1881, when she was new. Forty-five years later, she was a worthless derelict that nobody wanted any more.

The 1,707-ton wooden steamer, the *Yewbay,* built by Quayle & Martin at Cleveland, Ohio, in 1881 and launched as the *Cumberland,* official number 125918, measured 261' 8" (79.5 metres) in length, 38' 4" (11.5 metres) in beam, and 19' 6" (5.9 metres) in draft. Her magnificent superstructure included two smokestacks and four topmasts. In 1913, the *Cumberland* was renamed the *Collinge,* and three years later, in September, 1916, she was sold Canadian with the official Canadian number 138096. In December, 1916, the *Collinge* was renamed the *Stuart W.,* until finally, in 1923, close to the end of her career, the *Stuart W.* was renamed the *Yewbay* by her new owner, the Tree Line Navigation

Company of Montreal. A year after that, in April, 1924, she was reported out of commission.[541]

Her high value quickly declined after her launch: from $110,000 in 1881, this vessel was worth $100,000 in 1884, $90,000 by 1889, $80,000 in 1893, $70,000 in 1894, $60,000 in 1895, and $48,000 in 1899.[542] By 1924, the *Yewbay* was 43 years old, ancient by wooden vessel standards. There was only one way for her to go at that point.

In 1926, the hull of the *Yewbay* was finally towed out and scuttled in deep water off Kingston.[543]

The massive, impressive, four-masted steamer, Cumberland (later Yewbay), *towed barges up the St. Mary's River at Sault Ste. Marie. The vessel on the right is believed to be the barge,* B. F. Bruce. *The* Yewbay, *built in 1881, was scuttled off Kingston in 1926.* GREAT LAKES MARINE COLLECTION OF THE MILWAUKEE PUBLIC LIBRARY.

CHARLES HORN (May 15, 1926)

The wooden steamer, *Charles Horn,* like so many other vessels in the Kingston area, went by her final name for only the last few years of her lifespan. Originally named the *Marion* when she was built by Rieboldt & Wolter at Sheboygan, Wisconsin, in 1889, official #92102, the 1,206-ton steamer had a capacity to carry 1,000,000 feet of lumber. Her first enrollment was issued at Milwaukee, Wisconsin, on June 24, 1889. Originally built for the grain, coal, and lumber trade, although she later worked for a while in the salt trade out of Ludington, Michigan, the *Marion* was double-decked in 1890. By 1922, when she was sold and renamed the *Charles Horn,* she was cut down to a single deck again. She measured 202' 2" (60.8 metres) in length, 34' 7" (10.4 metres) in beam, and 13' 1" (3.9 metres) in draft. Her original McGregor of Milwaukee twin boilers (8' x 14' each) were replaced by a larger, single boiler (15' x 12') built by the Manitowoc Boiler Works in 1912. Her 1889 fore & aft compound S. F. Hodge & Company of Detroit engine could fire up 700 horsepower.[544]

In her very first season afloat, the *Marion* made the history books. On September 7, 1889, she collided with the steamer, *Philip D. Armour,* also newly-launched, in the St. Clair River, sustaining heavy damage to herself and sinking the *Armour.* The *Marion* aimed her damaged bow towards the Canadian shoreline of the river and grounded herself there to prevent sinking. When a hardhat diver examined her at Port Huron the next day, her injuries were labelled as "unimportant,"[545] although damage amounted to $12,000. The two-year salvage of the *Armour* from that deep, swift-moving water by the famous Reid Towing and Wrecking Company became an epic Great Lakes tale of stubborn determination and technical innovation.[546]

The grain-laden *Charles Horn* (named after a Chicago lumber company CEO who lived from 1877 until 1931) caught on fire about 26 miles, or 40 kilometres, off Point Petre Light on May 15, 1926, sending her crew of 17 scampering to the lifeboats. They were later rescued by the steamer, *Robert J. Buck.* The 37-year-old wooden steamer, *Charles Horn,* supposedly sank in 140' (42 metres) of water.[547]

The aging, wooden steamer, Charles Horn, *sank in 140' (42 metres) of Lake Ontario water off Point Petre after catching fire on May 15, 1926.* AUTHOR'S COLLECTION.

BURT BARNES (September 2, 1926)

The year 1926 was in the midst of the noble experiment called Prohibition in the U.S.A. Laws against alcohol produced abundant Coca Cola newspaper ads, one of which pictured a young couple sipping this "delicious and refreshing" beverage while sitting on the running board of that 1920's mass-produced item that everyone simply had to have, the "horseless carriage," or automobile, and the caption read, "For the picnic take a case on your running board."[548]

The year 1926 was also one of the final years for commercial sailing vessels on the Great Lakes. They were a rapidly dying breed, an "endangered species," and it was often no picnic as the last of these vessels drifted into history.

The graceful lines of the schooner, *Burt Barnes,* sank under the Lake Ontario's waves some time after her crew abandoned ship at 4:00 P.M. on Thursday, September 2, 1926. The *Barnes* had taken on 210 tons of coal at Sodus Bay, New York, and was heading for Picton when strong, 50-mile-per-hour (80-kilometre-per-hour) winds did the improbable: they snapped all three masts, one after another, leaving the schooner without propulsion. The drifting crew last viewed their sinking vessel, mastless and lying low due to waterlogging, just off Point Petre. Captain Patrick McManus (a captain in his own right, but acting as mate on the *William Jamieson* when that vessel sank three years earlier; read that story elsewhere in this chapter) and his three crew, Phillip Haskill, Ernest Zimmerman, and Edward Howard, all from Picton, drifted in their cramped, three-person yawlboat all the way across Lake Ontario, with only a loaf of bread and two pounds of butter to eat, landing at Braddock Point, New York, 32 hours later. Captain McManus, who had served the lakes for 40 years and was tired of having schooners sink from under him, retired after this particularly nasty episode in his life. "I have been in several shipwrecks," he stated, "but that experience was the worst I have ever had."[549]

Captain McManus, interviewed by a reporter after he and his crew had spent the night at the Coast Guard station at Summerville, New York, stated:

> There was a sudden squall, and off went the top mast. Then the foremast crashed and the mizzenmast heaved to the decks. It was a terrible storm, with the waters beating high over the boat and not a stitch of sail left. The boat dipped and plunged, gradually filling with water through the hatches. All Wednesday night we tossed about on that sea. The schooner...started to go down Thursday forenoon and she was listing heavily when I told the boys to abandon ship at noon. It seemed like suicide to go out in their open yawl in such a storm, but we seemed facing death anyway. We could not start the [yawlboat's] engine and the waves were so high we could not use the oars. Twice I thought we were gone as we rolled into that trough of the sea, and the boat seemed to be turning over. I guess the boys were all praying under their breaths. I know that I was and I told God if I ever

lived through this that I would never set foot inside of a schooner again, and I never shall. There was not a boat in sight during the trip. We simply tossed about, wet, cold and hungry. Finally we sighted land at Braddock's Point and drifted in.[550]

Under full sail leaving harbour, the schooner, Burt Barnes, *made a beautiful picture of poster quality.* GREAT LAKES MARINE COLLECTION OF THE MILWAUKEE PUBLIC LIBRARY.

The 134-gross-ton schooner, *Burt Barnes,* built by G. S. Rand and launched at Manitowoc in 1882 (official #3193) was sold to the Graham Brothers of Kincardine, Ontario, in 1904 (Can. #150489). In 1924, after a close call when the *Barnes* was dismasted on Lake Huron, the ship was sold to the Swift Coal Company of Kingston. This three-masted beauty of a boat measured 95' 5" (28.6 metres) by 24' 5" (7.3 metres) by 7' 3" (2.2 metres). The *Burt Barnes* was named after the father of John W. Barnes of Manitowoc, the ship's first owner.[551]

MARY A. DARYAW   (October 15, 1927)

Built as the *Kewaunee,* #14065, at Port Huron, Michigan, in 1866 by J. P. Arnold, this vessel lived a long and fruitful life in spite of two major accidents. On April 20, 1893, severe gales cast her ashore near Racine Harbour; 12 days of work finally released her. On November 26, 1922, she stranded for two days at Four Mile Point near Kingston in the same storm which destroyed the *Katie Eccles* and the *Horace Taber,* and which also grounded her sister ship, the *Lyman M. Davis.*[552] In April, 1921, she was sold to the Daryaw brothers of Kingston and renamed the *Mary A. Daryaw,* after one brother's wife (1882-1949).[553]

In the spring of 1927, the aging but still graceful schooner, *Mary A. Daryaw,* continued crossing Lake Ontario with full cargoes. Wherever she went, she impressed people because working schooners had become quite rare.[554]

However, her days were numbered. The *Mary A. Daryaw* accidentally burned to a complete loss while at dock in Kingston on October 15, 1927.[555]

The increasing rarity of schooners made the Mary A. Daryaw, *complete with her forest of rigging lines, lengthy bowsprit, ready headsails, anchors catted on the bow, donkey boiler, and iron jackass, a curiousity by 1927.* AUTHOR'S COLLECTION.

GRACE M. FILER   (1928)

Built in 1874 at Chicago by W. W. Bates & Co., the schooner, *Grace M. Filer,* official number 85312, was named after the two-year-old daughter (1872-1912) of Delos Filer. This 237-gross-ton vessel, launched on March 11, 1874, and measuring 125' 5" (37.6 metres) in length, 27' 3" (8.2 metres) in beam, and 9' (2.7 metres) in draft, was sold to Joe Fagan of Belleville, Ontario, in 1913, becoming C.111968. As late as 1935, the *Filer* was still listed as being owned by Joe Fagan, along with Francis A. Smith, also of Belleville.[556]

The *Grace M. Filer* last operated in 1924, after which she lay abandoned in Belleville, Ontario, harbour.[557]

> **During the winter of 1928, workmen set off a blast of dynamite in an effort to demolish the sunken schooner.**
> **Holes were cut in the ice and weighted bags, carrying dynamite, were placed on the bottom of the bay, surrounding the vessel. Hundreds of spectators watched the blast as tons**

of ice, rocks, and heavy pieces of oak were tossed high in
the air as the blast was set off.[558]

After the dynamiting, the "rotted hull" was reportedly removed.[559]

J. B. NEWLAND   (1929)

The schooner, *J. B. Newland,* named after Joshua Baldwin Newland (1820-
1893),[560] a Great Lakes lumberman who was once harbourmaster at Manitowoc,
Wisconsin, was launched at Manitowoc on Monday, July 25, 1870.

> **The J. B. Newland is the name of a beautiful fore-and-aft
> schooner just completed by Mr. Jasper Hanson of this city,
> and which was successfully launched from the shipyard at
> the foot of Buffalo street last Monday afternoon. She is
> owned by Messrs. Rudolph & Slauson of Racine, and will be
> ready to leave our harbor** [of Manitowoc] **in a few days.**[561]

The Custom House Report of August 18, 1870 also named Jasper Hanson
as this vessel's builder, although some other sources have differed. The145-net-
ton *J. B. Newland,* official #75366, measured 108' 6" by 26' 2" by 8' 2" (32.6
by 7.8 by 2.5 metres) and was used in the lumber trade on Lake Michigan. Her
carrying capacity was 300 tons. She was rebuilt in 1882, and it is probable that
her two masts became three at this time. In 1914, she was sold to Canadian
interests who kept her name; her new official number became C.103820.

By 1923, at the age of 53, the *J. B. Newland* lay idle due to her structural
instability. In 1929, this schooner was towed into the lake off Kingston and
scuttled.[562] After a long career, this modest workhorse quietly went to sleep.

The schooner, J. B. Newland, *spent the final years of her long life carrying cargoes
on Lake Ontario.* GREAT LAKES MARINE COLLECTION OF THE MILWAUKEE PUBLIC LIBRARY.

FRONTENAC   (December 11, 1929)

Spencer Shoniker loves his daughters, his wife, his boat, and shipwrecks in eastern Lake Ontario's Kingston region, and locating a virgin shipwreck provides yet another enormous thrill.

In September, 1995, acting on a suggestion from a friend who happened to be a local fishing charterboat captain, Spencer searched the waters west of Kingston with his scuba charter vessel, the *Brooke-Lauren,* named after his two daughters, and came across the location of the historic tugboat, *Frontenac,* which had been submerged for almost 70 years in about 115 feet (34.5 metres) of water.

The first divers exploring this shipwreck were absolutely stunned by the impressive sights that are rare on well-explored shipwrecks, but still in place on newly-discovered ones such as the *Frontenac:* porcelain plates, cups, and saucers arranged neatly in wooden boxes, the ship's wheel, and the tug's brass compass in a wooden box. Other impressive items on this intact, upright, vessel are the large, four-bladed propeller, the rudder, ship's anchors, a huge winch fully loaded with braided steel cable, fallen dorades (or air vents), and chain running graciously down the noble bow which rises majestically from the lake bottom.

Spencer Shoniker was careful to take only divers he could trust to Kingston's newest shipwreck location, with all its intact glory, and most divers emerged from their underwater exploration sharing his strong appreciation for the area's maritime history.

The tugboat, Frontenac, *seen here in drydock at Kingston to effect some repairs and maintenance upon the vessel's hull, worked in eastern Lake Ontario waters for almost 30 years.* THE MARINE MUSEUM OF THE GREAT LAKES AT KINGSTON, 982.2.218.

One early diver, however, lost control. In what he later described as his snap decision to prevent anyone from stealing the ship's compass, he removed that beautiful artifact from the shipwreck site in a late season dive and placed it about 80' (24 metres) off the wreck. This may indeed have been his true intention, but it disappointed and angered the *Frontenac's* discoverer, who located the compass the following spring and returned it to its original position on the hull. In some areas, the practice of removing artifacts from a shipwreck, hiding them underwater off the wreck, and returning to the site at a later date to recover them, has become common, if unscrupulous, behaviour.

What is the story behind the tugboat, *Frontenac?* Secondary sources of information have frequently excluded tugboats from their collections of shipwreck stories, wrongly giving the impression that tugs are inferior vessels of less historic significance than larger commercial ships. Tugboat histories, then, demand the researcher to investigate primary sources of information more intensely than usual.

The 111-ton tugboat, *Frontenac,* constructed by the Calvin Company, slid down the launchramp at Garden Island near Kingston in 1901. Measuring 89 feet (26.7 metres) in length and 22 feet (6.6 metres) in beam,[563] the new vessel was built mainly for river and wrecking work, as well as towing log rafts in the summer. In one of her final jobs for the Calvin Wrecking Company, the *Frontenac,* along with the steamer, *Cornwall,* took the damaged steamer, *Rock Ferry,* which had run aground on Charity Shoal off the head of Wolfe Island, across the border to Ogdensburg, New York, for repairs in October, 1912.[564]

The 89-foot tugboat, Frontenac, *was built in 1901.* PUBLIC ARCHIVES OF CANADA.

The Donnelly Wrecking Company purchased the *Frontenac* in 1912.[565] A circa-1920 newspaper advertisement for the Donnelly Salvage & Wrecking Co., Ltd., Kingston, Ontario, described the technical capabilities of their five vessels, the screw tug, *Frontenac,* the steamer, *Cornwall,* the steamer, *Saginaw,* the lighter, *Harriet D.,* and the screw tug, *William Johnston.* According to this ad, the *Frontenac* was "fitted with 100-ton pulling steam winch, 2 2-ton anchors and 2,500 feet of 1½ inch steel cable. Syphons, one 6-inch and one 4-inch. Steam connections and steel hose for steam pumps."[566]

The tug, *Frontenac,* was sold to the Sin-Mac Lines in early 1929.[567]

Late in the 1929 shipping season, right when newspapers were crackling with the excitement of the opening of the longest suspension bridge in the world, namely the Ambassador Bridge between Windsor, Ontario, and Detroit, Michigan,[568] and the shock of Russia's new 72-week calendar which excluded Saturdays and Sundays to fit their non-stop, round-the-clock five-day industrial work week,[569] the new 1,160-ton vessel, *Sarniadoc,* loaded with grain, ran aground in a blizzard near Main Duck Island.[570] Launched earlier that year at Glasgow, Scotland, for the Patterson Steamship Company of Fort William, Ontario, the 259-foot (77.7-metre) *Sarniadoc,*[571] although broken in two and initially declared a total loss,[572] was too new to be abandoned by her optimistic owners.

There had been great difficulty in rescuing the *Sarniadoc's* 22 crewmembers. Now, the nearby wrecking tug, *Frontenac,* was going to help lighter the cargo.

Planning to work as a team, the two Kingston wrecking tugs, the *Rival* and the *Frontenac,* cleared Portsmouth harbour at 1:45 P.M. on Wednesday, December 11, 1929, to remove some of the *Sarniadoc's* cargo of grain. The *Rival* towed the barge, *Cobourg.* The vessels arrived at the wreck site by 5:00 P.M., only to be dissuaded from performing any labour by the increasingly strong and dangerous winds and seas. They wisely retreated to Portsmouth.

On the return trip, at 8:15 P.M., between Main Duck Island and Pigeon Island, the *Frontenac's* whistle frantically blew distress signals. She was taking on water and settling swiftly!

The *Rival* cut her tow and swung back to remove the *Frontenac's* crew, no easy task considering that the waves were sweeping over the sinking vessel and the *Rival's* nose had to be run right up against the doomed hull. Less than ten minutes later, the *Frontenac* sank.[573]

After almost 30 years of hard labour, the wooden hull of the *Frontenac,* in spite of her complete rebuild in Anglin's drydock the previous spring,[574] had finally given in to the strain of the heavy seas.

By the time the *Rival* picked up the *Cobourg* and returned to Portsmouth, ice covered most of the tug. Captain Mallen, who had come to Kingston from Morrisburg specifically to command the *Frontenac,* returned home. Captain

Omar Marin, master of the *Rival,* himself just recently rescued from a sinking tugboat, the *Russell,* off Brighton, Ontario, now took the role of rescuer.[575]

Tug Frontenac of Kingston Wrecked Near Duck Islands

Foundered When Returning With Tug Rival From Attempts to Lighter Cargo of Wrecked Sarniadoc

MANAGER WON'T TALK

Captain Mallen of Morrisburg Was in Charge of Craft — All Members of Crew Taken Off

Gets Life Sentence For Stealing a Pie

VICTORIA, Texas, Dec. 12. —Thomas McGrew began a life sentence to-day because he stole 30 cents and a pie. McGrew, a negro, was tried under the old Texas "repetition of offenses' law, which provides a life term for a third felony conviction.

Headlines on the front page of the Kingston Whig-Standard, *Thursday, December 12, 1929.*

The Frontenac's *bow remains upright, strong, and defiant in 115'.* PHOTO BY CRIS KOHL

The local press, without mention of the *Frontenac,* later reported:

> **Canadian mariners in this district are complaining of the complete lack of life-saving facilities along the Canadian side of the Great Lakes chain, and we are asking for some means of saving shipwrecked sailors.**
>
> **The wreck of the steamer Sarniadoc a week ago on the reefs between the Duck Islands is one of many such disasters in that area in the past few years, local sailors declare. Yet, they protest, there is no means of going to the aid of wrecked ships, this country being dependent upon United States coastguard stations which line the American side of the Great Lakes chain....[576]**

The *Sarniadoc,* incidentally, was released from her grounding at Main Duck Island, repaired, and returned to service for several more years on the Great Lakes. This ship was sold for off-lakes use in the British war effort in 1940, and she was sunk by enemy action in the Caribbean on March 15, 1942.[577]

The recent discovery of the *Frontenac* poses a dilemma: besides being an important piece of physical history belonging to the people of Ontario, its attractive, intact state makes it desirable as an object for divers' exploration and appreciation; however it would take only one dishonest person to greedily destroy the integrity of this site forever, and detract from its appeal to visitors. Perhaps artifacts that are "at risk" should be removed, conserved, and publicly exhibited. That debate is long-standing; no solution has been found or seems forthcoming. Great pains are presently taken to assure that nothing is removed from the wreck of the *Frontenac,* and that its location is kept a secret. Spencer's delight has, for now, also become his Pandora's box.

Plates and cups from the Frontenac's *galley remain in boxes.* PHOTO BY CRIS KOHL.

365John Greenwood. *Namesakes 1920-1929*. Cleveland: Freshwater Press, Inc., 1984: 288. The *Daily British Whig* (Kingston) of Monday, November 22, 1920, stated that the *John Randall* was built by Captain John Randall, the father of the present commander, "about fifteen years ago at Smith's Falls, Ontario."

366*John Randall*. Ship Information and Data Record, Runge Collection, Milwaukee Public Library.

367Mills, op. cit., Supplement One. The *Daily British Whig* (Kingston), on Friday, November 26, 1920, reported that "...the steamer Randall was rebuilt in 1905 at the Kingston foundry. At that time, she received a new steel frame and engine. In 1912, a new boiler was placed in the steamer...." The rebuild date, 1905, is likely a reporting error, since the ship was launched that year.

368*Daily British Whig* (Kingston), Friday, November 26, 1920.

369*Daily British Whig* (Kingston), Saturday, November 20, 1920.

370*Daily British Whig* (Kingston), Wednesday, November 17, 1920.

371Ibid.

372At one point, the *Daily British Whig* (Kingston) of Friday, November 26, 1920, listed the engineer's name as "'Jack O'Grady."

373*Daily British Whig* (Kingston), Wednesday, November 24, 1920.

374Ibid. The *Daily British Whig* (Kingston), on Friday, November 26, 1920, reported that "...Captain [John] Randall sailed her [the John Randall] for eight years, and then his son Harry, who served his apprenticeship under him, took over the steamer...."

375*Daily British Whig* (Kingston), Friday, November 19, 1920.

376*Daily British Whig* (Kingston), Saturday, November 20, 1920.

377Ibid.

378*Daily British Whig* (Kingston), Monday, November 22, 1920.

379Ibid.

380*Daily British Whig* (Kingston), Wednesday, November 24, 1920.

381*Daily British Whig* (Kingston), Friday, November 26, 1920.

382*Daily British Whig* (Kingston), Thursday, November 25, 1920.

383Ibid.

384*Daily British Whig* (Kingston), Wednesday, November 24, 1920.

385*Daily British Whig* (Kingston), Thursday, November 25, 1920.

386Metcalfe, *Canvas & Steam on Quinte Waters*, op. cit., 85.

387*Daily British Whig* (Kingston), Wednesday, November 24, 1920.

388*Daily British Whig* (Kingston), Friday, November 26, 1920.

389*Daily British Whig* (Kingston), Saturday, November 27, 1920.

390*Daily British Whig* (Kingston), Friday, November 26, 1920.

391Kohl, *Dive Ontario! The Guide to Shipwrecks and Scuba*, op. cit., 74.

392*Daily British Whig* (Kingston), Saturday, November 20, 1920.

393Mills, op. cit., 109.

394*Schoolcraft*. Ship Information and Data Record, Runge Collection, Milwaukee Public Library.

[395]Ibid.

[396]Greenwood, *Namesakes, 1920-1929,* op. cit., 68.

[397]Ibid.

[398]Reprinted in the *Belleville Intelligencer,* November 19, 1879.

[399]Mills, op. cit., 120.

[400]Metcalfe, *Canvas & Steam on Quinte Waters,* op. cit., 134.

[401]Mills, op. cit.

[402]Kohl, Dive *Ontario Two! More Ontario Shipwreck Stories,* op. cit., 42.

[403]Greenwood, *Namesakes 1920-1929,* op. cit., 232.

[404]*Russell Sage.* Master Sheet, Institute for Great Lakes Research, Bowling Green State University, Ohio.

[405]*Chicago Inter Ocean,* June 22, 1881.

[406]*Atlasco.* Ship Information and Data Record, Runge Collection, Milwaukee Public Library.

[407]Ibid.

[408]*Russell Sage.* Master Sheet, Institute for Great Lakes Research, Bowling Green State University, Ohio.

[409]*Atlasco.* Ship Information and Data Record, Runge Collection, Milwaukee Public Library.

[410]Greenwood, *Namesakes, 1920-1929,* op. cit., 315.

[411]*Daily British Whig* (Kingston), Monday, August 8, 1921. Also reported in *The Daily Intelligencer* (Belleville), Wednesday, August 10, 1921, which attempted to give a reason for the many women and children on board the barges: "...Capt. Clark and the crew of the Macassen rescued all on board the two barges, including nineteen men, women, and children, it being a French-Canadian crew...." The implication is that French-Canadian sailors often took their families on board with them.

[412]*Daily British Whig* (Kingston), Tuesday, August 9, 1921.

[413]*Daily British Whig* (Kingston), Wednesday, August 10, 1921.

[414]*Daily British Whig* (Kingston), Friday, August 12, 1921.

[415]*Daily British Whig* (Kingston), Monday, August 15, 1921.

[416]*Daily British Whig* (Kingston), August 25, 1921.

[417]*Daily British Whig* (Kingston), September 9, 1921.

[418]*Daily British Whig* (Kingston), September 17, 1921.

[419]*Daily British Whig* (Kingston), September 19, 1921.

[420]*Daily British Whig* (Kingston), Monday, August 22, 1922.

[421]*Daily British Whig* (Kingston), October 5, 1922, and Monday, October 16, 1922.

[422]*Condor.* Master Sheet, Institute for Great Lakes Research, Bowling Green State Univeristy, Ohio.

[423]Metcalfe, *Canvas & Steam on Quinte Waters,* op. cit., 56.

[424]Rev. Peter J. Van der Linden, ed., and the Marine Historical Society of Detroit. *Great Lakes Ships We Remember II.* Cleveland: Freshwater Press, 1984: 183.

[425]*Daily British Whig* (Kingston), Wednesday, August 17, 1921.

[426]*Daily Intelligencer* (Belleville), Thursday, August 18, 1921.

[427] *H. N. Jex.* Ship Information and Data Record, Runge Collection, Milwaukee Public Library.

[428] *Lawrence.* Master Sheet, Institute for Great Lakes Research, Bowling Green State University, Ohio.

[429] *Daily Intelligencer* (Belleville), Tuesday, September 27, 1921.

[430] *Daily Intelligencer* (Belleville), Monday, September 12, 1921.

[431] *Daily Intelligencer* (Belleville), Thursday, September 15, 1921.

[432] *Daily Intelligencer* (Belleville), Wednesday, September 21, 1921.

[433] *Daily British Whig* (Kingston), Tuesday, September 6, 1921.

[434] *Daily Intelligencer* (Belleville), Tuesday, September 6, 1921.

[435] *Daily British Whig* (Kingston), Friday, September 9, 1921.

[436] *Daily Intelligencer* (Belleville), Saturday, September 10, 1921.

[437] "Wreck Commissioners' Enquiries and Judgments." November, 1921. On file at the Marine Museum of the Great Lakes, Kingston, Ontario.

[438] Ibid.

[439] Ibid.

[440] *Detroit Free Press,* September 27, 1921.

[441] *Daily British Whig* (Kingston), Friday, September 9, 1921.

[442] *Daily Intelligencer* (Belleville), Saturday, September 10, 1921.

[443] *Oliver Mowat.* Ship Information and Data Record, Runge Collection, Milwaukee Public Library.

[444] Greenwood, *Namesakes, 1920-1929,* op. cit., 253.

[445] *Daily Intelligencer* (Belleville), Wednesday, September 7, 1921.

[446] *British Whig* (Kingston), Wednesday, December 6, 1882.

[447] *Detroit Free Press,* October 24, 1889.

[448] Conversation with an early underwater explorer who requested anonymity.

[449] *Daily Intelligencer* (Belleville), Friday, November 25, 1921.

[450] Ibid.

[451] *Daily Intelligencer* (Belleville), Wednesday, November 16, 1921.

[452] Ibid.

[453] Greenwood, *Namesakes 1920-1929,* op. cit., 287.

[454] *Daily British Whig* (Kingston), Tuesday, November 29, 1921.

[455] *Daily British Whig* (Kingston), Monday, November 28, 1921.

[456] Ibid.

[457] *Chicago Herald and Examiner,* Sunday, November 27, 1921.

[458] *Daily British Whig* (Kingston), Wednesday, November 30, 1921. Captain John Randall stated that his son "knew better than any other man just what the steamer could do and just where the margin of safety was and he was too wise to take any chances of overloading."

[459] This latter ship's named was misspelled as the *"Paslow"* and the *"Phalow,"* in both contemporary newspaper accounts as well as modern secondary sources of information. The 170' (51-metre) wooden-hulled steamer, *Louis Pahlow,* built in 1882 and named after the German

foreman (1838-1921) of the Milwaukee Ship Yard Company where the ship was constructed, was sold for scrap in 1938, after an incredible 56 years of service on the inland seas.

[460]*Daily British Whig* (Kingston), Wednesday, November 30, 1921.

[461]*Daily British Whig* (Kingston), Monday, November 28, 1921.

[462]The 120-foot (36-metre) steamer, *Hinckley,* built for and named after Captain A. R. Hinckley (1856-1936) at Chaumont, New York, in 1901, was destroyed by the forces of nature after stranding on Stony Point, New York, on July 29, 1929.

[463]The steamer, *Isabella H.,* coincidentally was owned by Captain Hinckley, who also owned and mastered the steamer, *Hinckley,* which had accompanied the *City of New York* on her final trip. The *Isabella H.,* launched at Grand Haven, Michigan, as the *McCormick,* was renamed after Captain Hinckley's daughter (1877-1944), when he purchased the ship in 1915. The vessel foundered in shallow water off Oswego on September 28, 1925.

[464]Metcalfe, *Canvas & Steam on Quinte Waters,* op. cit., 55.

[465]*Daily British Whig* (Kingston), Monday, November 28, 1921.

[466]Ibid.

[467]Ibid. Also, *Daily British Whig* (Kingston), Thursday, December 1, 1921.

[468]*Daily British Whig* (Kingston), Tuesday, November 29, 1921.

[469]*Daily British Whig* (Kingston), Wednesday, November 30, 1921.

[470]Ibid.

[471]*Daily British Whig* (Kingston), Tuesday, November 29, 1921.

[472]Ibid.

[473]*Daily Intelligencer* (Belleville), Thursday, December 1, 1921, and the *Daily British Whig* (Kingston), Wednesday, November 30, 1921.

[474]*Daily British Whig* (Kingston), Friday, December 2, 1921.

[475]*Daily Intelligencer* (Belleville), Thursday, December 1, 1921, and the *Daily British Whig* (Kingston), Wednesday, November 30, 1921.

[476]*Daily British Whig* (Kingston), Wednesday, November 30, 1921.

[477]Ibid.

[478]*Daily British Whig* (Kingston), Thursday, December 1, 1921.

[479]*Daily British Whig* (Kingston), Monday, November 28, 1921.

[480]Greenwood, *Namesakes 1920-1929,* op. cit.

[481]*City of New York.* Ship Information and Data Record, Runge Collection, Milwaukee Public Library.

[482]Ibid.

[483]*Daily British Whig* (Kingston), Tuesday, November 29, 1921.

[484]*Daily British Whig* (Kingston), Monday, November 28, 1921.

[485]*Daily Intelligencer* (Belleville), Monday, November 27, 1922.

[486]*Daily British Whig* (Kingston), Tuesday, November 28, 1922.

[487]*Daily British Whig* (Kingston), Thursday, November 30, 1922.

[488]Greenwood, *Namesakes, 1920-1929,* op. cit., 93.

[489]*Amoskeag.* Master Sheet, Institute for Great Lakes Research, Bowling Green State University, Ohio, and *Horace Taber,* Ship Information and Data Record, Runge Collection, Milwaukee Public Library.

[490]Art Amos. *Rudders, A Comparison Study.* Midland, Ontario: Ontario Marine Heritage Committee, 1993: 33.

[491]*Kingston Whig-Standard,* Friday, May 11, 1984.

[492]Art Amos, op. cit.

[493]*Daily British Whig* (Kingston), Tuesday, November 28, 1922.

[494]*Daily Intelligencer* (Belleville), Tuesday, November 28, 1922.

[495]Ibid.

[496]Metcalfe, *Canvas & Steam on Quinte Waters,* op. cit., 90.

[497]Kohl, *Dive Ontario Two! More Ontario Shipwreck Stories,* op. cit., 222-223.

[498]*Daily British Whig* (Kingston), Tuesday, November 28, 1922.

[499]*Daily British Whig* (Kingston), Wednesday, November 29, 1922, and the *Daily Intelligencer* (Belleville), Thursday, November 30, 1922.

[500]*Daily Intelligencer* (Belleville), Thursday, November 30, 1922. This information was telephoned to the newspaper that afternoon, so two *Eccles* news articles appeared in the same issue.

[501]Ibid.

[502]*Kingston Whig-Standard,* Friday, July 21, 1961.

[503]*Kate Eccles.* Master Sheet, Institute for Great Lakes Research, Bowling Green State University, Ohio, and *Katie Eccles,* Ship Information and Data Record, Runge Collection, Milwaukee Public Library.

[504]*Daily Intelligencer* (Belleville), respectively, Saturday, December 2, 1922, Tuesday, December 5, 1922, and Monday, December 4, 1922.

[505]*Daily Intelligencer* (Belleville), Wednesday, December 6, 1922.

[506]*Kingston Whig-Standard,* Friday, July 21, 1961.

[507]Greenwood, *Namesakes, 1920-1929,* op. cit., 340.

[508]Ibid.

[509]Metcalfe, *Canvas & Steam on Quinte Waters,* op. cit., 134.

[510]Greenwood, *Namesakes, 1920-1929,* op. cit., 90.

[511]*Picton Gazette,* Thursday, May 17, 1923.

[512]*Daily British Whig* (Kingston), Wednesday, May 16, 1923.

[513]*Daily Intelligencer* (Belleville), Thursday, May 17, 1923.

[514]Greenwood, *Namesakes, 1920-1929,* op. cit., 307.

[515]*William Jamieson.* Master Sheet, Institute for Great Lakes Research, Bowling Green State University, Ohio.

[516]*Kingston Whig-Standard,* August 20, 1963.

[517]Ibid.

[518]Kohl, *Dive Ontario! The Guide to Shipwrecks and Scuba Diving,* op. cit., 66-67.

[519]Mills, op. cit., 122.

520*Picton Gazette,* Thursday, August 2, 1923.

521Ibid.

522Greenwood, *Namesakes, 1920-1929,* op. cit., 170.

523Ibid., 150.

524*Daily Intelligencer* (Belleville), Tuesday, October 14, 1924.

525*Picton Gazette,* Thursday, October 23, 1924.

526Ibid.

527*Bermuda.* Master Sheet, Institute for Great Lakes Research, Bowling Green State University, Ohio, and *Senator Derbyshire,* Ship Information and Data Record, Runge Collection, Milwaukee Public Library.

528Kohl, *Dive Ontario Two! More Ontario Shipwreck Stories,* op. cit., 40-41.

529*Daily British Whig* (Kingston), Wednesday, August 13, 1851.

530*Daily British Whig* (Kingston), Saturday, October 31, 1863.

531*Daily British Whig* (Kingston), Friday, December 1, 1865.

532*Daily British Whig* (Kingston), Saturday, September 27, 1902.

533*Daily British Whig* (Kingston), Friday, June 19, 1925.

534*Mapleglen.* Ship Information and Data Record, Runge Collection, Milwaukee Public Library.

535Kohl, *Dive Ontario Two! More Ontario Shipwreck Stories,* op. cit., 35-37.

536*Daily British Whig* (Kingston), Monday, June 22, 1925.

537*Maplegreen.* Ship Information and Data Record, Runge Collection, Milwaukee Public Library.

538Mills, op. cit., 41.

539*Maplegorge.* Ship Information and Data Record, Runge Collection, Milwaukee Public Library.

540*Daily British Whig* (Kingston), Thursday, July 9, 1925.

541*Yewbay.* Ship Information and Data Record, Runge Collection, Milwaukee Public Library.

542Ibid.

543Greenwood, *Namesakes, 1920-1929,* op. cit., 352.

544*Charles Horn.* Ship Information and Data Record, Runge Collection, Milwaukee Public Library, and *Marion,* Master Sheet, Institute for Great Lakes Research, Bowling Green State University, Ohio.

545*Detroit Free Press,* September 11, 1889.

546Cris Kohl, *Shipwreck Tales: The St. Clair River (to 1900),* Chatham, Ontario: self-published, 1987: 97-99.

547Master Sheet and Ship Information and Data Record for the *Marion/Charles Horn,* op. cit., as well as Greenwood, *Namesakes, 1920-1929,* op. cit., 177.

548*Daily Intelligencer* (Belleville), Saturday, September 4, 1926.

549Ibid.

550*Detroit Free Press,* Sunday, September 5, 1926.

551*Burt Barnes.* Ship Information and Data Record, Runge Collection, Milwaukee Public Library. Also,Rev. Peter J. Van der Linden, ed., and the Marine Historical Society of Detroit, *Great Lakes Ships We Remember III,* Cleveland: Freshwater Press, 1994: 25-26.

[552]*British Daily Whig* (Kingston), November 27 and 28, 1922, and the *Daily Intelligencer* (Belleville), of the same dates.

[553]Greenwood, *Namesakes, 1920-1929,* op. cit., 92.

[554]Richard Palmer. "The Age of Sail Ended on Ontario," *Inland Seas,* Vol. 46, No. 1, Spring, 1990: 6-10. Quoted in this article is a Rochester, New York, journalist, who, in 1927, captured the nostalgic feeling of sadness because the world of the Great Lakes was changing into a less beautiful one: "Perhaps Rochester will see one or two of the old vessels such as the *Mary A. Daryaw* again, but it is doubtful. They have been down under the rapidly onrushing stem of progress for only a few generations but what they stood for is as dead as Atlantis. But to see one again is to realize as better men since Melville have said that 'men have left the sea and gone into steamboats' and that most of the beauty and adventure has gone as payment for efficiency."

[555]*Mary A. Daryaw.* Ship Information and Data Record, Runge Collection, Milwaukee Public Library.

[556]*Grace M. Filer.* Ship Information and Data Record, Runge Collection, Milwaukee Public Library.

[557]Greenwood, *Namesakes, 1920-1929,* op. cit., 120.

[558]Metcalfe, *Canvas & Steam on Quinte Waters,* op. cit., 75.

[559]Greenwood, *Namesakes, 1920-1929,* op. cit.

[560]Greenwood, *Namesakes, 1920-1929,* op. cit., 193.

[561]*Milwaukee Sentinel*, "Manitowoc Items," Tuesday, August 2, 1870.

[562]Greenwood, *Namesakes, 1920-1929,* op. cit., 193.

[563]Mills, op. cit., 44.

[564]*Daily British Whig* (Kingston), Tuesday, October 20, 1912.

[565]Metcalfe, *Canvas & Steam on Quinte Waters,* op. cit., 65.

[566]This undated advertisement, likely from the *Daily Whig* (Kingston), was provided by researcher Ian Marshall.

[567]Metcalfe, *Canvas & Steam on Quinte Waters,* op. cit.

[568]*Daily Ontario* (Belleville), Saturday, December 7, 1929.

[569]*Daily Ontario* (Belleville), Wednesday, November 20, 1929.

[570]*Kingston Whig-Standard,* Wednesday, December 4, 1929.

[571]*Sarniadoc.* Ship Information and Data Record, Runge Collection, Milwaukee Public Library.

[572]*Daily Ontario* (Belleville), Tuesday, December 3, 1929.

[573]*Kingston Whig-Standard,* Friday, December 13, 1929.

[574]*Kingston Whig-Standard,* Thursday, December 12, 1929.

[575]*Daily Ontario* (Belleville), Saturday, December 14, 1929, and *Kingston Whig-Standard,* Friday, December 13, 1929.

[576]*Daily Ontario* (Belleville), Thursday, December 12, 1929.

[577]John Greenwood, *Namesakes 1930-1955,* Cleveland: Freshwater Press, Inc., 1978: 330.

Chapter Nine
Since 1930

CORNWALL (December, 1930)

The paddlewheeler, *Cornwall,* has an incredibly varied history. An entire book could be written on this one vessel alone, but here is her story in a nutshell. This iron-hulled sidewheeler, launched in 1855 at Montreal by builder William Gilbert, experienced several name changes in her career: *Kingston* (1855-1873), *Bavarian* (1873-1895), *Algerian* (1895-1906), and finally, *Cornwall* (1906-1930). Sometimes these name changes coincided with a major cataclysm, such as an accident or a rebuild, in the ship's life: as the *Kingston,* she burned at Grenadier Island in the St. Lawrence River on October 26, 1872, after which she was rebuilt; as the *Bavarian,* she burned on November 6, 1873, 15 miles (23 kilometres) off Oshawa on Lake Ontario, with the loss of 20 lives, after which she was rebuilt; as the *Algerian,* she partially burned in 1905, after which she was rebuilt. She was also rebuilt in 1895 and, finally, in 1915,when she was converted to a wrecking tug with the dimensions of 176' 6" (52.9 metres) in length, 27' 1" (8.1 metres) in beam, and 9' 9" (3 metres) in draft, with a gross tonnage of 588 and a registered tonnage of 304.[578]

The luxury passenger steamer, Kingston, *of the mid-1800's, metamorphosed into the wrecking tug,* Cornwall, *of the early 1900's* (above). PUBLIC ARCHIVES OF CANADA.

Later in life, she transformed amazingly from her early appearance, which boasted "luxurious couches,...walnut wood,...a handsome pianoforte,...stained glass..."[579] all of which catered to the élite, such as England's Prince of Wales, later King Edward VII, who used this ship as his floating palace which conveyed him between Toronto and Montreal during his visit in the summer of 1860.[580]

Later, as a wrecking tug, the *Cornwall* was described as a

> **Powerful light draft steel steamer, outfitted with a 40-ton steel derrick, fitted with clam shell outfit. Complete wrecking outfit on board ready at all times, 3 12-inch Rotary steam pumps and boilers. Diving outfits. Compressors, Lifting Jacks. 11-inch wrecking hawser. Syphons, two 6-inch, one 4-inch, one 24-inch. Steam connections and steel hose for steam pumps.**[581]

By the late 1920's, the vessel had outlived her usefulness, and, in late 1930, she was towed west of Kingston to the ships' graveyard off Amherst Island and dynamited.[582] She was last listed in *Merchant Vessels* in 1931.[583]

The remains of the *Cornwall* were located by Kingston historian and diver, Rick Neilson, who, in 1982, located and interviewed an aging former employee of the Donnelly Wrecking Company who helped scuttle the *Cornwall* in December, 1930. With patience and determination, Neilson ran zigzag patterns with his boat and depth sounder until he found the wreck in September, 1990.[584]

The *Cornwall* sits upright and dynamite-damaged in about 73' (21.9 metres) of water. Her engine was removed before scuttling, but the two Marine Fire Box type boilers, built in Buffalo in 1892 and measuring 9' by 16', or 2.7 by 4.8 metres, are in place, as are the ten-bladed, 20' (6-metre) paddlewheels. Scattered around the site are woodwork, a windlass, a ladder, barrels, pipes, and tools.[585]

Picton diver, Doug Pettingill, examines the secondary boiler mounted atop one of the two larger ones on the scuttled remains of the Cornwall. PHOTO BY CRIS KOHL.

DUNDEE (1930's)

The small schooner, *Dundee,* was one of three vessels which were abandoned in the "boneyard" of Belleville harbour in the early part of this century. Captain John Smith, who perished in the sinking of the *George A. Marsh* in August, 1917, "had once refitted the schooner *Dundee* in Toronto" in about 1912.[586] In the early spring of 1995, the schooner, Dundee, surfaced again, one last time:

> **A few piles of dark wood stabbed with rust-covered nails is all that remains of the schooner Dundee.**
>
> **The piles sit at the end of South George Street [Belleville].**
>
> **The last remnants of the Great Lakes vessel that rolled off the dry dock in 1885 were pulled from the shallow waters of the Bay of Quinte last weekend as part of the parkland development....the ship was built by the Kelly family in Toronto in 1885. It was a 60-foot, three masted schooner that likely hauled grain from the Quinte area to U. S. ports....[587]**

The town considered erecting a plaque at the former *Dundee* site.

HARVEY J. KENDALL (1931)

The wooden steam barge, *Harvey J. Kendall,* rolled down the launchramp at Marine City, Michigan, on April 10, 1892. She measured 141' 7" (42.5 metres) by 30' 9" (9.2 metres) by 9' 2" (2.7 metres), and was converted to a self-unloading bulk freighter in 1917 at Ogdensburg, New York.[588] Named after a St. Clair River tugboat and freighter captain (1858-1933), the *Kendall* was dismantled and abandoned in 1931, the namesake dying two years before the benefactor.[589] The hull the lies in Button Bay, Wolfe Island, near Kingston, and which is marked on the charts as having about 7' (2.1 metres) of water above it, is reputedly that of the *Harvey J. Kendall.*

The steamer, Harvey J. Kendall, was abandoned in 1931. AUTHOR'S COLLECTION.

GRANGER   (May 28, 1933)

The sloop, *Granger,* caught on fire while in the Rideau River at Kingston at 5:15 A.M. on Sunday, May 28, 1933. When firefighters arrived, the ship was a mass of flames. The cause of the fire was unknown.

> ...A punt was secured and firemen carried the end of the hose out to a flat scow moored near the Granger. Between the flat scow and the Granger lay an old hulk. After getting the hose up on the flat scow, the firemen had to carry it over the hulk and on to the Granger....There was danger of the flames spreading to scows nearby....[590]

The hulk which retarded the firefighters' progress was not identified.

FLORENCE   (November 14, 1933)

So unseasonably cold was the sudden snap of weather in mid-November, 1933, that fishermen of the district struggled to recover their fishing nets, which froze in the thick ice of the Bay of Quinte and adjoining waters. Whitefish had just commenced running, and most of the frozen nets were full of trapped fish. Some fishermen resorted to chopping the nets out of the ice, with varying degrees of failure and success.[591]

It was in conditions like this that the tugboat, *Florence,* sprang a leak and sank about a mile (1.6 kilometres) off Timber Island near Point Traverse on November 14, 1933.

The Florence *plied Great Lakes waters for almost half a century before sinking near Kingston.* GREAT LAKES MARINE COLLECTION OF THE MILWAUKEE PUBLIC LIBRARY.

> Angry, snow-shipped waves sent the tug Florence, of
> Toronto, to the bottom of Lake Ontario.... It was the last
> trip of the season for the Toronto-bound tug....
>   Point Traverse... Its waters are regarded ominously by
> sailors, as many vessels have met their doom there....the
> sailors...reached the fishing colony at the point. It is an
> isolated spot, 20 miles from a telephone....[592]

Captain Williard and his crew (First Mate Floyd Eves, Fireman Dave
Williard, Chief Engineer William Wright, Second Engineer Fred Davidson, and
Cook William Shackles) rowed desperately to reach uninhabited Timber Island,
where they built a fire and dried their clothes. Then they rowed the lifeboat to
Point Traverse, three miles (4.5 kilometres) away, where fisherman Claude
Dulmadge welcomed them to the fire in his shack. Later, a visiting fish buyer
gave the *Florence's* crew a ride into Picton in his truck.[593]

Salvage attempts moved the *Florence* from her original depth of about 80'
(24 metres) to shallower water, namely about 40' to 50' (12 to 15 metres) closer
to Timber Island. While portions of the vessel, such as the screw (propeller),
were salvaged, her bow, boiler, engine, and a hatch ladder, are still in place.[594]

The 113-gross-ton wooden tug, *Florence,* measuring 91' (27.3 metres) in
length, 19' 8" (5.9 metres) in beam, and 9' (2.7 metres) in draft, and built by the
Maritime and Industrial Company at Levis, Quebec in 1885, worked in Quebec
(1885-1903, 1908-1923), Amherstburg, Ontario (1903-1908), New Brunswick
(1923-1927), Windsor, Ontario (1927-1932), and Toronto (1932-1933).[595]

*Trenton scuba diver, Kathy Everson, investigates chain and the upper portion of the
steam engine on the tugboat,* Florence, *which sank in 1933.* PHOTO BY CRIS KOHL..

SIMLA   (September 6, 1937)

In 1926, the Kingston newspaper praised the fact that several abandoned hulks had been towed out into Lake Ontario and scuttled in 1925:

> ...A number of the old-timers were removed last year being towed out into deep water and sunk. Now the lower Harbour looks better.[596]

In spite of the enthusiasm over the aesthetics, it was over ten years before the next fleet of derelicts was removed from Kingston's backwaters and scuttled.

The *Simla,* the first to be scuttled in 1937, was one of the last steamers on the Great Lakes built of wood. In 1923, a Buffalo newspaper reported:

> The Canadian-built and owned ship Simla is the newest wooden steamer on the lakes, having been built in 1903.[597]

Built by Calvin & Company at Garden Island near Kingston in 1903, and launched on May 9th of that year, the oak-hulled propeller-driven bulk freighter, *Simla,* official number 112144, was fitted with a triple expansion engine rated at 700 horsepower, built by the Polson Iron Works in Toronto, which also built her two new Scotch boilers.[598] This power plant was later installed in the *Mapleheath.*[599] The *Simla* measured an impressive 225' 6" (67.5 metres) by 34' 8" (10.4 metres) by 15' (4.5 metres), with a gross tonnage of 1,197. Sold to Canada Steamship Lines Ltd. in 1921, the *Simla* saw little activity after that date, remaining tied to the wharf at Portsmouth (Kingston) until fire burned her to the waterline on Nov. 23, 1936.[600] Her sunken hull lay in place until 1937.

The *Simla,* on September 6, 1937, became the first of many obsolete vessels to be raised and scuttled off Nine Mile Point by Sincennes McNaughton Tugs Ltd., under the direction of local manager, Capt. M. B. Donnelly.[601]

The abandoned steamer, Simla, *lead the 1937 fleet of derelicts.* AUTHOR'S COLLECTION.

PALMBAY   (September 21, 1937)

The steamer, *Palmbay,* was the second derelict in the 1937 project to be raised from Kingston harbour, towed out into the lake, and scuttled.

Launched as the *Pueblo* by the Milwaukee Ship Yard Company in 1891, official number 150152, the 1,493-gross-ton ship measured 236' 1" (71 metres) in length, 36' 3" (10.9 metres) in beam, and 19' 3" (5.8 metres) in draft. Her fire box type boiler was built by the Davis Brothers of Milwaukee, and her fore and aft compound engine, capable of producing 500 horsepower, came from the King Iron Works in Buffalo.[602]

The *Pueblo* was sold to Canada Cement Transport of Montreal in the spring of 1913, becoming official number C.133822. In 1916, her name was changed to *Richard W.,* and her final name change, to *Palmbay,* occurred in 1923, when her owner was listed as the Palmbay S. S. Company of Montreal.[603]

The *Palmbay* was reportedly severely damaged by fire while laying idle at Kingston on January 16, 1926.[604]

After the *Palmbay* and other wooden vessels were abandoned in Kingston harbour, water traffic continued to move around their hulks. It was suspected that, on November 23, 1936, sparks from the passing steamer, *Rapids Prince,* ignited a fire on board the superstructure of the abandoned *Palmbay,* which in turn spread to the nearby derelicts, *Simla, Stormount,* and Simon Langell.[605]

The remains of the steamer, *Palmbay,* were raised, towed out to the Nine Mile Point graveyard and scuttled on September 21, 1937.[606]

The steamer, Pueblo, *later renamed the* Palmbay, *had been abandoned at Kingston for over ten years.* GREAT LAKES MARINE COLLECTION OF THE MILWAUKEE PUBLIC LIBRARY.

Raising the derelict steamer, Palmbay, *from Portsmouth Harbour (Kingston), on September 21, 1937.* MARINE MUSEUM OF THE GREAT LAKES, KINGSTON, 982.19.422..

STORMOUNT   (September 27, 1937)

The third long-abandoned hull to be raised from Kingston's harbour, re-moved, and scuttled was that of the large and old steamer named the *Stormount.*

Launched as the steamer, *Avon,* in 1877 at Buffalo, New York, this vessel, official number 105733, was built by the Union Dry Dock Company. For many years, the *Avon* was owned and operated by the Union Steamboat Company, carrying package freight from Buffalo to Chicago and Milwaukee and return. In the fall of 1892, she was sold to the Union Transit Company, for whom she travelled mainly between Buffalo and Duluth, Minnesota. The *Avon* was rebuilt at Kingston, Ontario, in 1918, and ended up being sold there to the Montreal Transportation Company on February 24, 1919, official Canadian number 140962. They changed her name to *Stormount.* At this point in her life, the *Stormount's* dimensions were 254' 3" (76.3 metres) in length, 35' 3" (10.6 metres) in beam, and 14' 7" (4.4 metres) in draft. She still retained her original steeple compound engine, built by the King Iron Works of Buffalo. However, her old boiler had been replaced in 1903 by a Kingsford Manufacturing Company fire box type from Oswego, New York.[607]

Unfortunately, the *Stormount* struck the rocks and sank outside the Morrisburg Canal along the St. Lawrence River on November 2, 1920. She was lightered and salvaged by the Donnelly Wrecking Company of Kingston, but she was so badly damaged that she was taken over by her underwriters. Initial hopes were that she wuld be repaired over the winter and be ready for the 1921 shipping season,[608] but she was declared a total loss and abandoned in Kingston's harbour.

The *Stormount* was one of the four derelicts that caught on fire on November 23, 1936. A year later, after almost 17 years of sitting on the bottom of the harbour, the steamer, *Stormount,* had a cofferdam placed around her on September 25, was raised on September 27, and was towed out and dynamited to the bottom of Lake Ontario on September 30, 1937.[609]

The steamer, Avon, *later renamed* Stormount, *at left in this scene of Oswego, New York, harbour.* GREAT LAKES MARINE COLLECTION OF THE MILWAUKEE PUBLIC LIBRARY.

Raising of the derelict steamship, Stormount, *from Kingston Harbour on September 27, 1937.* MARINE MUSEUM OF THE GREAT LAKES, KINGSTON, 982.19.421.

SAINT LOUIS   (October 9, 1937)

The famous shipyard of Louis Shickluna at St. Catharines, Ontario, built the three-masted, oak-hulled vessel named the *Saint Louis*. The vessel measured 133' 3" (40 metres) in length, 26' 2' (7.9 metres) in beam, and 11' 9" (3.5 metres) in draft. She slid down the launchramp on June 8, 1877, and remained in service for almost half a century. In early 1926, fire destroyed her at Kingston.[610]

The *Saint Louis* was a ship of few headlines throughout her life. There was, however, one occasion when people inquiring about her made the news. It was just after the storm that tragically sank the *George A. Marsh* in August, 1917:

> The Whig since the storm on Tuesday has been beseiged with inquiries about the schooner St. Louis supposed to have been caught in the storm. There were rumours that she had been lost, following the fate of the Marsh....[611]

Four days later, the fate of the *Saint Louis* was reported:

> The schooner St. Louis, which was held up at Charlotte on account of the big storm, has arrived in port with a cargo of coal for the Montreal Transportation Company. Capt. Patterson was all ready to clear for Kingston the night of the storm, but he did not like the looks of the weather so decided to remain in port.[612]

A few years afterwards, the *Saint Louis* joined the ranks of the derelicts. The ship was raised in Kingston Harbour on October 7, 1937, and, two days later, was towed out and scuttled 300' (90 meters) to the west of the white spar buoy, approximately two miles (three kilometres) south of Nine Mile Point.[613]

The barkentine, Saint Louis, *was scuttled on October 9, 1937.* AUTHOR'S COLLECTION.

SIMON LANGELL   (October 15, 1937)

The wooden propeller, *Simon Langell,* was built by a man named Simon Langell (1835-1920) at St. Clair, Michigan, and launched on April 14, 1886. The *Simon Langell's* 845 gross tons were distributed along her length of 195' 3" (58.6 metres), her beam of 34' 6" (10.4 metres) and her draft of 13' 7" (4 metres). The ship had nine successive owners between 1886 and 1919, when she was finally sold to a Canadian named Robert S. Misener from Sarnia, Ontario. He operated this aging freighter for five years, at which point the 845-ton *Simon Langell* transferred to her final owner, the Langell Transportation Company of Sarnia.[614]

In 1920, the *Langell's* 1886 Glove Iron Works boiler was replaced with an 1899 William Denney & Brothers, Ltd., fore box type boiler built in Dunbarton, Scotland. The steam engine remained the old 1886 fore and aft compound built by the Globe Iron Works in Cleveland, Ohio.[615]

The vessel, however, was laid up at Kingston in 1926, and never ran again. On November 23, 1936, the *Simon Langell,* docked at Portsmouth Harbour, Kingston, alongside the steamers *Simla, Stormount,* and *Palmbay,* caught fire after the latter ship ignited. The *Langell* burned beyond repair.[616]

The derelict remains of the *Simon Langell* were raised from the harbour on October 15, 1937,[617] and she was scuttled in deep water off Nine Mile Point on Simcoe Island, where her bones rest in the company of other wooden freighters which were among the last to operate on the Great Lakes.

The steamer, Simon Langell, *was one of the last wooden freighters to operate on the Great Lakes.* GREAT LAKES MARINE COLLECTION OF THE MILWAUKEE PUBLIC LIBRARY.

Raising the derelict, Simon Langell, *from Portsmouth harbour on October 15, 1937.*
MARINE MUSEUM OF THE GREAT LAKES, KINGSTON, 982.19.417.

SARNOR   (November 1, 1937)

The steamer, *Sarnor,* ended any hopes of revitalizing her career as a Great Lakes carrier when she caught on fire, likely set by vandalous boys, in Kingston harbour on March 15, 1926,[618] the same blaze that destroyed the old sailing ship, *Saint Louis.*

The 1,319-gross-ton *Sarnor,* built at West Bay City, Michigan, by James Davidson in 1888 and launched as the *Brittanic,* official number 3400, measured 227' 6" (68.1 metres) in length, 36' 2" (10.8 metres) in beam, and 21' 3" (6.4 metres) in draft. Her fore and aft compound engine, initially one built in 1888 by King Iron Works, Buffalo, New York, was later replaced by one constructed by H. G. Trout, also of Buffalo. As the *Brittanic,* this ship worked mainly in the coal and iron ore trade.[619]

The *Brittanic's* last American owner, Henry McMorran of Port Huron, Michigan, sold the vessel in 1912 as a recovered wreck to Canadian interests, namely the Lake Erie & Quebec Transportation Company of Montreal, who renamed her the *Sarnor,* official Canadian number 133824, in early 1913.[620]

The *Brittanic* had been rebuilt at the David Lester Shipyard, Marine City, Michigan, in 1896,[621] following a tragic incident in which the ship, loaded with iron ore, sank in the Detroit River with the loss of one life on August 9, 1895.[622] The *Sarnor's* final owner was listed as Canada Steamship Lines Ltd., and a man named A. B. MacKay.[623]

In the 1937 clean-up of Kingston harbour, the burnt remains of the steamer, *Sarnor,* were raised, removed, and scuttled in deep water off Nine Mile Point on November 1, 1937.[624]

The old steamer, Sarnor, *as she appeared at the Buffalo Dry Dock Company's facilities on June 1, 1917. Her 29 years of existence, mishaps, and hard work were taking their toll on her oak hull. Things would get worse for her.* AUTHOR'S COLLECTION.

Raising the hulk of the steamer, Sarnor, *from Kingston harbour, November 1, 1937.* MARINE MUSEUM OF THE GREAT LAKES, KINGSTON, 982.19.425.

HATTIE HUTT   (November 6, 1937)

The gracious schooner, *Hattie Hutt,* was one of the most photographed ships on the Great Lakes, with a wide range of photographs taken of her between 1888 and 1923, near the end of her career.

Built in 1873 at Saugatuck, Michigan, by J. Martel for Mr. F. B. Stockbridge of Grand Rapids, Michigan, and launched as the *F. B. Stockbridge,* official number 120117, this elegant, 265-gross-ton schooner was constructed especially with the lumber trade in mind, and she worked in that capacity on Lake Michigan for many years. She measured 127' 8" (38.3 metres) in length, 26' 2" (7.9 metes) in beam, and 9' 6" (2.9 metres) in draft.[625]

On December 28, 1881, this vessel was renamed the *Hattie Hutt* when Mr. Louis Hutt, of Hutt & Johnson, a Chicago lumber mill and forwarding company, purchased the vessel. Being a romantic gentleman, he renamed this ship after his dear wife, Hattie (1839-1913).[626]

In 1908, the *Hattie Hutt* was sold Canadian. Her name was retained, while her new official number became 112190. She was sailed by Captain Frank Granville, her owner, of Chatham, Ontario, until 1923, the year she was sold to James Oliver of Kingston[627] and used as a tow barge on various Lake Ontario ports. However, she was still listed as the property of Frank Granville on the Canadian Registry of 1932. She was dropped from registry in 1936.[628]

Abandoned since the late 1920's, the forgotten *Hattie Hutt* was raised from Kingston harbour on November 6, 1937,[629] and scuttled off Nine Mile Point.

She was a popular subject for photography as she cruised along the St. Clair or Detroit Rivers. This was the classic schooner, Hattie Hutt. AUTHOR'S COLLECTION.

Raising the hulk of the old, forgotten schooner, Hattie Hutt, *from Kingston harbour on November 6, 1937, with the dredge,* Islander, *alongside. The* Hattie Hutt *was one of many derelicts upon which small, modern pleasure craft were damaging themselves.* MARINE MUSEUM OF THE GREAT LAKES, KINGSTON, 982.19.420.

AUGUSTUS   (November 15, 1937)

The schooner-barge, *Augustus,* was the last of the derelicts to be removed from Portsmouth harbour at Kingston and scuttled in deep water in Lake Ontario in 1937.

Constructed by the Calvin company at Garden Island, near Kingston, in 1893, the 802-ton schooner, *Augustus,* measured 177' 5" (53.2 metres) in length, 39' 6" (11.9 metres) in beam, and 15' (4.5 metres) in draft.[630] Her deep draft made her a particularly spacious wooden workhorse.

This huge vessel worked most of her life hauling heavy cargoes, particularly lumber, in the Kingston area, but, by the late 1920's, she was lying abandoned with many other aging wooden ships at Kingston.

The *Augustus* was one of eight derelict ships slated in the late summer and early autumn of 1937 for removal and scuttling.[631]

On November 15, 1937, the derelict barge, *Augustus,* was raised and removed from Portsmouth harbour and scuttled in about 90' (27 metres) of water abreast of Snake Island.[632]

WILLIAM JOHNSTON (1941)

One ship worked Kingston waters, off and on, for an incredible 101 years!

Built originally by Calvin Company as the wooden sidewheel steam tug, *Raftsman,* at Garden Island in 1840,[633] this vessel measured 100' (30 metres) in length and 22' (6.6 metres) in beam.[634] The *Raftman's* main concern in the 1840's was towing log rafts between Montreal and Quebec City. Returning to the Kingston area in 1851, this vessel's engines were removed at Garden Island and she sat idle at the dock there until she sank.[635]

Raised in the mid-1850's, the *Raftsman* was used as a small barge, with an engine and propeller being installed in 1878, when the ship was renamed the *William Johnston.* This 54.85-ton steam tug measured 73' by 20' by 6' 6" (21.9 by 6 by 1.9 metres).[636] The Donnelly Wrecking Company of Kingston purchased the *Johnston* in 1912 and converted her to a wrecking tug:

SCREW TUG "WILLIAM JOHNSTON"

Fitted with 100 ton pulling steam winch, two 2-ton anchors and 2500 ft. of 1$^1/_2$ inch steel cable. Sythons one 4-inch, one 2$^1/_2$ inch. Steam connections and steel hose for steam pumps.[637]

Sin Mac Tug Lines bought Donnelly's in 1929, and the *William Johnston* worked for them for the remainder of her lifespan. In 1941, having outlived her seaworthiness, the vessel was scuttled in deep water off Nine Mile Point.[638]

The wrecking tug, William Johnson, *at dock.* AUTHOR'S COLLECTION.

GEORGE T. DAVIE   (April 18, 1945)

Little is known about the loss of this vessel other than this:

THREE RESCUED AS BARGE SINKS

The composite barge George T. Davie, owned by the pyke Salvage Co., Kingston, which was carrying 1,040 tons of hard coal from Oswego, N.Y., to Kingston, sank in 85 feet of water off Nine Mile Lighthouse Wednesday afternoon [April 18, 1945].

Capt. J. Ruth who was in command of the barge; G. Conaghan, l. More and H. Moore, members of the crew of the vessel, were thrown in the water when the barge capsized and sank. They were rescued by the crew of the salvage tug Salvage prince, in command of Capt. A. Brown.

This barge was to have brought its next load of coal to Colliver & Huff at Picton, and owing to its sinking, delivery of fuel to this firm has been delayed ten days. It is expected a cargo, from another company, will arrive this week-end.[639]

This 680-ton vessel reportedly sank three miles north of Pigeon Island.[640]

HILDA   (November 7, 1967)

The *Hilda* was a bulk freight barge owned by the Pyke Towing and Salvage Company of Kingston. Built originally by the Polson Iron Works of Toronto in 1898, the *Hilda* measured 164' by 30' by 12' 3" (49.2 by 9 by 3.7 metres). In later years, the *Hilda* worked in shallow ports such as Deseronto and Napanee, both near Kingston. She was scuttled in Lake Ontario on November 7, 1967.[641]

S. M. DOUGLAS   (1986)

The iron hull of the steamer originally named the *White Star* is the reason for her longevity. Built at Montreal in 1897 by W. C. White, this ship was in service, off and on, until the mid-1980's. In 1899, the *White Star* was acquired by the Oakville Navigation Company for use in the Toronto-Hamilton area. A fire at Hamilton on March 1, 1926, destroyed the *White Star,* but her burned-out hull was converted into a coal barge for use in the Kingston area until she was abandoned in 1940. A Brockville sand company purchased the remains of the White Star in 1949, renamed her the *S. M. Douglas,* and rebuilt her as a sandsucker, until she again lay idle in 1973.[642] Considered for a while as a breakwater at Kingston, and also as an additional scuba dive site after the successful scuttling of the ferry, *Wolfe Islander II,* in September, 1985,[643] the *Douglas* was towed out into deep water and scuttled at an undisclosed site in about 1986. An unsubstantiated report indicates that she was located by scuba divers in December, 1995. The *S. M. Douglas* measured 160' 6" (48.1 metres) in length, 25' 4" (7.6 metres) in beam, and 8' 1" (2.4 metres) in draft.[644]

WOLFE ISLANDER II   (September 21, 1985)

The *Wolfe Islander II* ferry is probably the most frequently visited shipwreck in the Kingston area. But had things been different in China, or had opponents to her controversial scuttling had their way, she would not be where she is today.

Built in Collingwood, Ontario, in 1946, official number 157269,[645] the 164' (49.2 metre) ship, with the proposed name, *Ottawa Maybrook,* was intended as a gift from the Canadian government to China to assist her recovery from 15 years of war and civil difficulties. However, when China declared itself a communist state after World War II, Canada cancelled her gift, opting instead to use the vessel at Kingston. Replacing the *Wolfe Islander,* a vessel which had been operating since 1905, the renamed *Wolfe Islander II* ferry plied the two-mile (three-kilometre) route between Wolfe Island and Kingston from 1946 until late 1975, carrying residents, students, tourists, vehicles, and a future shipwreck book writer.

The *Wolfe Islander II* had her dramatic moments: a deckhand was accidentally killed in the spring of 1947 when the rigging holding the lifeboat upon which he was sitting collapsed. Both he and the lifeboat plunged into the water from the third deck, the boat landing on top of him. On the other hand, the *Wolfe Islander II* was the scene of births on two separate occasions in the late 1940's, from island ladies who waited too long before heading to a hospital on the mainland. Both babies were boys, delivered on comfortable bunks in the crew's quarters.[646]

In December, 1975, the *Wolfe Islander III* replaced the *II,* which stayed in the area on stand-by duty. The semi-retired *Wolfe Islander II* served admirably as a spectator craft during the 1976 Olympic Regatta. Then she sat idle.

In 1984, the Marine Museum at Kingston acquired the *Wolfe Islander II* ferry, with the intention of restoring her as a floating exhibit.[647] However, in the spring of 1985, the museum unexpectedly acquired the much larger, newly decommissioned Canadian Coast Guard vessel, the *Alexander Henry,* and display plans for the old ferry were shelved. The Museum sold the *Wolfe Islander II* for the sum of $1.00 to the Comet Foundation, which had plans for turning the ship into a scuba dive attraction. The people on Wolfe Island felt betrayed.

To raise money to help offset the $8,000 scuttling expense, bits and pieces of the *Wolfe Islander II* ferry, such as a bilge pump, signal flags, mahogany doors, firepails, and life preservers, were sold at auction, raising about $1,700. For a fee of only $5.00 each, people could engrave their signatures in one of the ship's 33 portholes, which remained on the vessel when she was sunk.[648]

Eleventh-hour threats from a member of the Wolfe Island council argued that the proposed scuttling showed "a complete disregard for our heritage on Wolfe Island"[649] and contravened provisions in the township's plans, as well as provided potential liability problems, but Kingston diver/lawyer, Wayne Gay, heading the Wolfe Islander Sinking Committee, was satisfied that all zoning bylaws and other legal aspects had been satisfied.[650] Sport shop owners, Steve and Terry Alford, along with Wayne Gay, spearheaded the scuttling project.

The *Wolfe Islander II* was sunk in an "all-weather" area about three miles (4.8 kilometres) east of Kingston at 11:48 A.M., Saturday, September 21, 1985, with a flotilla of over 100 horn-sounding boats in attendance.[651] Seacocks had been opened and a pump-equipped boat poured water into the ferry to help sink her faster. Rusty dust burst through vents to the surface as air trapped below deck was forcibly replaced by water. Scuba divers explored her that same day, and the vessel has continued to be a very popular attraction.

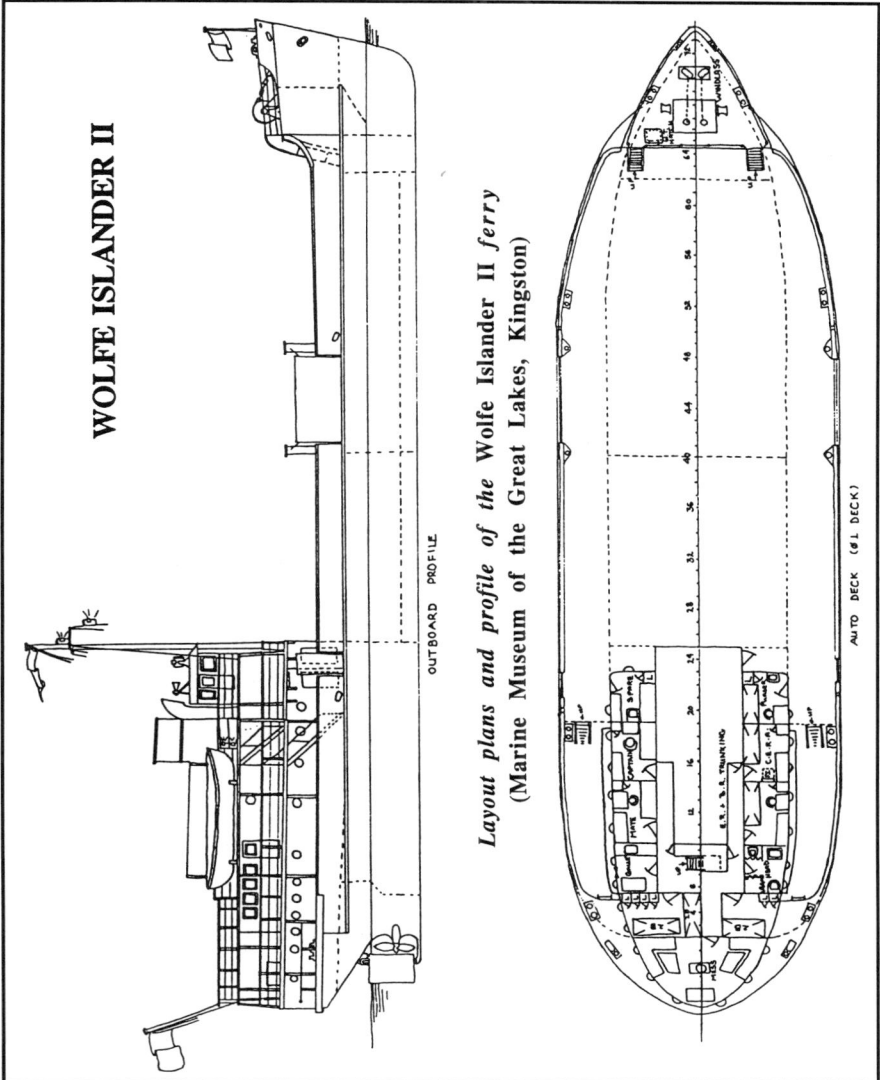

WOLFE ISLANDER II

OUTBOARD PROFILE

AUTO DECK (#1 DECK)

Layout plans and profile of the Wolfe Islander II *ferry* (Marine Museum of the Great Lakes, Kingston)

The ferry sits upright in about 83' (24.9 metres) of water, with her superstructure rising to about 35' (10.5 metres) of the surface. Visiting divers can explore her open deck area, complete with davits, bollards, dorades, smokestack, railings,[652] and even a motorcycle, a later addition. More experienced divers can also explore the *Wolfe Islander II's* interior. All doors and hatches have been removed in the interest of diver safety, but it is still possible to get temporarily lost in the maze of below deck rooms and corridors. Use caution and common sense for a fun dive. The *Wolfe Islander II* lives on as "the focal point of one of the greatest inland diving areas on the continent."[653]

Kingston area artist Robert Aucoin's conception of the sunken Wolfe Islander II ferry, on descriptions from divers. (Used with permission of Mr. Aucoin.)

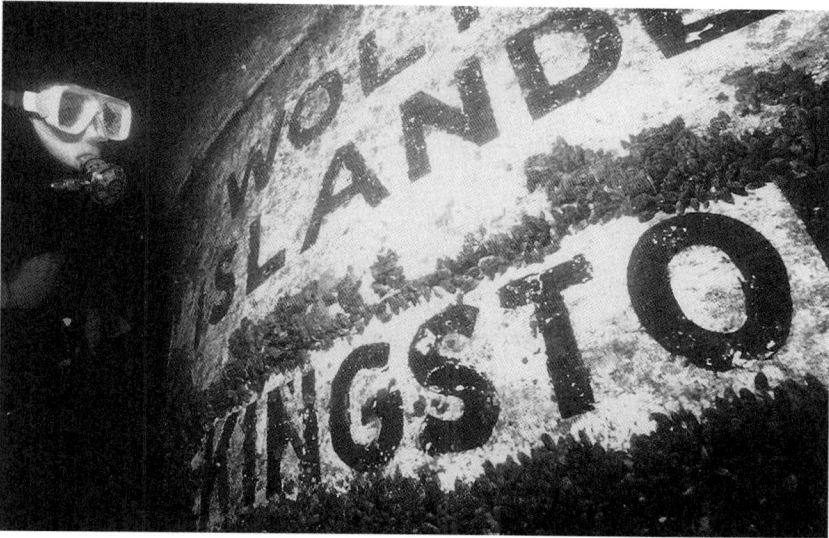

Trenton scuba instructor, Marcy McElmon, reads the ship's name and port of call on the transom of the Wolfe Islander II. *Again, as with the Roman numeral draught markings on the bow of the* Aloha, *visiting scuba divers have rubbed off any attempted accumulation of aesthetics-inhibiting zebra mussels.* PHOTO BY CRIS KOHL.

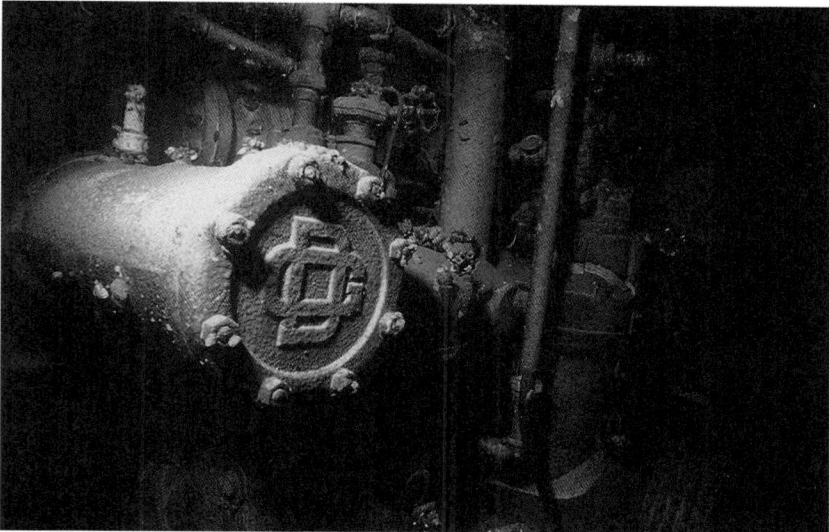

The engine room of the Wolfe Islander II *has a vast and interesting array of original mechanical components still in place. Scuba divers can drop down from straight above, since the metal hatch cover has been removed.* PHOTO BY CRIS KOHL.

"Are we having fun yet?" Scuba diver Marcy McElmon poses inside one of the Wolfe Islander II's *dorades, or air vents, on the upper deck.* PHOTO BY CRIS KOHL.

EFFIE MAE   (October 17, 1993)

Scuba diving on shipwrecks in the Kingston area has become increasingly popular in the past few years. With that incremental interest came the appearance of more and more special scuba charter boats that would taxi visiting divers to and from the various shipwreck sites in the area.

One of the most popular scuba charter boats Kingston ever had, one which ferried thousands upon thousands of people to these historic sites, was the *Effie Mae.* Ironically enough, she herself eventually became a shipwreck site visited by thousands of underwater explorers.

Construction of the 40' (12 metre), modern, bare, trawler hull, which became the *Effie Mae,* was ordered by Ken and Lois Jenkins of Port Credit, Ontario, and that hull was built of wood in Shelburne, Nova Scotia, and shipped by train to Port Credit. The couple completed building the vessel in their back yard: diesel engine, fuel tanks, below-deck fittings, superstructure, everything. She was finally launched in 1968 amidst great fanfare.[654]

After a dozen years of exploring the Great Lakes, the *Effie Mae* became the first scuba liveaboard charter boat in the Kingston area. Ken's navigational skills were well-known, as was his ability to bring the *Effie Mae,* time after time, to the precise locations of shipwrecks in the days before Loran C or G.P.S. In 1982, the *Effie Mae* became the first boat to take divers to the legendary, well-preserved schooner, *Annie Falconer* (see chapter six) off Point Traverse.[655]

The charter boat, Effie Mae *of Quinte, was always loaded with scuba divers on spring, summer, and early fall weekends in the Kingston area throughout the 1980's. This image was taken in the early 1980's when Ken and Lois Jenkins were the owners/operators. The vessel was anchored for lunch. Another innovation that made the* Effie Mae *different from other charter boats was the fact that facilities existed for the filling of scuba tanks with compressed air between dives.* PHOTO BY CRIS KOHL.

When Ken's health faltered in 1987, he reluctantly sold his beloved ship. He died of cancer the following year. Ted and Donna Walker, the new owners, carried on the fine charter business. From personal experiences, I can say that the *Effie Mae* was usually booked solidly a year in advance throughout the 1980's.

Transferring to the west coast in 1990, at the start of the economic recession in Canada, the Walkers could find no suitable buyer for the *Effie Mae,* and, in 1993, the decision was made to strip the vessel of any saleable items and to donate the hull to the care of the marine conservation group in Kingston called Preserve Our Wrecks (P.O.W.).

After quickly applying for permission to various government agencies, cleaning up the vessel, and adding 6,000 pounds of concrete block to the engine compartment for ballast, Preserve Our Wrecks decided upon an appropriate location to sink the hull: adjacent to the historic 1917 wreck of the schooner-barge, *Aloha* (see chapter seven).[656]

Finally, on Sunday, October 17, 1993, while bobbing on huge lake swells, the *Effie Mae* joined the *Aloha* as a new dive site in the Kingston area. In 1994, the *Effie Mae* was moved slightly away from the wreck of the *Aloha* to prevent the possibility of damaging the larger historic shipwreck.[657]

Trenton scuba diver, Marcy McElmon, explores the below deck area of the Effie Mae. *Literally thousands of meals for scuba divers were prepared in this galley when the ship was operational. The* Effie Mae *rests within 100' (30 metres) of the schooner-barge,* Aloha, *in about 55' (16.5 metres) of water.*[658] PHOTO BY CRIS KOHL.

---

[578]*Kingston.* Master Sheet, Institute for Great Lakes Research, Bowling Green State University, Ohio.

[579]*Toronto Globe,* July 7, 1873.

[580]Erik Heyl, "The Steamboat *Kingston,* Was She Rebuilt into the Steamboat *Bavarian?"* *Inland Seas,* Vol. 16, No. 4, Winter, 1960, p. 309.

[581]From an undated advertisement, likely from the *Daily Whig* (Kingston), which was provided by researcher Ian Marshall.

[582]Rick Neilson, "The Sidewheeler, *Cornwall,"* *Diver Magazine,* Vol. 17, No. 4, June, 1991, p. 33.

[583]*Algerian.* Ship Information and Data Record, Runge Collection, Milwaukee Public Library.

[584]*Kingston Whig-Standard,* Monday, December 31, 1990.

[585]Kohl, *Dive Ontario Two! More Ontario Shipwreck Stories,* op. cit., 32.

[586]*British Daily Whig* (Kingston), Monday, August 13, 1917.

[587]*Intelligencer* (Belleville), Saturday, March 18, 1995.

[588]Van der Linden, ed., *Great Lakes Ships We Remember II,* op. cit., 168-169.

[589]Greenwood, *Namesakes, 1930-1955,* op. cit., 221.

[590]*Kingston Whig-Standard,* Monday, May 29, 1933.

[591]*Ontario Intelligencer* (Belleville), Monday, November 20, 1933.

[592]*Toronto Telegram,* Tuesday, November 14, 1933.

[593]*Ontario Intelligencer* (Belleville), Wednesday, November 15, 1933.

[594]Kohl, *Dive Ontario! The Guide to Shipwrecks and Scuba Diving,* op. cit., 84-85.

[595]*Florence.* Master Sheet, Institute for Great Lakes Research, Bowling Green State University, Ohio.

[596]*Daily British Whig* (Kingston), Tuesday, March 16, 1926.

[597]*Buffalo Sunday Courier,* November 18, 1923.

[598]*Simla.* Master Sheet, Institute for Great Lakes Research, Bowling Green State University, Ohio.

[599]*Kingston Whig-Standard,* Thursday, March 1, 1973.

[600]Van der Linden, ed., *Great Lakes Ships We Remember,* op. cit., 248.

[601]*Kingston Whig-Standard,* Tuesday, September 21, 1937. Three photographs published in this issue depicted clearly how the derelict Simla was raised and how decrepit her appearance was when she was refloated. The article also listed the other seven vessels which would be removed shortly from Portsmouth Harbour: *Palmbay, Simon Langell, Augusta, Starmount, Sarnor, Hattie Hutt,* and *St. Louis.*

[602]*Palmbay.* Ship Information and Data Record, Runge Collection, Milwaukee Public Library.

[603]Ibid.

[604]Greenwood, *Namesakes, 1930-1955,* op. cit., 351.

[605]Van der Linden, ed., *Great Lakes Ships We Remember,* op. cit.

[606]Marine Museum of the Great Lakes, Kingston. Date on photograph caption, negative #982.19.422 and #982.19.423, both picturing the raising of the *Palmbay.*

[607]*Stormount.* Ship Information and Data Record, Runge Collection, Milwaukee Public Library.

[608]*Daily British Whig* (Kingston), Friday, November 19, 1920.

[609]*Kingston Whig-Standard,* Friday, July 23, 1971.

[610]Greenwood, *Namesakes, 1930-1955,* op. cit., 370.

[611]*Daily British Whig* (Kingston), Friday, August 10, 1917.

[612]*Daily British Whig* (Kingston), Tuesday, August 14, 1917.

[613]Marine Museum of the Great Lakes, Kingston. Information on photograph caption, negative #982.19.415, picturing the raising of the *Saint Louis.*

[614]*Simon Langell.* Master Sheet, Institute for Great lakes Research, Bowling Green State University, Ohio.

[615]Ibid.

[616]Van der Linden, ed., *Great Lakes Ships We Remember,* op. cit.

[617]Marine Museum of the Great Lakes, Kingston. Information on photograph caption, negative #982.19.417, picturing the raising of the *Simon Langell.*

[618]*Daily British Whig* (Kingston), Monday, March 15, 1926.

[619]*Sarnor.* Ship Information and Data Record, Runge Collection, Milwaukee Public Library.

[620]Ibid.

[621]Greenwood, *Namesakes, 1930-1955,* op. cit., 54.

[622]David Swayze, *Shipwreck!,* Boyne City, Michigan: Harbor House Publishers, 1992: 40.

[623]Greenwood, *Namesakes, 1930-1955,* op. cit.

[624]Marine Museum of the Great Lakes, Kingston. Information on photograph caption, negative #982.19.425, picturing the raising of the *Sarnor.*

[625]*Hattie Hutt.* Ship Information and Data Record, Runge Collection, Milwaukee Public Library.

[626]Greenwood, *Namesakes, 1930-1955,* op. cit., 254.

[627]*Daily British Whig* (Kingston), Tuesday, April 3, 1923.

[628]*Hattie Hutt.* Ship Information and Data Record, Runge Collection, Milwaukee Public Library.

[629]Marine Museum of the Great Lakes, Kingston. Information on photograph caption, negative #982.19.420, picturing the raising of the *Hattie Hutt.*

[630]Swainson, op. cit.

[631]*Kingston Whig-Standard,* Tuesday, September 21, 1937.

[632]Marine Museum of the Great Lakes, Kingston. Information on photograph caption, negative #982.19.413, picturing the removal of the *Augustus.*

[633]Swainson, op. cit.

[634]Mills, op. cit., 98.

[635]*Kingston Whig-Standard,* Thursday, May 4, 1972 (part of the "The Ships of Yesteryear" series.)

[636]Swainson, op. cit.

[637]This undated advertisement, likely from the *Daily Whig* (Kingston), was provided by researcher Ian Marshall.

[638]*Kingston Whig-Standard,* Thursday, May 4, 1972 (part of the "The Ships of Yesteryear" series.)

[639]*Picton Gazette,* Wednesday, April 25, 1945.

[640]Swayze, op. cit., 66.

[641]John Greenwood, *Namesakes, 1956-1980,* Cleveland, Freshwater Press, Inc., 1981: 474.

[642]Van der Linden, *Great Lakes Ships We Remember II,* op. cit., 392.

[643]*Kingston Whig-Standard,* Wednesday, October 30, 1985.

[644]*White Star.* Master Sheet, Institute for Great Lakes Research, Bowling Green State University, Ohio.

[645]*Wolfe Islander* [this should read *"Wolfe Islander II"*; the *Wolfe Islander* was another vessel]. Ship Information and Data Record, Runge Collection, Milwaukee Public Library.

[646]*Daily British Whig* (Kingston), Tuesday, April 7, 1964.

[647]*Kingston Whig- Standard,* Wednesday, October 31, 1984.

[648]*Kingston Whig-Standard,* Saturday, September 14, 1985.

[649]*Kingston Whig-Standard,* Tuesday, September 17, 1985.

[650]*Kingston Whig-Standard,* Friday, September 20, 1985.

[651]*Kingston Whig-Standard,* Monday, September 23, 1985.

[652]Kohl, *Dive Ontario! The Guide to Shipwrecks and Scuba Diving,* op. cit., 48-50.

[653]*Kingston Whig-Standard,* Tuesday, October 27, 1987.

[654]Ken Mullings, "Diving a Dive Boat, the Sinking of the *Effie Mae,"* *Dive Ontario,* Spring, 1994: 13.

[655]Ibid.   [656]Ibid., 14.   [657]Ibid., 15.

[658]Kohl, *Dive Ontario Two! More Ontario Shipwreck Stories,* op. cit., 27.

Chapter Ten

A Potpourri of Miscellaneous Shipwrecks

The following Kingston area shipping losses were reported sparingly in a variety of sources: contemporary newspaper reports which omitted details for a number of possible reasons (e.g. the vessel was possibly unregistered, or was too small or too old to merit mention as a commercial loss, or certain issues of contemporary newspapers were missing when archival microfilm copies were being made, and thus details of a vessel's demise were possibly lost to history forever). Also consulted for this compendium were secondary sources of information, namely the books, J. B. Mansfield's (editor), *History of the Great Lakes,* Willis Metcalfe's *Canvas and Steam on Quinte Waters,* Karl Heden's *Directory of Shipwrecks of the Great Lakes,* and *Canadian Coastal and Inland Steam Vessels, 1809-1930* by John Mills; plus Paul Ackerman's "Lake Ontario Dive Chart" (1990), and a newspaper article published in the *Picton* (Ontario) *Gazette* on April 8, 1964, by Willis Metcalfe, listing many vessels which wrecked on Prince Edward County shores:

The crew of the 92-ton schooner, *Acorn,* a ship built in 1844, almost died before a passing steamer rescued them. Their vessel had wrecked on Main Duck Island after a deckload of lumber shifted.

On April 24, 1882, the 67-ton Kingston sloop, *Alice Mary,* sprang a leak and sank while enroute from Amherst Island to Kingston. This vessel and cargo, both a total loss, were valued at $4,000.

The 60-ton ship, *Allie,* ran aground near Belleville, Ontario, on September 30, 1873, and became a total loss.

The 221-ton, 141' (42-metre) paddlewheeler, *America,* built at Niagara, Ontario, in 1840, foundered off Kingston in 1874.

The three-masted, 278-gross-ton schooner, *Abbie L. Andrews,* built at Toledo, Ohio, in 1873, was abandoned in Kingston's inner harbour early in the twentieth century. Positive identification was made of this vessel, one of 14 submerged hulks at that site, in late 1994 by the Marine Museum of the Great Lakes at Kingston. The other two vessels identified to date are the *Chicago* and the *Glengarry.*

The two-masted schooner, *H. M. Ballou,* caught fire and burned to a total loss at Belleville, Ontario, in 1907. Her career included other dramatic moments, such as when, on July 13, 1900, a sudden, powerful wind squall capsized the ship off the north shore of Smith's Bay, near Waupoos. The three men on board survived. Earlier, this schooner accidentally plowed into a small boat used for fishing, claiming the life of one of the two men in that small boat; the other man saved himself by jumping up and clinging tightly to the stays on the *Ballou's* bowsprit!

The 92' (27.6-metre), two-masted schooner, *Minnie Blakely,* launched in 1873 and the last sizeable commercial vessel built in Port Credit, Ontario, ran hard aground on a rock in the Bay of Quinte near Ox Point in May of 1882. Her load of ashes became saturated with water, ruining the wooden hull's integrity and spelling the vessel's doom. The location of her demise was marked for many years on navigation charts as "Minnie Blakely Shoal."

The schooner, *Blanche,* was lost with all hands in 1889 off Salmon Point.

The small, 30-ton ship named the *John Bright* burned to a total loss at Belleville, Ontario, on October 9, 1879. This vessel was valued at $6,000.

In 1813, a sailing vessel burned off Main Duck Island, but it is unclear whether that ship was of the British transport type, or was actually named *British Transport.*

The 126-ton schooner, *Hannah Butler,* loaded with a $5,500 cargo of 8,000 bushels of grain, grounded on a rocky reef off Salmon Point on November 26, 1887, and became a total loss. The vessel, valued at only $2,200, was worth far less than her cargo. Two years earlier, this vessel had accidentally plowed ashore near the Point Traverse lifesaving station; her removal by a Kingston tug provided a school holiday for the Point Traverse children so they could watch the salvage!

In December, 1895, the 144' (43-metre), 309-ton sidewheel steamer, *Hiram A. Calvin,* burned at the Garden Island shipyards where she had been launched in 1868.

An autumn gale in 1864 piled the four-year-old clipper-bowed schooner, *Carrier Dove,* onto the rocky south shore near Point Petre. This vessel, built at Cherry Valley (near Picton, Ontario), regularly plied the shipping route from Prince Edward County to Oswego, New York.

The scow schooner, *Catherine,* broke up in South Bay, near Picton, Ontario.

The 352-ton Canadian barge, *Chicago,* built at Montreal in 1872, lies submerged and abandoned in Kingston's inner harbour, along with 13 other vessels. Positive identification was made of this vessel, and two others, namely the *Abbie L. Andrews* and the *Glengarry,* by the Marine Museum of the Great Lakes at Kingston in late 1994.

The small schooner, *F. F.* (for Francis Farrington) *Cole,* was built and launched at Point Petre by Leige VanDusen. Captain John Hineman was the sole person aboard when his 19-ton vessel was driven ashore near Poplar Bar, Point Traverse; the Point Traverse Lifesaving Crew rescued him from his stranded ship, but the vessel was a total loss.

One account of the schooner, *Minerva Cook,* ended her career dramatically in 1886 by capsizing during a ruthless gale and washing ashore, mastless and lifeboatless, on her side at Poplar Bar, a small, but dangerous islet off the south shore of Point Traverse. All seven people, including Captain Kennedy of Kingston and his sister, Elizabeth Kennedy, who happened to be the cook on board the *Cook,* remained on board in the dangerously pounding surf. Also on board was a large, black, Newfoundland dog named Nero and two horses, one of which drowned when the vessel went over. The other horse, named Sugar, had attempted swimming to shore, but was called back by Captain Kennedy. Elizabeth Kennedy, meanwhile, had been washed off the stranded schooner three times by the vicious waves, each time being rescued and returned to the ship by the dog, Nero, and her brother, who had a way with animals. Finally, the captain tied her to the horse's back so she would not be knocked off by the waves, and the steed started swimming towards shore, accompanied by the dog, Nero. All three vanished from sight, amidst the furiously breaking waves, white foam, and pounding surf, as the horrified onlookers remained with the stranded ship. Shortly thereafter, the Point Traverse lifesaving crew rescued the six people on the doomed vessel, and a few days later, Sugar, the horse, was located roaming in the woods near the shore, but there was no trace of his rider. The lifeless body of Nero washed up on shore, and, several weeks later, the body of Elizabeth Kennedy appeared on the shore east of Poplar Bar. A desperate attempt to save the only lady on board the *Minerva Cook* had ended in disaster. However, another report is slightly less dramatic: Mansfield states simply that the *Minerva Cook* sank in a collision with the bark, *Clayton,* in 1858. One point of agreement, however, is that the *Minerva Cook* was built at Garden Island,near Kingston by Delane Dexter Calvin in about 1841.

On December 3, 1904, an early season ice floe crushed the wooden hull of the 137' (41.1-metre) merchant schooner, *Thomas Dobbie.* Originally launched as the *Comanche* at Oswego, New York, in 1867, this ship was abandoned in place off Forester's Island near Deseronto, Ontario. This may be the vessel labelled the steam barge, *Dobey,* which reportedly sank at the same location in 1907.

The steam barge, *William Egan,* ended her career when she was abandoned in Kingston harbour.

The small, five-ton tug, *Eleanor,* sprang a leak and was lost in about 90' (27 metres) of water between Main Duck Island and Nine Mile Point on Feb. 29, 1892. She was returning from Oswego, New York, at the time of her demise.

In 1848, the small schooner, *Ellen,* foundered off Salmon Point with the loss of eight lives.

The old barges, *England, Ireland,* and *Scotland,* ended their days in the early part of the 20th century abandoned at Cow Island in the Bay of Quinte, off the Rossmore shoreline east of the Bay Bridge. A construction company located some of the timbers from these old wrecks in 1964.

Strong southwest winds dragged the anchored schooner, *Enterprise,* ashore on November 24, 1882, at West Point, where she became a total loss. This 91-ton, 90' (27-metre), round-sterned vessel had been constructed at Port Hope in 1855 by William Manson. A 200-pound anchor from the *Enterprise,* located by an Ottawa woman while sailing on Little Sandy Bay in July, 1941, is presently on display at the Marine Museum at South Bay.

The *Flora Jane,* constructed as a small schooner by Tait in Picton, Ontario, in 1886, met her demise in South Bay near Cooper's storehouse.

A blinding snowstorm on November 28, 1887, caused the 137-ton Kingston schooner, *Forest Queen,* to run aground at Indian Point, opposite the western end of Amherst Island in the Bay of Quinte, and become a total loss. This small vessel was valued at $1,000.

The tugboat, *Lady Franklin,* ran ashore north of the Point Petre lighthouse on April 29, 1873.

The Canadian barge, *Glengarry,* long ago abandoned in Kingston's inner harbour, was identified in late 1994 by the Marine Museum of the Great Lakes at Kingston as part of a project hoping to identify and survey the 14 submerged vessels at that site. The 277-net-ton *Glengarry* was built in 1873 in Lancaster, Ontario. The other two vessels identified to date are the *Abbie L. Andrews* and the *Chicago.*

The broken up shipwreck lying in Young's Cove, Picton harbour, is either the two-masted schooner, *Mary Gormally,* or the schooner, *Olivet.*

The *Hattie Ann* was one of several old vessels abandoned in the shallows of Belleville Harbour in the 1930's.

The small, two-masted schooner, *Hibernia,* built in 1863 by David Tait at the mouth of Black Creek near Picton, Ontario, was valued at $5,600. This 120-ton vessel foundered in a storm on November 18, 1879, and sank near Amherst Island opposite Bath, Ontario. Scuba divers from nearby Kingston reportedly located her remains in the summer of 1967.

The two-masted schooner, *Clara Hill,* ran ashore at Salmon Point, near Outlet in Athol Bay. One report mentions the steambarge, *John J. Hill,* as being stranded at Salmon Point on April 1, 1895 (April Fool's Day!), but this has not been verified. There may be confusion due to the same surnames. A schooner named the *John H. Hill* sank in Lake Erie on June 22, 1885.

The small schooner, *Agnes Hope,* became a total loss while enroute from Oswego, New York, to Belleville, Ontario, on November 6, 1884.

The Belleville schooner, *Florence Howard,* built in 1859, foundered after her seams opened in June, 1877, at Picton Harbour.

The body of a woman cook washed ashore on False Duck Island in 1874 or 1875 and was removed to nearby Point Traverse for burial. Belief was that she had worked on the schooner, *Maggie Hunter,* which had disappeared with all five crewmembers a few weeks earlier somewhere between Oswego and Kingston. Today, we would find it hard to believe that individual people's movements and whereabouts could be difficult to track; however, after this body came ashore, authorities could offer only two possibilities as to the identity of this deceased person: it was either Miss Eliza Kennedy of Kingston, or Miss Ellen or Eliza Cook. The only other evidence that this vessel sank was the finding of her jibboom with stays attached. No other bodies were ever located. A newspaper article in the *Kingston Whig-Standard* on July 21, 1961, suggested that the recently located shipwreck off False Duck Island "may be the *Maggie Hunter,* another coal boat en route to Kingston which sank with all hands. But little information can be gathered regarding this ship." This shipwreck, however, proved to be the schooner, *Fabiola.*

The 389-ton schooner, *International,* of Chicago, while sailing towards Kingston with a load of corn in 1865, foundered in a severe gale near Salmon (or Wicked, as it was called in early days) Point, Ontario, with the loss of three of her crew.

Flames totally destroyed the small, 52-ton, Kingston schooner, *Ionia,* on July 11, 1881, at Port Metcalfe on Wolfe Island. The ship and cargo were valued at $1,750.

The new 88' (26,4-metre), 96-ton schooner, *Jura,* stranded on the Duckling Reef off Point Traverse in 1862, the same year Captain John Shaw built the ship. The vessel was trapped, immobile on the rocks, until a strong, southerly breeze freed her, only to have her drift to the foot of the cliff at Cape Vesey and smash to pieces. Kingston scuba divers Barbara Carson, Audrey Rushbrook, Stephannie Kadgielawa and Sylvia Johnson located the *Jura's* wreckage on July 31, 1966, and reportedly brought to the surface timbers and iron spikes from the unfortunate ship.

The small, 49-ton, propeller-driven steamer, *Josephine Kidd,* burned to a complete loss four miles (six kilometres) from Big Bay, in the Bay of Quinte area, on November 4, 1882.

The steamer, *Lamonde,* reportedly was abandoned in Picton harbour, across from the Prince Edward Yacht Club on the upper side of Young's Point.

On July 16, 1900, the small, 52' (16-metre), Canadian schooner that went by the name of *Madcap* reportedly sank off Glenora Bay with a cargo of peas.

The small, two-masted schooner, *Sir Charles Metcalfe,* built at South Bay, Ontario in 1850, plied Lake Ontario waters until October 15, 1861, when, cruising from Oswego, New York towards Kingston, Ontario, with a load of hard coal, she foundered somewhere near the Duck Islands.

The schooner, *Lady Moulton,* sank after a collision with the bark, *Sir Edmund Head,* reportedly off Point Petre, in May of 1869.

The small vessel, *New Dominion,* was abandoned in about 1920 in the shallows of Belleville Harbour, along with several other old ships.

The 70-ton steamer, *Norfolk,* built at Port Rowan, Ontario, in 1868, and valued at $7,000 at the time of her demise, burned to a total loss at Napanee, Ontario, in the early spring of 1877. The narrow *Norfolk* measured 80' (24 metres) in length and 15' (4.5 metres) in beam.

The schooner, *Olivia,* while enroute from Mill Point, Ontario, to Oswego, New York, capsized on Lake Ontario in October, 1871. The crew clung to the sides of the ship until they managed to free the lifeboat, get in, and drift seven miles (12 kilometres) down the lake. The schooner, meanwhile, sank.

The 79-ton *Ontario* foundered about 15 miles (23 kilometres) southeast of the Point Petre Light on September 10, 1881.

Upbound from Belleville to Cleveland with a load of iron ore or pig iron in 1880, the schooner, *Peerless,* built in 1853 in Prince Edward County, sprang a leak and foundered off Point Petre. Captain James Savage ensured that he and every crewmember reached the safety of Point Petre's shore in a lifeboat.

The two-masted, 196-ton schooner, *Persia,* with a length of 99'6" (30 metres), slid down the Hamilton, Ontario, launchway in 1867. The vessel, a confirmed stone hooker not interested in hauling other freights, was thoroughly overhauled in the winter of 1893-94, but sank off Point Petre in the spring of 1894 with a cargo of stone bound for Toronto. The crew and their ship's mascot, a pet raccoon which had become quite a seasoned sailor over the previous few years on board, reached shore safely in their yawlboat. It is not known whether the raccoon returned to the wilds, or if he signed on with another ship.

The schooner, *Peruvian,* foundered off Forester's Island near Deseronto, Ontario, with a load of iron in December, 1898.

The tug, *Phoenix,* ran aground near Point Traverse in 1863, caught fire, and burned to a total loss.

The 190-ton vessel named the *Pioneer* foundered about ten miles (16 kilometres) from Main Duck Island Light on June 12, 1871.

The old schooner, *Wilfred Plunkett,* originally named the *Kate of Oakville* when she was launched in 1868, burned at Belleville in 1909 and was abandoned in place. Two unlucky instances almost spelled the end for this vessel. On May 27th, 1889, powerful storm winds drove the *Kate of Oakville* ashore at South Bay while she was loading stone; she was, however, released with only minor damage. In the summer of 1895, the *Kate of Oakville* capsized one dark night at the mouth of Carnahan's Bay in the Bay of Quinte during another violent, windy storm. With no cargo to act as ballast, and making no headway at the time, the vessel went keel up, rolling over completely. Her masts broke off when they struck the bottom of the bay. Rolling back onto her side, the ship began filling with water which gushed through hatches and gangways. The cook and a sailor in the forecastle drowned, while the survivors, clinging desperately to the overturned ship, were picked up by the steamer, *Varuna,* in the morning. The incapacitated sailing vessel was towed to Hepburn's shipyard in Picton for repairs. In 1905, after a major rebuild, the ship was renamed the *Wilfred Plunkett,* but served for only four years under her new name before her fiery demise.

The two-masted schooner, *Primrose,* built near the Outlet River, Athol Bay, in 1846, near Picton, Ontario, foundered off Point Petre in about 1856.

The schooner, *Red Bird,* ended her career in 1888 when she sank in the Bay of Quinte just east of Belleville.

On November 13, 1898, the schooner, *Red River,* burned to a total loss while laid up for the winter in Kingston Harbour. Her value was $5,500.

The towbarge, *Isabella Reid,* of the A. W. Hepburn fleet, burned to a total loss at the "ways" below Picton, Ontario, on March 11, 1918.

The small, 73' (22-metre), 72-ton schooner, *Restless,* launched in 1859 as the *Dream* at Cleveland, Ohio, ended her restless career 30 years later. Among her experiences were capsizing on Lake Michigan (when two of her crew died), running ashore in Georgian Bay, capsizing in Lake Erie, smuggling liquor near the end of the Civil War (circa 1864-65), and hauling grain in the Belleville area. In the winter of 1888-89, she was retired from service, beached at Belleville, and eventually used as firewood.

In a severe storm in about 1901, the steamer, *Richelieu,* loaded with almost 2,000 bushels of Prince Edward County tomatoes intended for U. S. markets, foundered in the Lower Gap area in about 65' (20 metres) of water. The entire crew and the single passenger on board managed to reach land in a lifeboat.

The remains of the small, locally-owned schooner, *Ripple,* repose at the head of South Bay near Picton, Ontario.

The 128' (38.4-metre) steel bulk freighter, *Roberval,* launched at Toronto's Polson Iron Works in 1907, sank with all hands during a tyrannous storm about halfway between Oswego, New York, and Main Duck Island, on September 25, 1916. Her mast and large kingpost boom arrangement (used for self loading and unloading cargo at ports that lacked onshore handling equipment; a forerunner of future vessels known as "self-unloaders") had evidently been ripped off the ship by the vigorous waves and savage gales before the vessel sank.

The 111-ton vessel, *A. G. Ryan,* sank off Captain John's Island in the Bay of Quinte, in late September, 1886. This wooden vessel was rigged as a "steam schooner."

If you don't succeed the first time, try, try again. The three-masted barquentine, *St. George,* took this saying literally when she, along with several other vessels, ran aground near Poplar Bay during a severe autumn storm on November 27, 1860. It took until the following spring to refloat this ship after lightering. The *St. George* enjoyed one more season of service, but again was driven ashore at almost the same location on October 1, 1861. This time, the ship broke up and became a total loss.

The schooner, *Seabird,* possibly the square-nosed, 300-ton vessel once owned by local resident, Captain John Walters (yes, his namesake, the schooner, *John Walters,* is the shipwreck which lies broken up in the shallows off Russel Island in the underwater park near Tobermory, Ontario) is one of seven old ships whose abandoned remains were found in Picton harbour, between the docks and the pumping station, by survey engineers in 1946. Captain Walters used the *Seabird* to convey home to South Bay the remains of the young sailor, Moses Dulmage, who had died from exposure when autumn gales forced his rowboat to drift across Lake Ontario on October 31, 1879. The 121-ton *Seabird* was abandoned as a wreck in Picton harbour on May 30, 1889.

The Kingston schooner, *Shannon,* reportedly foundered on Lake Ontario about 20 miles (31 kilometres) from Oswego, New York, on June 20, 1874.

A small, local steamer named the *H. B. Sherwood,* from Napanee, Ontario, burned to a complete loss in the Bay of Quinte on September 17, 1884. The vessel was valued at $5,000.

The small steamer, *Silver Spray,* built at Milford, Ontario, in 1880 by Capt. John Fegan, proved to be too small and unseaworthy for regular crossings of the "Gap" between Milford and Kingston. The vessel lay abandoned at Picton for a number of years before burning to the water's edge.

The scow sloop named the *Sovereign* worked strictly in local commerce, sailing between the ports of Kingston and Trenton , and, for a while, the Rideau Canal, delivering loads of wood used for fuel. This vessel, which never went so far as to cross Lake Ontario during her career, sank near Belleville on the Bay of Quinte.

The small, two-masted schooner, *W. J. Suffle,* reportedly caught on fire in the Bay of Quinte when her crew became careless heating tar for her deck seams.

The small steam tug, the *Surprise,* worked in transporting fish the 22 miles (31 kms.) from Main Duck Island to Cape Vincent, New York, and ended her career in the Main Duck harbour.

The 324-ton bark, *George Thurston,* was wrecked on the west shore of Prince Edward County on November 17, 1869. The namesake of this vessel was a Kingston shipbuilder; one of his many claims to fame was the construction of the barque, *Arabia,* which is a popular scuba dive site near Tobermory, Ontario.

A schooner named the *Volunteer* reportedly became a total loss when she collided with the Belleville Bay bridge.

The 278-ton, 228' (68-metre) steamer-turned-to-towbarge, *Warrenko,* reputedly an American blockade runner during her early career, sank at her dock at the foot of Kingston's Gore Street on July 7, 1938, when the steamer, *Spruce Bay,* plowed into her. The *Warrenko* had been docked with her end projecting from the wharf, and the *Spruce Bay,* which was undamaged in the collision, kept towards shore. Built in Liverpool, England, by Faucet and Preston in 1864, the *Warrenko's* initial name, the *Let-her-be* ("she was called *Let-her-be* because there wasn't a boat around that could catch her") changed to the *Chicora* when she worked in the passenger trade between Toronto and Queenston. In 1924, her engines were removed and she was sold as a towbarge to Captain Grant Pyke, of thd Pyke Salvage and Wrecking Company of Kingston.

The steambarge, *Belle Wilson,* reportedly sank in August, 1888, at her mooring in Picton Harbour. Built in Picton in 1881, her length was 103' (31 metres).

Sometimes a vessel and her master work so well together that whatever affects the one influences the other. Call it coincidence or name it the supernatural, but Captain John Cornelius, owner and master of the sloop, *Wood Duck,* passed away at his home in Napanee at exactly the same time that his aging vessel sank in the Napanee River. The *Wood Duck* had also sunk at Rathbun's dock in Kingston on December 17, 1896, blocking the wharf for quite a while until the vessel could be removed. The familiar *Wood Duck* spent most of her career hauling wood from Deseronto to Picton and Napanee for the Rathbun Company.

NEAR-SHIPWRECKS:

The 102.3' (31-metre), two-masted schooner, *Acacia,* built by William O'Mara at Smiths Falls, Ontario, in 1873 (her builder's certificate was issued at Kingston on September 13, 1873), experienced a long history of commercial work, mostly hauling lumber, in the Kingston area. She also had a few encounters that nearly put a premature end to her career, such as this one reported in the May 12, 1903, *Picton Gazette:*

> The schooner, Acacia, which was ashore near the Main Duck's Island was released by the Donnelly Wrecking Company and arrived in Kingston on Thursday morning. There was a hole in her bottom, and her seams were opened by the heavy strain of the sea. She will go into dry dock for repairs.

The schooner, Acacia, *(centre of photo) and another local schooner,* Wilfrid Plunkett *(at right; vessel partially obstructed at left is unidentified). The* Plunkett's *story is told on page 227.* GREAT LAKES MARINE COLLECTION OF THE MILWAUKEE PUBLIC LIBRARY.

The *Acacia* reportedly foundered on July 12, 1908, and was finally listed again in one 1909 shipping directory as "a recovered wreck." Her value made the list at $10,000 in 1875, when she was only two years old and still rated "A1" by the insurance company; in 1879, her value was $6,500; in 1882, $5,500; in 1890, after a rebuild in 1888, $6,500; and a mere $2,500 in 1906. She was last listed in a Canadian vessel directory in 1937, although she had likely been inactive, probably abandoned, for years already. Metcalfe suspected that the *Acacia* ended her days at Wolfe Island; revelation of her final disposition is still awaited.

The *BAVARIA:* One incredibly unusual experience befell the full-rigged, three-masted, lumber-loaded schooner, *Bavaria,* while being towed out of Kingston, along with two unrigged schooner-barges, the *Norway* and the *Valencia,* by the steambarge, *D. D.. Calvin,* on November 30, 1889. Mountainous seas in a late season storm stressed the towlines to the point of parting, and the enormous waves and violent wind rendered the *Calvin* incapable of assisting her charges.

The *Norway* and *Valencia* dropped anchor and rode out the storm as best as they could; water seeped into the hulls, forcing the crews onto the cabin rooftops, where they perched for 24 miserably cold hours before the returning *Calvin,* accompanied by the steamer, *Armenia,* provided succor. The *Bavaria,* however, was nowhere in sight.

Two days later, searchers on board the *Armenia* located the *Bavaria* aground on Galloo Island, in New York state waters just across the international boundary line about nine miles southwest of Main Duck Island. As their ship drew nearer to the strangely inactive *Bavaria,* inexplicable discomfort overcame the *Armenia's* crew. Something here was drastically wrong. No relieved voices from the hushed hull responded to their shouts; no figures strode the stranded deck. The silent schooner offered only the creaking of her timbers as the weakened waves of the storm's aftermath lapped at her hull.

Other than water in her hold, nothing seemed amiss, broken, or disturbed on the vessel: the galley oven contained bread that had been in the process of baking, a new, unattached spar remained in place on the deck, the captain's papers and money were found in his desk, and, below deck in one of the cabins, a caged canary still chirped cheerily. Missing from the *Bavaria* without a trace were the yawlboat, Captain John Marshall, and all seven of his crewmembers!

Writers with runaway imaginations have suggested supernatural or extraterrestrial influences in the loss of these eight men. The logical answer is that the *Bavaria's* crew, seeing water entering the hold, erred in their estimation of their vessel's danger, and abandoned ship prematurely. The schooner had been rolling so uncontrollably from the troughs to the crests of the immense waves that the crew could not even pull out the stowed sails, hoist them, and attempt to regain steerage, or control of their ship's direction and speed.

The crews of her accompanying vessels had last seen the *Bavaria* driven by the northwest winds to the other (eastern) side of Main Duck Island. The captain of the passing schooner, *Cavalier,* upon reaching Kingston, related his attempts to pick up the *Bavaria's* skipper clinging to the overturned hull of the yawlboat, and a nearby crewmember clinging to a floating timber, but the storm's forces prohibited any such rescues. In the end, none of the bodies was ever recovered; the cold, winter waters seem to have condemned them to the lake bottom forever.

Built at nearby Garden Island in 1878 for Calvin & Breck of Kingston, the 410-gross-ton *Bavaria* measured 145' (43.5 metres) in length with a beam of 26.1' (7.8 metres). She was no stranger to hardship, as this news item from Kingston's *British Whig,* dated November 4, 1882, indicates:

> The sailors on the schooner Bavaria, just arrived at Garden Island, had a hard experience in the gale of Saturday night last. The vessel then passed down Lake Erie in a terrible sea -- the worst the Captain says he has ever encountered. The waves dashed over the vessel, sweeping away everything moveable. At one time, four sailors went out on the boom to reef the gibs. Such was the storm that the end of the boom, 26 feet from the water, dipped several times; at one time, the men were taken eight feet below the surface. Captain Dix never expected to see his men again, but they clung to the ropes and came up safely.

Repaired and returned to service in 1890, the *Bavaria* stranded in Georgian Bay in October, 1898, but was recovered. The once-controversial vessel, last listed in 1906 as owned by Alex Kidd of Sarnia, faded quietly into history.

The mysterious three-masted schooner, Bavaria, *dropping sail upon entering Kincardine harbour.* GREAT LAKES MARINE COLLECTION OF THE MILWAUKEE PUBLIC LIBRARY.

On May 13th, (a Saturday, not a bad luck Friday!), 1933, the package freighter, *Calgarian,* transporting Plymouth automobiles and bicycles, modes of conveyance for all budgets, ran aground on the West Reef off Salmon Point lighthouse. Some tedious unloading of the stranded vessel freed her without any hull damage.

The huge, three-masted barge, *Ceylon,* ran aground east of Gull Pond in 1913; abandoned by her crew, the ship, valued at $45,000, was pulled off, repaired, and returned to service the following spring. This 1,079-net-ton, 211' (63.3-metre) vessel, built at Garden Island, near Kingston, by A. Brine in 1891, was renamed *J.G. René,* sold for use in Nova Scotia in 1920, and was abandoned on the East Coast in 1943. The length and bulk of this ship made her difficult to steer, and she wore out nine rudderstocks in her lifetime.

The bulk freight schooner, *Colonel Cook,* stranded on the south side of Amherst Island on July 15, 1888, but was soon released. This auspicious event would not be worth the mention were it not for the historic infamy of this ship. Launched as the schooner, *Augusta,* in 1855 at Oswego, New York, this vessel gained notoriety in 1860 as the ship which rammed the passenger steamer, *Lady Elgin,* in Lake Michigan, then left the scene of the accident. Although unaware that the *Lady Elgin* was mortally wounded, and fearing that she herself would founder, the *Augustus* limped into port, unaware that 300 people had died when the *Lady Elgin* sank. Hatred forced the *Augustus* to change her name to the *Colonel Cook* and, for many years, leave the Great Lakes for the Atlantic Ocean. The *Colonel Cook* eventually met her demise on Lake Erie when she foundered well offshore on April 27, 1895.

The 126' (37.5-metre), 320-ton, aptly-named *Concretia,* a concrete lighthouse tender constructed in Montreal in 1918 during the steel scarcity of World War One (1914-1918), ran ashore in School House Bay on Main Duck Island in December, 1919, but was towed off the following spring. When this vessel was finally scrapped at Kingston in 1940, she saw use as a dock and as a breakwater. She was reportedly raised in 1980 and rebuilt as the barquentine, *Onaygorah.*

The 70' (21-metre), steel tugboat, *J. A. Cornett,* sank in 50' (15 metres) of water on July 10, 1949 about two miles (three kilometres) south of the Point Traverse Light. Commercial fishermen Cecil and Earl Lobb rescued the men on the sinking tug. Salvage operations by the vessels, *Rival* and *Cobourg,* were successful, and the *Cornett* returned to service a few weeks later.

The vessel that sparked controversy just before being purposely torched as a public spectacle in Toronto on June 29, 1934, the schooner, *Lyman M. Davis,* came close to meeting a more standard, less witnessed, but nobler demise on November 27, 1922, when she stranded on Waupoos Island, Ontario, in the Kingston area. The vessel was soon recovered and returned to service, much to many people's delight and many others' chagrin 12 years later.

A transatlantic visitor, the British freighter, *Dewstone,* stranded at False Duck Island Reef three miles off Point Traverse in 1928. This ship, registered in London, England, and enroute to that place from Toronto, was refloated by the Donnelly Salvage Company of Kingston.

The two-masted, 132-ton schooner, *Gazelle,* a fine-lined, clipper-bowed vessel built by Henry Doviel at Sodus, New York, in 1847, served until the early 1900's in the Toronto-Kingston area. Her last owner, Claude Cole of Main Duck Island, finally dismantled and burned the vessel as firewood at Main Duck harbour. One unique feature of this ship, in connection with her name, was the deer antlers decorating the truck (the top) of her foretopmast while she plied the lakes. This vessel is believed to be the one which capsized on October 5, 1885, while enroute from Deseronto to Kingston, but was later returned to service.

The schooner, *Great Western,* of Port Hope, Ontario, capsized and washed ashore on Simcoe Island on September 30, 1880. This was possibly the vessel that was recovered and renamed the *F. H. Burton.*

The submarine chaser, *Lovincourt,* ran hard aground in dense fog on the False Duck Island shoal on August 28, 1948. The Pyke Salvage Company tug, *Salvage Prince,* released the ship undamaged a few days later.

The towbarge, *Maple Hearst* (not to be confused with the bulk freighter, *Maplehurst,* which sank in Lake Superior in late 1922 with the loss of 11 lives), grounded on Salmon Point on July 1, 1921, but was released by Kingston salvage tugs several days later after lightering thousands of bushels of her grain cargo.

The 249' (75-metre) steamer, *A. McVittie,* built by the Detroit Dry Dock Company in Wyandotte, Michigan, in 1890, was sold to Canadian interests in 1917 near the end of her career. Two years later, she suffered severe stress during a particularly nasty storm on Lake Ontario in October, 1919. She was declared unseaworthy and laid up at Kingston, Ontario, where, five years later, she was cut up for scrap.

The three-masted, 143' (43-metre), 332-ton schooner, *Norway,* loaded with timber, encountered fierce gales which drove her ashore on Main Duck Island, with the loss of all hands (nine people) on November 7, 1882. The vessel, later recovered, suffered $6,500 worth of damage, but continued to serve the Great Lakes until she was scrapped in 1919. The *Norway* had been constructed by the Calvin & Breck Shipyard at Garden Island, Ontario, in 1873.

The small schooner, *Parthenon,* spent the winter of 1886-87 just off the south shore of Point Traverse, having been grounded there by an autumn storm. Her four crew had not been injured in this mishap. Captain John Parkinson of South Bay, agreed to free and deliver the vessel to her owners for a fee of $100.00. However, even with assistance from two other men, it took him two weeks to release the ship after the ice had melted in the spring. As they started sailing the ship to their destination, bad luck hit again, for the centerboard box had become wedged tight with some stones it had picked up over the winter on her rocky perch, and, without the ability to lower her centreboard for stability, the *Parthenon* drifted well off her course. One source states that Mr. Robert MacDonald purchased the vessel, converted her into a steamer, and renamed her after himself. However, documentation exists establishing the construction by Hepburn of the fore-and-after, 96' (29-metre) schooner named the *Robert MacDonald* right from the time of her launch in Picton in 1890, through her rebuild in 1907 as a propeller-driven steamer, and finally to her sinking and abandonment in Picton harbour in 1919.

On April 19, 1938, dense fog prompted the eight-year-old, 260' (78-metre) , diesel-powered, steel bulk freighter, *Redriver,* to run hard aground on the rocky shore at Gull Pond near Point Petre. However, the Quebec ship was soon released by a Kingston tug. The *Redriver* continued to ply Great Lakes and St. Lawrence River waters until 1962, and the vessel was sold for scrap in 1965.

The tugboat, *Sarnia City,* stranded at Poplar Bar near Point Traverse on October 8, 1930. This vessel may have been recovered and returned to service.

The small schooner named *Sassy Jack* (also referred to as *Saucey Jack)* came to temporary grief in a furious snowstorm in the autumn of 1870, ashore on Poplar Bar off Point Traverse. Enroute to Kingston with a load of grain from Port Dover, Ontario, on Lake Erie, the *Sassy Jack* grounded so heavily that the five crew and the captain's wife reached the solid safety of the beach with few difficulties. Once on shore, however, they faced the prospect of freezing to death in the blinding snowstorm. Fortunately, a local resident rounding up stray cattle for the winter found the survivors and led them to safety. The *Sassy Jack* spent that winter on the rocky beach. Refloated the following spring, the ship reportedly grounded on Timber Island several months later, but her final disposition is unknown.

The schooner, *Star,* stranded near Yorkshire Island, near Main Duck Island, in December, 1874, but was released.

On May 15, 1927, the two-year-old, Scottish-built freighter, *William C. Warren,* strayed off course at Salmon Point and ran aground, but was released the following day with only minor damage to the vessel. God only knows what happened to the reef. Outliving numerous near-disasters, including grounding at Presqu'ile in Lake Huron in late 1947 and in Port Colborne's outer harbour in November, 1948, the *Warren* was finally scrapped in 1965.

The three-masted towbarge, *Valencia,* valued at $20,000 and owned by the D. D. Calvin Company, ran ashore at Point Traverse, with the crew being rescued by the steam tug, *D. D. Calvin.* The date of this accident is not known, but this 183' (55-metre) vessel, built by the owners on Garden Island near Kingston in 1888, was eventually rescued from that shoreline and returned to service. Transferred to the lower St. Lawrence River in 1921, this ship was scrapped five years later.

UNIDENTIFIED SHIPWRECKS:

The nicknamed "K.P.H." shipwreck (for "Kingston Psychiatric Hospital," off which this vessel is located) rests in about 65' (19.5 metres) of water. This unidentified flat barge, a bit over 100' (30 metres) in length, is of a composite construction, namely steel-framed and wood-sheathed, as well as wood-decked. This vessel has 6'-8' (1.8-2.4 metres) of headroom below deck, an area which contains two huge boilers, coal chutes, piping, and machinery. The stern is completely broken open, with loose board littering the area. The four-bladed propeller is intact, although mostly sunk into the lake bottom, and the large, upright steering post (which is hollow and so large in diameter that some scuba divers have mistaken it for a large funnel or smokestack!) still has a thick, wooden, triangle-shaped rudder attached to the bottom of it. The shipwreck seems to attract a vast quantity of silt, both above and particularly below the deck. Zebra mussels cover most of this shipwreck at this point in time, making the chances of future identification of this vessel a bit slimmer.

The nicknamed "Ricky's tug" lies about seven miles (11 kilometres) west of Kingston in about 70' (21 metres) of water in the ships' graveyard. The background of this 80' (24-metre) tugboat is unknown. Located originally by Ed Donnelly, it was possibly the late Ken Jenkins (owner-operator of the former scuba charter boat, *Effie Mae,* in the Kingston area from 1968 until 1987) who nicknamed this shipwreck after local diver and historian, Rick Nielson. This shipwreck, which sits upright but minus major components, was likely scuttled.

Near "Ricky's tug," the shipwreck nicknamed the "Titanic" (due to its impressive size) sits in about 75' (22.5 metres) of water in the ships' graveyard near Kingston. A huge barge, with two enormous boilers and a vast amount of anchor chain, is intact enough to be penetrated by experienced, trained, and prepared scuba divers. This is one of the many shipwrecks usually buoyed annually by the marine conservation and education group named Preserve Our Wrecks (P.O.W.) from Kingston.

Other unidentified shipwrecks in the Kingston area include the "Mark I" in about 65' (19.5 metres) of water, and the "Mark II," both believed nicknamed after their discoverer or the first scuba diver to explore them thoroughly.

Numerous wooden stock anchors, as well as others of more modern vintage, have recently been located in several areas around Kingston.

To date, eleven of the fourteen abandoned, submerged vessels in Kingston's inner harbour remain to be identified.

BIBLIOGRAPHY

BOOKS

Amos, Art. *Rudders, A Comparison Study.* Midland, Ontario: Ontario Marine Heritage Committee, 1993.

Barry, James P. *Ships of the Great Lakes, 300 Years of Navigation.* Berkeley, California: Howell-North Books, 1973.

-------------*Wrecks and Rescues of the Great Lakes, A Photographic History.* LaJolla, California: Howell-North Books, 1981.

Berton, Pierre. *Flames Across the Border, 1813-1814.* Toronto: McClelland and Stewart Ltd., 1981.

Bowen, Dana T. *Lore of the Lakes.* Cleveland: self-published, 1940.

-------------*Shipwrecks of the Lakes.* Cleveland: self-published, 1952.

Boyd, Marion Calvin. *The Story of Garden Island.* Kingston: Edited by Margaret A. Boyd, 1983.

Boyer, Dwight. *Great Stories of the Great Lakes.* New York: Dodd, Mead & Co., 1966.

Canadian Encyclopedia. Edmonton: Hurtig Publishers, 1988 (second edition).

Charlebois, Peter. *Sternwheelers and Sidewheelers, the Romance of Steamdriven Paddleboats in Canada.* Toronto: NC Press Ltd., 1978.

Cochrane, Hugh. *Gateway to Oblivion, The Great Lakes' Bermuda Triangle.* New York: Avon Books, 1981.

Encyclopedia Canadiana. Toronto: Grolier of Canada, 1968 (third edition).

Gourley, Jay. *The Great Lakes Triangle.* Greenwich, Connecticut: Fawcett Publications, Inc., 1977.

Greenwood, John O. *Namesakes 1900-1909.* Cleveland: Freshwater Press, Inc., 1987.

-------------*Namesakes 1910-1919.* Cleveland: Freshwater Press, Inc., 1986.

-------------*Namesakes 1920-1929.* Cleveland: Freshwater Press, Inc., 1984.

-------------*Namesakes 1930-1955,* Cleveland: Freshwater Press, Inc., 1978.

-------------*Namesakes 1956-1980,* Cleveland: Freshwater Press, Inc., 1981.

Grun, Bernard. *The Timetables of History.* New York: Simon & Schuster/Touchstone, 1975 (third revised edition).

Hatcher, Harlan. *The Great Lakes.* London, New York, Toronto: Oxford University Press, 1944.

-------------and Erich A. Walter. *A Pictorial History of the Great Lakes.* New York: Bonanza Books, 1963.

Heden, Karl E. *Directory of Shipwrecks of the Great Lakes.* Boston: Bruce Humphries Pubs., 1966.

Heyl, Eric. *Early American Steamers, Vols. I-VI.* Buffalo, New York: published by the author at 136 West Oakwood Place, 1961-1969.

Kohl, Cris. *Dive Ontario! The Guide to Shipwrecks and Scuba.* Chatham, Ontario: self-published, 1990; revised edition, 1995.

-------------*Dive Ontario Two! More Ontario Shipwreck Stories.* Chatham, Ontario: self-published, 1994.

-------------*Shipwreck Tales; The St. Clair River (to 1900).* Chatham, Ontario: self-published, 1987.

Lockery, Andy. *Marine Archaeology and the Diver.* Toronto: Atlantic Publishing, 1985.

Loyal She Remains, A Pictorial History of Ontario. Toronto: The United Empire Loyalists' Association of Canada, 1984.

Mansfield, J. B., ed. *History of the Great Lakes,* Two volumes. Chicago: J. H. Beers & Co., 1899; reprint edition, Cleveland: Freshwater Press, 1972.

Metcalfe, Willis. *Canvas & Steam on Quinte Waters.* South Bay, Ontario: The South Marysburgh Marine Society, 1979.

-------------*Marine Memories.* Picton, Ontario: The Picton Gazette, 1975.

-------------*Memories of Yesteryear.* Picton, Ontario: The Picton Gazette, 1977.

Mika, Nick and Helma, with Derek F. Crawley, Kathy Harding, Capt. J. R. McKenzie, and Francis K. Smith. *Kingston, Historic City.* Belleville, Ontario: Mika Publishing Company, 1987.

Mills, John M. *Canadian Coastal and Inland Steam Vessels, 1809-1930.* Providence, Rhode Island: The Steamship Historical Society of America, Inc., 1979.

Oleszewski, Wes. *Ghost Ships, Gales & Forgotten Tales.* Marquette, Michigan: Avery Color Studios, 1995.

Pound, Arthur. *Lake Ontario.* Indianapolis & New York: Bobbs-Merrill Company, 1945.

Ratigan, W. *Great Lakes Shipwrecks and Survivals.* New York: Galahad Books, 1960.

Swainson, Donald. *A Shipping Empire, Garden Island.* Kingston: Marine Museum of the Great Lakes at Kingston, 1984.

Swayze, David. *Shipwreck!* Boyne City, Michigan: Harbor House Publishers, 1992.

Townsend, Robert B., ed. *Tales from the Great Lakes.* Toronto: Dundurn Press, 1995.

Treasure Ships of the Great Lakes. Detroit: Maritime Research & Publishing Company, 1981.

Van der Linden, Rev. Peter J., ed., and the Marine Historical Society of Detroit. *Great Lakes Ships We Remember.* Cleveland: Freshwater Press, 1979; revised 1984.

-------------*Great Lakes Ships We Remember II.* Cleveland: Freshwater Press, 1984.

-------------*Great Lakes Ships We Remember III.* Cleveland: Freshwater Press, 1994.

Young, Anna G. *Great Lakes Saga.* Owen Sound: Richardson, Bond & Wright Ltd., 1965.

PERIODICALS

Alford, Terry. "Kingston's Newest Wreck Dive." *Diver Magazine,* Vol.12, No.1, March, 1986, pp.18-21.

----------"Time Capsule in Kingston, Queen of Kingston's Wrecks." *Diver Magazine,* Vol. 14, No. 1, March, 1988, pp. 19-20.

Argonautica. The Newsletter of the Canadian Nautical Research Society, Vol. XII, No. 3, July, 1995, pp. 29-30.

Chase, Gordon. "A Double Dose of Disaster for Harry Randall." *Save Ontario Shipwrecks Newsletter,* Fall, 1986, pp. 17-18.

Cruikshank, E. A. "The Contest for the Command of Lake Ontario in 1814." *Ontario History,* Vol. 21, 1924, pp. 99-159.

Fleming, Roy F. "The Burning of the *Ocean Wave.*" *Inland Seas,* Vol. 13, No. 3, Fall, 1957, pp. 226-228.

Golding, Peter. "Inner Space Adventure, *Comet* in Lake Ontario." *Diver Magazine,* Vol. 5, No. 4, June, 1979, pp. 21-24.

----------"The Wreck of the *George A. Marsh.*" *Diver Magazine,* Vol. 5, No. 8, Nov./Dec., 1979, pp. 38-40.

Harvey, Robert. "Survey Report---S.O.S. Quinte, *Annie Falconer.*" *Save Ontario Shipwrecks Newsletter,* Spring/Summer, 1985, pp. 11-14.

----------, and Ken Mullings. "Report from S.O.S. Quinte." *Save Ontario Shipwrecks Newsletter,* Winter, 1984, pp. 17-18.

Hector, Bruce. "Kingston Wrecks." *Diver Magazine,* Vol. 17, No. 1, March, 1991, pp. 32-33.

Heyl, Erik. "The Steamboat *Kingston,* Was She Rebuilt into the Steamboat *Bavarian?*" *Inland Seas,* Vol. 16, No. 4, Winter, 1960, pp. 309-312.

Kohl, Cris. "Lake Ontario's Lost Team: *Condor & Atlasco.*" *Diver Magazine,* Vol. 22, No. 7, October/November, 1996, pp. 24-25.

----------"*Manola*--Half a Shipwreck." *Diver Magazine,* Vol. 21, No. 9, Feb., 1996, p. 28.

----------"Shipwrecks Threatened by Freshwater Barnacles." *Diving Times.* Vol. 12, No. 2, Summer, 1989.

Lewis, Walter. "The *Comet/Mayflower.*" *Inland Seas,* Vol. 41, No. 2, Summer, 1985, pp. 112-120.

Malcomson, Robert. "HMS *Psyche.*" *Seaways' Ships in Scale,* Vol. IV, No. 6, November/December, 1993, pp. 16-20.

----------"HMS *St. Lawrence.*" *Seaways' Ships in Scale,* Vol. V, No. 1, January/February, 1994, pp. 44-51.

Miller, John. "*Hattie Hutt.*" *Telescope,* Vol. 11, No. 6, June, 1962, p. 133.

Morgan, Ian. "Silent Giant of Great Lakes Warfare, H.M.S. *St. Lawrence,* 1814." *Canadian Diving Journal,* Summer, 1983, p. 16.

Mullings, Ken. "Diving a Dive Boat, the Sinking of the *Effie Mae.*" *Dive Ontario,* Spring, 1994, pp. 13-15.

-----------"The Fate of the *Falconer.*" *Diver Magazine,* Vol. 18, No. 6, Sept., 1992, pp. 18-19.

-----------"Quinte's Favourite Dive Site." *Save Ontario Shipwrecks Newsletter,* Spring/Summer, 1988, pp. 20-22.

Neilson, Rick. "The Sidewheeler, *Cornwall.*" *Diver Magazine*, Vol. 17, No. 4, June, 1991, pp. 32-33.

"P.O.W. Kingston 1812 Freshwater Fleet Research Project." *Save Ontario Shipwrecks Newsletter,* Summer, 1989, pp. 30-32.

Palmer, Richard. "The Age of Sail Ended on Ontario." *Inland Seas,* Vol. 46, No. 1, Spring, 1990, pp. 6-10.

-----------"Great Canadian Shipbuilder: Louis Shickluna." *Inland Seas,* Vol. 41, No. 1, Spring, 1985, pp. 11-19, 57.

-----------"Great Lakes Time Line, Lake Ontario." *Inland Seas,* Vol. 41, No. 4, Winter, 1985, pp. 295-299.

-----------"The Longest Pull." *Inland Seas,* Vol. 40, No. 3, Fall, 1984, pp. 200-204.

Preston, R. A. "The Fate of Kingston's Warships." *Historic Kingston,* Vol. 1, October, 1959, pp. 3-14.

Ryan, V. Pat. "Beloved Shipwreck." *Canadian Diving Journal,* Summer, 1983, pp. 10-13, 15.

Soegtrop, Michael, and Eva Woloszczuk. "Kingston." *Diver Magazine,* Vol. 7, No. 1, January/February, 1981, pp. 23-24.

Stacey, C. P. "The Ships of the British Squadron on Lake Ontario, 1812-1814." *The Canadian Historical Review,* Vol. 34, 1953, pp. 311-323.

Warwick, Peter D. A. "Pioneer Shipbuilder of the Great Lakes." *Canadian Geographical Journal,* Vol. 94, No. 3, June/July, 1978, pp. 26-29.

Wishart, Bruce. "Sir James Yeo and the *St. Lawrence,* 'A Remarkable Fine Ship'." *The Beaver,* February-March, 1992, pp. 12-22.

MISCELLANEOUS

Ackerman, Paul. Midwest Explorers League, Chicago: "Lake Ontario Dive Chart" (1990).

British Military Records, Public Archives of Canada (PAC), Ottawa, RG8, C-Series, Vol. 730-735, microfilm reels C-3243 and C-3244.

Hilton, Nancy, ed. *A 10 Year Summary of Sport Diving Fatalities in Ontario, 1979-1988.* Ontario Underwater Council, 1185 Eglinton Avenue East, NORTH YORK, Ontario M2C 3C6, telephone: (416) 426-7033.

Kohl, Cris. *Scuba Dive Log Books* for the years 1982, 1983, 1984, 1986, 1988, 1991, 1992, 1994, 1995, and 1996.

"Master Sheets." Institute for Great Lakes Research. Bowling Green State University, Ohio. For the following vessels: *Aberdeen, Acacia, Aloha, Atlasco, Frank C. Barnes, City of Sheboygan, Comet, Cornwall,*

Senator Derbyshire, S.M. Douglas, Katie Eccles, Annie Falconer, Florence, John E. Hall, Charles Horn, Wm. Jamieson, H. N. Jex, Simon Langell, George A. Marsh, Navajo, John R. Noyes, Psyche, Quinte, Simla, Horace L. Taber.

Mullings, Ken. "Monitoring the *Falconer,* An Archaeological Site Update of the Fore-and-Aft Schooner, *Annie Falconer.*" Kingston: Preserve Our Wrecks, 1992, plus 1993, 1994, and 1995 updates.

"Runge, Herman G., Collection." The Great Lakes Marine Collection of the Milwaukee Public Library. Ship Information and Data Records. For the following vessels: *Acacia, Aloha, Atlasco, Burt Barnes, Bavaria, Cabotia, Bertie Calkins, City of New York, City of Sheboygan, Comet, Cornwall, Mary A. Daryaw, Senator Derbyshire, Katie Eccles, Empire State, Annie Falconer, Grace M. Filer, Florence, John E. Hall, C. Hickox, Charles Horn, Hattie Hutt, H.N. Jex, Manola, Mapleglen, Maplegorge, Maplegreen, George A. Marsh, Oliver Mowat, J.B. Newland, John R. Noyes, Oatland, Overland, Palmbay, John Randall, Prince Regent, St. Lawrence, Sarniadoc, Sarnor, Stormount, Horace Taber, Wolfe Islander II, Yewbay.*

Reports from the Ontario Underwater Council Concerning Ontario Diving Fatalities, 1989, 1990, 1991, 1992, 1993, 1994, 1995. Ontario Underwater Council, 1185 Eglinton Avenue East, NORTH YORK, Ontario M2C 3C6, telephone: (416) 426-7033.

Teepell, David M. "1868-1922 Wrecks." Not dated. A 17-page, non-circulating shipwreck list, compiled "solely from the Department and Fisheries statement of Wrecks and Casualties Annual Report 1868 to 1923", available for perusal at the Marine Museum of the Great Lakes, 55 Ontario St., Kingston, Ontario, Canada K7L 2Y2.

Thompson, Douglas G. *The Annie Falconer, Archaeological Survey & Salvage Project, 1982.* Preserve Our Wrecks Kingston Ltd., January 31, 1983.

NEWSPAPERS

Various issues of the following newspapers were used:

Canadian Gazeteer
Kingston Chronicle
Daily British Whig (Kingston)
Daily Whig (Kingston)
Standard (Kingston)
Weekly British Whig (Kingston)
Whig-Standard (Kingston)
Quinte Weekly News
Hastings Chronicle (Belleville)
Intelligencer (Belleville)
Toronto Globe
Toronto Telegram

Hallowel Traveller (Picton)
Hallowel Free Press (Picton)
Picton Gazette
London (Ontario) *Free Press*
St. Catharines Journal
Syracuse (New York) *Standard*
Oswego Palladium
Detroit Evening News
Detroit Free Press
Chicago Herald and Examiner
Chicago Inter-Ocean
Milwaukee Sentinel

INDEX

Ships' names are in *italics*.

An asterisk [*] denotes a photograph.

ABOUT THE AUTHOR

(Photo by Sherry Stayer)

Cris Kohl, who hails from Windsor, Ontario, has three university degrees, including an M.A. (Master of Arts) degree in History, specializing in Great Lakes Maritime History. He also enjoys exploring (since 1974) and photographing (since 1982) the underwater world, particularly that of the Great Lakes. He is a certified Divemaster, Nitrox, and Full Cave Diver, presently completing his Trimix training.

He has written five books and scores of magazine and newsletter articles on Great Lakes shipwrecks and scuba diving. Serving as a scuba club president (1985-87) and as an executive member of a Save Ontario Shipwrecks chapter (1987-93), he has been on the Board of Directors of the Ontario Underwater Council since 1988.

Having explored the underwater world of Kingston's shipwrecks since the early 1980's, having researched and photographed those shipwrecks since the mid-1980's, and having written about many of them since the early 1990's, Cris Kohl was amply prepared when he commenced writing this book in May, 1996.

An educator by profession, Cris Kohl teaches high school English and History. His dedication to education, however, goes far beyond the classroom.

Cris Kohl's research, award-winning photography, vigour, and sense of drama have made him a popular speaker at local historical societies and major scuba shows.

HOW TO OBTAIN ADDITIONAL BOOKS

Additional copies of *Treacherous Waters: Kingston's Shipwrecks,* or other shipwreck books by Cris Kohl, are available at local bookstores and scuba dive shops. Books may also be ordered directly from the author at 16 Stanley Avenue, Chatham, Ontario, Canada, N7M 3J2. Telephone (519) 351-1966 or fax (519) 351-1753 for availability and prices.

HAPPY READING!